THE REVOLUTIONS OF 1989

"A concise and thoughtful summary of the 1989 revolutions in Eastern Europe."

David Turnock, *University of Leciester*

"Tismaneanu is one of the leading American analysts of the rise and fall of communism in Eastern Europe, and [this book] is a representation of the best that the field has written about the East European revolutions."

Norman Naimark, *Stanford University*

The Revolutions of 1989 is a collection of both classic and recent articles examining the causes and consequences of the collapse of communism in East and Central Europe, the most important event in recent world history.
  It includes discussion of:

- the economic, political and social nature of revolutions
- the role of dissidents and civil society in encouraging the breakdown of eastern European communist regimes
- comparisons with other revolutions
- the extent of the collapse of Leninist regimes in East-Central Europe.

Vladimir Tismaneanu is Professor in the Department of Government and Politics at the University of Maryland at College Park and editor of the journal *East European Politics and Societies*. His previous books include *In Search of Civil Society: Independent Peace Movements in the Soviet Bloc* (1990), *Reinventing Politics: Eastern Europe from Stalin to Havel* (1992) and *Fantasies of Salvation: Democracy, Nationalism and Myth in Post-Communist Europe* (1998).

Rewriting Histories focuses on historical themes where standard conclusions are facing a major challenge. Each book presents papers (edited and annotated where necessary) at the forefront of current research and interpretation, offering students an accessible way to engage with contemporary debates.

Series editor **Jack R. Censer** is Professor of History at George Mason University.

REWRITING HISTORIES
Series editor: Jack R. Censer

Already published
THE INDUSTRIAL REVOLUTION AND WORK IN
NINETEENTH-CENTURY EUROPE
Edited by Lenard R. Berlanstein

SOCIETY AND CULTURE IN THE SLAVE SOUTH
Edited by J. William Harris

ATLANTIC AMERICAN SOCIETIES
From Columbus through Abolition
Edited by J.R. McNeill and Alan Karras

GENDER AND AMERICAN HISTORY SINCE 1890
Edited by Barbara Melosh

DIVERSITY AND UNITY IN EARLY NORTH AMERICA
Edited by Philip D. Morgan

NAZISM AND GERMAN SOCIETY 1933–1945
Edited by David Crew

THE FRENCH REVOLUTION: RECENT DEBATES AND
NEW CONTROVERSIES
Edited by Gary Kates

Forthcoming
HOLOCAUST: ORIGINS, IMPLEMENTATION AND
AFTERMATH
Edited by Omer Bartov

STALINISM
Edited by Sheila Fitzpatrick

ISRAEL/PALESTINE QUESTION
Edited by Ilan Pappe

THE REVOLUTIONS
OF 1989

Edited by
Vladimir Tismaneanu

London and New York

First published 1999
by Routledge
2 Park Square, Milton Park, Abingdon, Oxon, OX14 4RN

Transferred to Digital Printing 2005

Simultaneously published in the USA and Canada
by Routledge
270 Madison Ave, New York NY 10016

Typeset in Palatino by
BC Typesetting, Bristol

British Library Cataloguing in Publication Data
A catalogue record for this book is available from the British Library

Library of Congress Cataloguing in Publicaiton Data
Tismaneanu, Vladimir.
The revolutions of 1989/Vladimir Tismaneanu.
p.   cm. — (Rewriting histories)
Includes bibliographical references and index.
1. Europe, Eastern—Politics and government—1989–   I. Title.
II. Series: Re-writing histories.
DJK51.T57   1999
947′.009′048—dc21   98-34372
                                                       CIP

ISBN 0–415–16949–6 (hbk)
ISBN 0–415–16950–X (pbk)

CONTENTS

CONTENTS

CONTRIBUTORS

Bruce Ackerman, professor of political theory, Yale University.

Daniel Chirot, professor of sociology, Henry Jackson School of International Affairs, University of Washington (Seattle).

S. N. Eisenstadt, professor of sociology, the Hebrew University, Jerusalem and professor, Committee on Social Thought, University of Chicago.

Timothy Garton Ash, journalist and historian, Oxford University.

Jeffrey C. Isaac, professor of political theory, Indiana University, Bloomington.

Ken Jowitt, professor of political science, University of California at Berkeley.

Tony Judt, professor of history, director of Remarque Institute, New York University.

Leszek Kolakowski, professor of philosophy, Oxford University.

Jacek Kuroń, political writer and activist, former minister of labour, one of the leaders of the Freedom Union Party, Poland.

Adam Michnik, historian and journalist, editor-in-chief of *Gazeta Wyborcza* (Poland).

Mircea Mihăieş, literary essayist and political commentator, editor of the monthly *Orizont* (Romania).

Jacques Rupnik, professor of political science at the Center for International Studies and Research, Fondation Nationale des Sciences Politiques, Paris.

G. M. Tamás, civic activist and political philosopher, University of Budapest, Hungary.

Vladimir Tismaneanu, professor of politics and director of the Center for the Study of Post-Communist Societies at the University of Maryland (College Park).

Katherine Verdery, professor of anthropology, University of Michigan, Ann Arbor.

Zhelyu Zhelev, historian and politician, former President of Bulgaria.

SERIES EDITOR'S PREFACE

Although the reactions to the disintegration of communism in Eastern Europe have been numerous, this volume provides a selection of understandings and responses that constitute in general a far more reflective and distanced approach than earlier ones. The contributions here focus on characteristics of the regimes before 1989, the reasons for their demise, and the prospects for the future. While little lamentation exists for prior governments, the articles here reveal a powerful debate emerging over the impact of their past history and over the abilities of the revolutionaries to overcome these restraints. As both participant and observer, Vladimir Tismaneanu is well positioned to guide us through political, intellectual and academic reactions.

ACKNOWLEDGEMENTS

All extracts and articles published in this volume have already been published. We would like to thank the following copyright holders for permission to reproduce their work:

Chapter 1   Reprinted from *The Crisis of Leninism and the Decline of the Left*, ed. Daniel Chirot (Seattle, WA: University of Washington Press, 1991), pp. 3–32. Copyright © 1991 University of Washington Press.

Chapter 2   Reprinted by permission of *Daedalus* (Journal of the American Academy of Arts and Sciences), from the issue entitled "The Exit from Communism," 121: 2 (Spring 1992): 43–56.

Chapter 3   Reprinted by permission of the publisher from Katherine Verdery, *What Was Socialism and What Comes Next* (Princeton, NJ: Princeton University Press, 1996), pp. 19–38. Copyright © 1996 Princeton University Press.

Chapter 4   Reprinted by permission of *Daedalus* (Journal of the American Academy of Arts and Sciences), from the issue entitled "The Exit from Communism," 121: 2 (Spring 1992): 21–41.

Chapter 5   Reprinted by permission of the author from Timothy Garton Ash, *The Magic Lantern* (London: Vintage, 1990), pp. 131–56. Copyright © 1990, 1993 Timothy Garton Ash.

Chapter 6   Reprinted by permission of *Social Research* (an international quarterly of the social sciences), 63: 2 (Summer 1996): 291–344.

Chapter 7   Reprinted by permission of *Daedalus* (Journal of the American Academy of Arts and Sciences), from the issue entitled "After Communism: What?," 123: 3 (Summer 1994): 1–19.

Chapter 8   Reprinted by permission of *Uncaptive Minds*, 7: 2 (Summer 1994): 19–34.

Chapter 9   Reprinted by permission of *Journal of Democracy*, 1: 1 (Winter 1990): 72–4. Copyright © 1990 Johns Hopkins University Press.

Chapter 10   Reprinted by permission of the publisher from Bruce Ackerman, *The Future of Liberal Revolution* (Newhaven, CT:

ACKNOWLEDGEMENTS

Yale University Press, 1992), pp. 113–23. Copyright © 1992 Yale University Press.

Chapter 11 Reprinted by permission of the publisher from Ken Jowitt, *New World Disorder: The Leninist Extinction* (Berkeley, CA: University of California Press, 1992), pp. 284–305. Copyright © 1992 The Regents of the University of California.

Chapter 12 Reprinted by permission of the publisher from *Journal of Democracy* 6: 2 (April 1995): 61–73. Translated from the French by Deborah M. Brissman. Copyright © 1995 Johns Hopkins University Press.

Chapter 13 Reprinted by permission of the author. Originally published in Polish in *Gazeta Wyborcza* in September 1993. English version (trans. Elzbieta Matynia) published in *Bulletin of the East and Central Europe Program of the New School for Social Research* (October 1994).

Chapter 14 Reprinted by permission of the author from *Partisan Review*, 59: 4 (1992): 711–17.

Chapter 15 Reprinted by permission of the publisher from *Journal of Democracy*, 7: 3 (July 1996): 3–6. Copyright © Johns Hopkins University Press.

INTRODUCTION

Vladimir Tismaneanu

By a felicitous coincidence, this volume appears precisely ten years after the world-shattering series of events widely known as the revolutions of 1989. During that year, what appeared to be an immutable, ostensibly inexpugnable system, collapsed with a breath-taking velocity. And this happened not because of external blows (although external pressure did matter), as in the case of Nazi Germany, but as a consequence of the development of insoluble inner tensions. The Leninist systems were terminally sick, and the disease affected first and foremost their capacity for self-regeneration. After decades of flirting with the ideas of intrasystemic reforms, it had become clear that communism did not have resources for readjustment and that the solution lay not within but outside, and even against the existing order.

The demise (implosion) of the Soviet Union, consummated before the incredulous eyes of the world in December 1991, was directly and intimately related to the previous dissolution of the East European "outer empire" provoked by the revolutions of 1989. No matter how we regard or value these events, it is now obvious that the historical cycle inaugurated by World War I, the Bolshevik seizure of power in Russia in October 1917 and the long European ideological warfare that followed had come to an end.[1] The importance of these revolutions cannot therefore be over-estimated: they represented the triumph of civic dignity and political morality over ideological monism, bureaucratic cynicism and police dictatorship. Rooted in an individualistic concept of freedom, programmatically skeptical of all ideological blueprints for social engineering, these revolutions were, at least in their first stage, liberal and nonutopian.[2] Unlike traditional revolutions they did not originate in a doctrinarist vision of the perfect society and rejected the role of any self-appointed vanguard in directing the activities of the masses. No political party headed their spontaneous momentum and in their early stage they even insisted on the need to create new political forms, different from ideologically defined, traditional party differentiations. The fact that the aftermath of these revolutions has been plagued by ethnic strifes, unsavory political bickering, rampant political and economic corruption, and the rise of illiberal parties and movements, including strong authoritarian, collectivistic trends, does not diminish their generous message and colossal impact. And, it should be noted, it was precisely in the countries where the revolutions did not occur (Yugoslavia) or were derailed (Romania) that the exit from state socialism was particularly convoluted, tottering and in the long run problematic. These facts should be kept in mind especially when we are confronted with discourses that question the success of these revolutions by referring exclusively to their ambiguous legacies. The "reactionary rhetoric," brilliantly examined by Albert Hirschman, uses the futility, jeopardy, and perversity arguments in order to delegitimize change *per se*, or make it look impossible or undesirable.[3] This line of reasoning, often encountered in some of the more sophisticated approaches, argues along the following logic: the postrevolutionary environment has unleashed long-dormant ugly features of the national political cultures, including chauvinism, residual Fascism, ethnoclerical fundamentalism, and militarism, and is therefore more dangerous than the *status quo ante*; or, nothing really changed and the powerholders have remained the same, simply affixing to themselves new masks; or, no matter what the men and women of the revolutions of 1989 had hoped, the results of their endeavors have turned out to be extremely disappointing, allowing for political scoundrels to make it and use the new opportunities to establish their domination.

Remembering the real message of these revolutions, revisiting their main interpretations and a number of key pronouncements made by the revolutionaries themselves, is therefore a politically, morally and intellectually useful exercise. We should not forget that what is now generally taken for granted, the end of Sovietism, was only a possibility, and not even a very likely one, at the beginning of 1989. True, some dissident thinkers (Ferenc Fehér, Agnes Heller, Václav Havel, Jacek Kuroń, Adam Michnik) thought that the system was slowly decaying and that it had no future, but even they were not considering the collapse an immediate possibility. The whole philosophy of dissent was predicated on the strategy of long "penetration" of the existing system, the gradual recovery and restoration of the public sphere (the independent life of society) as an alternative to the all-embracing presence of the ideological party-state.[4] Think of the subtitle of the extraordinarily influential collection of samizdat essays edited in the mid-1980s by Václav Havel: "citizens against the state."[5] If there is a main moral of the great revolutionary drama that unfolded in Eastern Europe in 1989, it is that history is never a one-way avenue, and that the future is always pregnant with more than one alternative. Indeed, as Jeffrey Isaac argues in the article included in this anthology, the revolutions of 1989 had more than one meaning and put forward a challenging agenda not only for the postcommunist societies, but for Western democracies as well.[6]

It is true, as Polish philosopher Leszek Kolakowski notices in the essay selected for this volume, that there were a number of thinkers (himself among them) who anticipated the inevitable collapse of Sovietism. But very few were those who really thought such an occurrence would be possible with such an alacrity and, as a general rule, without violence. The nature of post-totalitarian, but still authoritarian Leninist regimes was not one conducive to negotiations and a peaceful transfer of power from the ruling communist party to the opposition. Thus, one of the most surprising developments of 1989–1990 was the readiness of the communist elites in Hungary and Poland first to share and then to give up power. In so doing, they jettisoned the most cherished Leninist dogma regarding the communist party's "leading role" (monopoly on power) and allowed for democratic transitions to start and proceed in a gradual, peaceful way. In other countries, however, reforms were rejected in the name of the defense of "socialist gains of the people," but this confrontational line adopted by the ruling elites could not save them. The model of "barracks socialism" had outlived itself and the desperate efforts to rescue it by what was known as the "Gang of Four" (Romanian, East German, Bulgarian, and Czechoslovak leaders) had no chance to succeed in the long run. Veteran observers of the Soviet bloc, historians, political scientists, and journalists alike were struck by the extraordinary dynamics that in less than twelve months, and, with the exception of Romania, in a peaceful, nonviolent manner, put an end to Leninist tyrannies in Central and Eastern Europe.[7]

The meaning of those events, the role of dissidents (critical, unregimented intellectuals) in the resurrection of long-paralyzed civic societies, the overall crisis of those regimes, and the decline of the communist parties' hegemony have generated an enormous amount of interpretive literature. The initial general temptation was to acclaim role of dissidents in the breakdown of Soviet-style regimes and the rise of civic initiatives from below.[8] Euphoric accounts of the revolutionary wave, often compared to the 1848 "Spring of the Nations," abounded, and British historian and journalist Timothy Garton Ash offered some of the most eloquent articles along this line in his gripping contributions to the *New York Review of Books*, later collected in the volume *The Magic Lantern*.[9] One of these essays, emblematic for the approach that emphasizes the role of the critical intelligentsia in the destruction of the Leninist despotisms of Central Europe, is included in this volume. The dominant trend was to regard these revolutions as part of the universal democratic wave; indeed, a confirmation of the ultimate triumph of liberal democratic values over collectivist-Jacobin attempts to control human minds. This vision inspired the reflections on the future of liberal revolution by political philosopher Bruce Ackerman for whom the dramatic changes in East and Central Europe were part of a global revival of liberalism. In other words, their success or failure

3

would condition the future of liberalism in the West as well, because we live in a world of political, economic, and cultural-symbolic interconnectedness and interdependence.

Very few analysts insisted on the less visible, but nonetheless persistent illiberal and neo-authoritarian components of the anticommunist upheaval in the East. Taken away by the exhilarating effects of the revolutionary turmoil, most observers preferred to gloss over the heterogeneous nature of the anticommunist movements: not all those who rejected Leninism did it because they were dreaming of an open society and liberal values. Among the revolutionaries were quite a few enragés, ill-disposed towards the logic of compromise and negotiation. There were also populist fundamentalists, religious dogmatics, nostalgics of the precommunist regimes, including those who admired pro-Nazi dictators like Romania's Ion Antonescu and Hungary's Miklos Horthy. It was only after the disintegration of Yugoslavia and the velvet divorce that led to the breakup of Czechoslovakia into two countries (the Czech Republic and Slovakia) that scholars and policy-makers realized that the liberal promise of these revolutions should not be taken for granted and that the aftermath of communism is not necessarily liberal democracy. In the early 1990s it became increasingly clear that the postcommunist era was fraught with all sorts of threats, including bloody ethnic conflicts, social unrest, and the infectious rise of old and new sorts of populisms and tribalisms.[10] This volume brings together some of the seminal analyses of the revolutions of 1989 and their aftermath. Selecting the articles for this book, I tried to gather the most lucid, albeit controversial, approaches staying away from both the overly optimistic or the incurably catastrophic perspectives. The main hypothesis that most of the authors selected in this volume share is that the events of 1989 had revolutionary consequences. Some praise the role of civic society, critical intellectuals, and dissidents, others take issue with this approach, but none of them denies the important fact that these changes resulted in the end of Leninist regimes in East and Central Europe. Whether the term "revolution" is the most appropriate to describe these changes is of course an open question. What is beyond dispute, at least among the authors present in this book, is the world-historical impact of the transformations inaugurated by the events of 1989.

The volume highlights three major themes: the deep-seated meanings of the collapse of state socialist regimes in East Central Europe; the nature of revolutions at the end of the twentieth century; and the role of critical (public) intellectuals in politics. The book brings together significant, truly original, and provocative contributions offered by both interpreters and actors of one of the century's most formidable developments: the breakdown of once supremely self-confident regimes, the revival of civic, social, and economic life, and the search for non-ideological and non-Machiavellian forms of political organization and participation. My purpose in selecting these pieces within a daunting bulk of literature dealing with these topics is to allow students of East and Central European politics, history, and societies to avoid any myopic simplifications as well as unfounded speculative generalizations. The pieces I put together in this book do justice, I hope, to the tremendous complexity of the revolutionary upheaval of 1989 and explain a number of otherwise deeply disconcerting evolutions: the marginalization of the first postcommunist elites (often recruited from the dissident countercultures); the former communists' recovery and their return to leading positions in government; the ethical confusion of post-communism and the rampant cynicism that seems to bedevil all these societies.[11]

The main assumption for this volume is the shared belief among its contributors that what happened in East and Central Europe in 1989 transcends the boundaries of the region and has had long-term impact on international stability. Not only did the Soviet zone of influence and the Warsaw Pact come to an end as a result of these events, but they led to the fall of the Berlin Wall, that shameful symbol of contempt for civic rights, the disbandment of the German Democratic Republic (GDR), the reunification of Germany, and the conclusion of the Cold War through the victory of the liberal West. Nowadays, as I write these lines, all this seems normal, even banal, but ten years ago such a denouement of the East–West confrontation would have appeared as surreal. It is, therefore, of great intellectual and political significance to revisit the main interpretations of these most fascinating developments in recent European and world history. Why did the revolutions occur? Were they truly revolutions in the classical sense and, if so, what new ideas and practices did they propose? Is it true, as some writers argued, that these were nothing but efforts to "right" the wrongs of communism's experiments, or, better said, they were just endeavors to restore the precommunist situation? Were these revolutions primarily a consequence of the economic failure of Leninism, in other words of the inability of command (centrally planned) economies to catch up with the challenges of the postindustrial age? What was the impact of moral/cultural factors on the emergence of civic-society initiatives within late Leninist (post-totalitarian) regimes?What was the importance of the pre-1989 dissident and reform-communist traditions in different East Central European countries? How does one account for the nonviolent, self-limited nature of these revolutions and the absence of mass-scale vindictive attempts to punish the former powerholders? What was the real popular attitude toward the dissidents and how can one make sense of the transitions from "velvet revolutions" to "velvet counter-revolutions," or "restorations"? Students of European history and politics, as well as those interested in social movements, the relationship between morality and politics, the role of intellectuals in the breakdown of communism, political democratization, and post-Cold War international politics in general, will find this book useful. Indeed, it was the end of communism in East Central Europe that accelerated centrifugal-disintegrative processes in the USSR, catalyzed the national patriotic movements in the Baltics and Ukraine, and ushered in a new, post-Cold War and post-bipolar world. As Ken Jowitt has often argued, this has created a fundamentally new and dangerous situation in which the absence of norms and predictable rational behavior on the part of the involved actors could result in global chaos. This is not to deplore the end of the pre-1989 arrangements, but simply to point to the need to recognize that these revolutions, and the end of Leninism, have placed all of us in a radically novel situation. As several pieces in this volume argue (Daniel Chirot, S. M. Eisenstadt, Jeffrey C. Isaac, Katherine Verdery), understanding the revolutions of 1989 helps us grasp the meanings of the ongoing debates about liberalism, socialism, nationalism, civil society, and the very notion of human freedom at the end of this most atrocious century.[12]

As I mentioned before, the crucial question to be addressed is: Were the events of 1989 genuine revolutions? If the answer is positive, then how do we assess their novelty in contrast to other similar events (the French Revolution of 1789 or the Hungarian one of 1956)? If the answer is negative (as some today like to argue), then it is legitimate to ask ourselves: What were they? Simple mirages, results of some obscure intrigues of the beleaguered bureaucracies that mesmerized the whole mankind but did not fundamentally change the "rules of the game"? These last words, *the rules of the game*, are key for interpreting what happened in 1989 and, focusing on them, we can reach a positive assessment of those revolutions and their heritage. In my view, and here I agree with Bruce Ackerman, Daniel Chirot, S. M. Eisenstadt, Jacques Rupnik, and most of the East European contributors to this volume, the upheaval in the East, and primarily in the Central European core countries, represented a series of *political revolutions* that led to the decisive and irreversible transformation of the existing order. Instead of autocratic, one-party systems, the revolutions created emerging pluralist polities. They allowed the citizens of the former ideologically driven despotisms (closed societies) to recover their main human and civic rights and to engage in the building of open societies.[13] Instead of command, centrally planned economies, all these societies have embarked on creating market economies. In these efforts to meet the triple challenge (creating political pluralism, market economy, and a public sphere, i.e. a civil society) some succeeded better and faster than others (the contrast between the Czech Republic and Romania inspires Mircea Mihăieş's wry essay). But it cannot be denied that in all the countries that used to be referred to as the Soviet bloc, the once monolithic order was replaced by political and cultural diversity.[14] While it is true that we still do not know whether *all* these societies will become well-functioning liberal democracies, it is nevertheless important to emphasize that in all of them the Leninist systems based on ideological uniformity, political coercion, dictatorship over human needs, and suppression of civic rights have been dismantled.[15]

In focusing on the revolutions of 1989 we need to address the perceived failure of Western social science to anticipate (predict) the collapse of Leninism as a world system. The failure should not be seen as universal. Some authors (Ken Jowitt, Leszek Kolakowski) had long insisted on the moral and cultural decay of Soviet-style regimes and the twilight of the energizing-mobilizational, i.e. charismatic appeals of the official creed. The road to 1989–1991 was prepared by the less visible, often marginal, but critically significant in the long run, workings of what we call now civil society (Solidarity in Poland, Charter 77 in Czechoslovakia, unofficial peace, environmental, and human rights groups in the GDR, Democratic Opposition in Hungary). In examining the wreckage of Leninism we should thus avoid any one-dimensional, monistic approach. In other words, there is no single factor that explains the collapse: economics as much as politics, and culture as much as insoluble social tensions converged in making these regimes irretrievably obsolete. But these were not any kind of autocracies: they derived their only claim to legitimacy from the Marxist-Leninist "holy writ," and once this ideological aura ceased to function, the whole edifice started to falter.[16] They were, to use sociologist Daniel Chirot's apt term, "tyrannies of certitude" and it was precisely the gradual loss of ideological commitment among the ruling elites, what was once a truly Messianic ardor, that accelerated the process of inner disintegration of Leninist regimes.[17] In a way, the revolutions of 1989 were an ironical vindication of Lenin's famous definition of a revolutionary situation: those at the top cannot rule in old ways, and those at the bottom do not want to accept these ways any more. They were more than simple revolts because they attacked the very foundations of the existing systems and proposed a complete reorganization of society. It is perhaps worth remembering: Communist parties were not in power as a result of legal-rational procedures. No free elections brought them to the ruling positions, but rather they derived their spurious legitimacy from the ideological (and teleological) claim according to which they represented the "vanguard" of the working class and, consequently, they were the carriers of a universal-emancipatory mission.

Once the ideology ceased to be an inspiring force and influential members of the ruling parties, the offspring and beneficiaries of the nomenklatura system, lost their emotional commitment to the Marxist radical behests, the Leninist castles were doomed to fall apart. Here comes the role of what is often called the Gorbachev effect.[18] It was indeed the international climate generated by the shockwaves of the policies of glasnost and perestroika initiated by Mikhail Gorbachev after his election as General Secretary of the Communist Party of the Soviet

Union in March 1985 that allowed for an incredible amount of open dissent and political mobilization in East and Central Europe. While it is true that for the first two years of his leadership (1985–1987) Gorbachev's strategy toward Eastern Europe was one of encouraging intrasystemic moderate changes, without considering the possibility of communist parties losing their privileged positions, after 1988 things started to change considerably. It was Gorbachev's denunciation of the ideological perspective on international politics and the abandoning of the "class struggle perspective" that changed the rules of Soviet–East European relations. The Brezhnev doctrine of limited sovereignty was practically abandoned precisely twenty years after its initial formulation, in August 1968, when it was concocted as a justification of the Warsaw Pact crushing the Prague Spring (Alexander Dubček's experiment with "socialism with a human face"). As the joke was making the rounds in 1988 in Prague and other East European capitals: What is the difference between Gorbachev and Dubček? None, but Gorbachev doesn't know it yet.[19]

The Gorbachev factor, without which the revolutions of 1989 would have been barely thinkable, was itself the consequence of the loss of self-confidence among communist elites. Gorbachev was not the "liberator" of Eastern Europe, and even less was he a conscious, deliberate gravedigger of Sovietism. Initially, at least, he used his power to fix rather than ruin the system. Much of what happened as a result of his originally modest reforms was spontaneous and unpredictable, and there was an immense gap between the Soviet leader's neo-Leninist illusions and the practical conditions within these societies. Gorbachev's merit was to acknowledge that lest force be used the Leninist system could not be preserved in the countries of the former Warsaw Pact: unlike all his predecessors he refused to resort to tanks as the ultimate political argument and rejected the Leninist (or *Realpolitik*) position that might creates right. In so doing, Gorbachev fundamentally altered the rules of the game. Thanks to the "new foreign-policy thinking" (advocated by Gorbachev and his close associates Aleksandr Yakovlev and Eduard Shevardnadze, and resented by Politburo hard-liners headed by Yegor Ligachev) the margin of political experimentation in East Central Europe and in the former USSR expanded dramatically.

It is impossible within the confines of an introduction to discuss all the ethical and political legacies of the dissident movements, the nature of the 1989 upheaval, and the causes of what Adam Michnik calls the "velvet restoration": the current syndrome of disenchantment with the dissident tradition, the political marginalization of the once acclaimed heroes, and the return of more or less repentant or reconstructed communists to political prominence. Themes that deserve special exploration but that go beyond the scope of this volume are the fate of the former communists, the intricacies of the legal-political process of "decommunization" in different countries, and the conflicting views surrounding the concept and practice of political (retroactive) justice. Let me say that the controversies regarding the treatment of the former party and secret police activists and collaborators were among the most passionate and potentially disruptive in the new democracies. Some argued, together with the first post-communist and anticommunist Polish Prime Minister Tadeusz Mazowiecki, that one needed to draw a "thick line" with the past and fully engage in a consensual effort for building an open society. Others, for different reasons that went from fanatic anticommunism to cynical manipulation of an explosive issue, argued that without one form or another of "purification" the new democracies would be fundamentally perverted. The truth, in my view, resides somewhere in between: the past cannot and should not be denied, covered with a blanket of shameful oblivion. Real crimes did take place in those countries and the culprits should be identified and brought to justice. But legal procedures and any other form of retribution for past misdeeds should always take place on an individual base, and preserving the presumption of innocence is a fundamental right for any human being, including former communist apparatchiks. In this respect, with all its shortcomings, the lustration law in the Czech Republic offered a legal framework that prevented any form of "mob justice." In Romania, where no such law was passed and access to personal secret police files was systematically denied to citizens (while these files continued to be used and abused by those in power), the political climate continued to be plagued by suspicion, murky intrigues and dark conspiratorial visions.[20]

This volume documents the main interpretive lines concerning the revolutions of 1989, but does not offer a country-by-country perspective.[21] It is, however, important to notice, at least in this introduction that, while the structural causes of communism's collapse were similar, the dynamics, rhythm, and orientation of these revolutions depended to a large extent on the local conditions. In this respect, one may argue that it was the strength or the weakness of pre-1989 intraparty reformist trends as well as oppositional traditions that explain the striking distinctions between these events in different countries. In Poland and Hungary, the revolutions were gradualist and peaceful, and the radical changes resulted from negotiations between enlightened exponents of the ruling elites and moderate representatives of the opposition. In Czechoslovakia and the GDR the disappearance of the Soviet protective shield (Gorbachev's refusal to encourage the communist governments to use force against mass expressions of civic disobedience) led to complete disarray at the top and the crumbling of the party/government machines. The existence of unofficial civic initiatives and the strategic vision of Václav Havel and his fellow Charter 77 activists explain the velvetness of the November revolution in Prague and Bratislava. Based on the constitutional fiction according to which it was the "first German state of the workers and peasants," the

GDR could not outlive the end of the Socialist Unity Party's monopolistic hold on power. In a matter of several weeks, the electrifying slogan "We are the people!" chanted by hundreds of thousands in night demonstrations in East Berlin, Leipzig, Dresden and other major cities, turned into "We are one people!" thereby making the issue of German reunification urgent and inevitable. The initial voices of the East German revolution, all those poets, balladeers, and ecological and human rights activists who had spent years under strict *Stasi* (secret police) surveillance, suddenly found themselves without a constituency. To their disappointment they discovered that most East Germans were not hoping to improve the socialist experiment, or to embark on a search for an ecological-pacifist utopia, but rather were eager to enjoy what they thought to be the benefits of West Germany's welfare capitalist state. Of all the former Warsaw Pact countries, the GDR was the only one that owed its very existence to Soviet military presence and pure ideological considerations. It was also the only one that disappeared through unification with (incorporation into) the bigger and more powerful other state of the same nation. Indeed, whereas the velvet divorce of December 1992 led to the emergence of two independent, sovereign states (the Czech Republic and Slovakia), the end of the GDR amounted to the complete absorption of the former East Germany into the Federal Republic.

In Bulgaria, the Gorbachevites within the top echelons got rid of Todor Zhivkov's sclerotic leadership through a Moscow-endorsed coup d'état. Their plans to preserve the system failed however because of the swift development of oppositional democratic forces fully committed to a systemic transformation. But the absence of robust dissident traditions, the factionalism among the democrats, and debility of radical reformers among Bulgarian communists (rebaptized Socialists) led to a continuous fragmentation of the political spectrum and a state of political and social anarchy. In Romania, dictator Nicolae Ceauşescu used the military and secret police to quell the anticommunist demonstrations in Timişoara and Bucharest. Dissent in that country was even weaker than in Bulgaria: any form of collective endeavor to challenge Ceauşescu's uniquely personalistic autocracy had been long stifled by the *Securitate* (secret police). Alienated from his own party bureaucracy, internationally isolated and criticized both East and West, outraged by Gorbachev's reforms which he publicly denounced as a treason of socialism, Ceauşescu was an increasingly erratic despot: even the army and the secret police higher-ups were aware of the enormous risks of continuing to serve him and his clan. Thus, on December 22, 1989 a mass upheaval in Bucharest and other major cities succeeded in getting rid of the Ceauşescu couple (his wife Elena had become the regime's number two person). Their successors, however, were not anticommunist civic democrats, nor pro-Western liberals, but exponents of the second echelon of party and government bureaucracies. They immediately formed a National Salvation Front as the country's new political leadership and did their utmost to contain the rise of civic and political movements and parties committed to fulfilling the initial revolutionary expectations. The widening chasm between those who hoped that Romania would finally break with its communist past and the authoritarian, restorative policies of Ceauşescu's successors led to a climate of continuous strife, suspicion and confrontation in Romanian politics. It was only as a result of the electoral victory of the anticommunist Democratic Convention in November 1996 and the election of Emil Constantinescu as the country's president that Romania decisively embarked on the same political and economic reforms as its Central European neighbors.[22]

This inevitably sketchy introduction is intended to allow the reader to grasp the importance of the debates incorporated in this volume. Whereas some authors (Timothy Garton Ash, Daniel Chirot, Jeffrey C. Isaac) emphasize the role of critical intellectuals in formulating the revolutionary agenda, others (Ken Jowitt, Tony Judt, G. M. Tamás) insist on the debility of liberal traditions and the problematic nature of the early enthusiasm with such normative concepts and ideas as "civil society," "antipolitics," and "return to Europe." Some authors think that these were liberal revolutions advancing a global trend toward democracy (Bruce Ackerman), while others (especially G. M. Tamás and Tony Judt) propose a more skeptical view of the whole dissident saga and its genuine impact on those societies. Furthermore, this debate affects our perspective on the role of ideas and public intellectuals in historical changes, the very possibility of a new politics based on trust and morality, and the overall meaning of the antitotalitarian struggle of critical intellectuals in the East. It is the purpose of this volume to help readers understand that one of the most profound and enduring meanings of 1989 was the quest for a reinvention of politics along the lines spelled out by the dissidents. If this project fails and East Central Europe reverts to some version of corporatism or quasi-fascist authoritarianism, the consequences of such developments would affect the West as well. And this would happen sooner rather than later. These points are luminously made by Jacques Rupnik and Daniel Chirot, who emphasize both the immense hopes and the perils unleashed by the revolutionary wave of 1989 and its aftermath.

This book includes essays written by prominent Western scholars (historians, political scientists, sociologists, anthropologists). Some of them are well known for their lifelong interest in East and Central Europe. Others have started to reflect on the events in that region during and after the miraculous year 1989. All share, however, the belief that whatever happened in East Central Europe has a global significance: the collapse of communism and the birth of protopluralist, albeit still unstable, regimes invites serious reflection on the nature of politics and the future of liberal values at the end of this most convulsive and highly ideological century.

Sociologist S. N. Eisenstadt examines the revolutions of 1989 as anti-teleological, nonutopian, and nonideological forms of social activism. This approach is important because there are voices that consider these revolutions mere re-enactments of similar events in the past. In reality, as Eisenstadt argues, the revolutions of 1989 have brought something novel into the story: unlike previous revolutions they did take place in the absence of a coherent, tightly formulated revolutionary doctrine. More than that, their victory was directly related to a strong suspicion among the revolutionaries toward any form of ideological hubris. Suffice it to mention here Václav Havel's and George Konrád's strong attacks on ideology in their writings of the 1980s.[23]

Tony Judt argues that liberal dissidents never had a strong impact on their societies and that the region's precommunist illiberal traditions, enhanced by the lingering effects of Leninism, are a major obstacle for liberal democracy to thrive in the region. In Judt's view there is little usable past for exponents of pluralism to harken back to. Instead, there is a strong and unprocessed memory of real or perceived victimization, a lot of self-idealization and very little readiness for empathy and commiseration. At the opposite end of the interpretive spectrum stands Timothy Garton Ash. As one of the main chroniclers of the breakdown of Leninist regimes in Central Europe and of the role of critical intellectuals in the emergence of civil societies, Garton Ash insists on the revolutions of 1989 as "moral resurrections" and highlights the crucial status of public intellectuals like Havel or Michnik as paragons of a new political style. His article in this volume is important because it runs counter the ongoing temptation to discard the significance of dissent and treat former anti-communist dissidents as an extinct political force. The fact that many of the personalities mentioned by Garton Ash have lost their prominent positions in postcommunist governments is not necessarily an indication of their defeat. After all, seizing power was not the ultimate dissident dream: the antipolitical activists of the 1970s and 1980s were committed to the restoration of truth and morality in the public sphere, the rehabilitation of civic virtues, and the end of the totalitarian methods of control, intimidation, and coercion. In this respect, they succeeded. True, the new political order is not exactly a liberal heaven, and all sorts of unsavory phenomena have come to the fore: cynicism, corruption, the economic empowerment of the former nomenklaturas, chauvinist and nationalist outbursts of intolerance and hatred, new forms of exclusion and ethnic arrogance. But as Ken Jowitt argues, post-1989 East Central Europe is a political and economic laboratory in which the new institutional arrangements will be strongly influenced by the legacies of forty years of Leninism.

The volume also includes essays written by some of the most influential voices from the region. The reader will thus be able to compare Western academic interpretations with the political visions of those directly involved in these changes. Both Adam Michnik and Jacek Kuroń were among the most active members of Poland's anticommunist opposition. Both were founding members of the Committee for Workers' Defense (created in 1976), then political advisors to Lech Walesa during the first experience of legal Solidarity (1980–1981). Both served prison terms for their ideas and unbending commitment to freedom and truth. After the end of communism Michnik chose the career of journalism and became the editor in chief of *Gazeta Wyborcza*, Poland's most popular newspaper. Kuroń served as minister of labor in several postcommunist governments and has remained one of the most popular politicians in his country. Michnik's piece is important because it sheds light on the inner debates among the originally united anticommunist opposition: on the one hand the moderates, proponents of a Spanish-style transitional model, on the other those for whom the elimination of former communists for public functions is an indispensable premise for social recovery. In his thoughtful essay, Kuroń explains some of the major challenges associated with this unprecedented effort to get rid of Leninist totalitarian legacies. The reader should notice that both Kuroń and Michnik have consistently opposed any form of "anticommunist fundamentalism" (what Michnik calls "anticommunism with a Bolshevik face") and advocated a future, rather than past-oriented strategy for postcommunist Poland. In many respects, their views are consonant with arguments often made by Václav Havel in his post-1989 writings.[24]

Hungarian writer G. M. Tamás proposes a provocative vision of the meaning of dissent, insisting on the split between the universalistic philosophy of civic movements and groups on the one hand, and the persistence of illiberal sentiments among the majority of the population on the other. In other words, the moral paradigm of the dissidents, the very position of the civic activist as a symbol of emancipation was not shared by those who had found forms of adjustment within the old system. He may be right to some extent in the case of Hungary, where the liberal democratic opposition never became a mass movement like Poland's Solidarity. But even in the case of Czechoslovakia, the ideas of a Charter 77 generated a political style and vision that left an enduring imprint on the post-1989 developments. In other words, ideas do have a life of their own, and even if some of the dissident values appear now as somewhat naive, it is still important to emphasize the importance of the rediscovery of civic virtues and the affirmation of individual rights as advocated in the dissident concept of freedom. Former Bulgarian president Zhelyu Zhelev's discussion of the postcommunist rampant cynicism and moral squalor is also an important contribution to the discussion of the legacies of 1989: the main danger these days is not the restoration of Leninist institutions, including the terrorist ones (secret police, camps, propaganda, and censorship). The real danger is that people get tired and exasperated with the costs of the transition, distrust the politicians, and may embrace populist discourses of salvationist demagogy. But again, this discontent with the elites is not a peculiar East European phenomenon: one sees the rise of radical movements and parties in the West as well (the spectacular successes of Austria's Freedom Party is a striking example). In the East, however, pluralist institutions and practices are still fragile, and the neutralization of populist-ethnocentric parties and movements rooted in social anger is more problematic than in consolidated democracies.

To conclude, the revolutions of 1989 have fundamentally changed the political, economic, and cultural map of the world. Resulting from the widespread dissatisfaction with Leninist ideological domination, they allowed for a rediscovery of democratic participation and civic activism. After decades of state aggression against the private sphere, these revolutions reinstituted the distinction between what belongs to the government and what is the territory of the individual. Emphasizing the importance of political and civic rights, they created a space for the exercise of liberal democratic values. In some countries these values have become the constitutional foundation on which the institutions of an open society can be safely built. In others, the reference to pluralism remains somewhat perfunctory. But even in the less successful cases of democratic transitions (Albania, Bulgaria, Romania), the old order, based on suspicion, fear, and mass hopelessness, is irrevocably defunct. In other words, while the ultimate result of these transitions is not clear, the revolutions have succeeded in their most important task: disbanding the Leninist regimes and permitting the citizens of these countries to fully engage in the shaping of their own destinies.

NOTES

Acknowledgment I wish to acknowledge the research and editorial contributions made to this volume by Beata Czajkowska. It was she who not only helped me to select the pieces included in this volume, but also managed to deal with the labyrinthine world of copyrights. I also wish to thank Kevin Trowell for his assistance in putting together the final draft of the manuscript.

Washington, DC
March 25, 1998

1 See Eric Hobsbawn, *The Age of Extremes: A History of the World, 1914–91* (New York: Pantheon Books, 1994), pp. 461–99.
2 For the exhaustion of ideological-style secular religions, see Agnes Heller and Ferenc Fehér, *The Grandeur and Twilight of Radical Universalism* (New Brunswick, NJ: Transaction Books, 1991).
3 See Albert Hirschman, *The Rhetoric of Reaction: Perversity, Futility, Jeopardy* (Cambridge, MA: The Belknap Press of Harvard University Press, 1991).

4 See Miklós Haraszti, "The Independent Peace Movement and the Danube Movement in Hungary," in Vladimir Tismaneanu, ed., *In Search of Civil Society: Independent Peave Movements in the Soviet Bloc* (New York and London: Routledge, 1990), pp. 71–87.
5 See Václav Havel, *et al.*, *The Power of the Powerless: Citizens against the State in Central-Eastern Europe* (Armonk, NY: M. E. Sharpe, 1990).
6 See Jeffrey Isaac, *Democracy in Dark Times* (Ithaca, NY: Cornell University Press, 1997). For a particularly insightful analysis of the revolutionary upheaval of 1989 and its long-term consequences, see Ralf Dahrendorf, *Reflections on the Revolution in Europe* (New York: Random House, 1990).
7 For ideologically-driven modern despotisms, see Daniel Chirot, *Modern Tyrants: The Power and Prevalence of Evil in Our Times* (New York: Free Press, 1994).
8 See William Echikcson, *Lighting the Night* (New York: William Morrow, 1990); Vladimir Tismaneanu, *Reinventing Politics: Eastern Europe from Stalin to Havel* (New York: Free Press, 1993), paperback edition with a new afterword; Andrew Nagorski, *The Birth of Freedom: Shaping Lives and Societies in the New Eastern Europe* (New York: Simon & Schuster, 1993).
9 See Timothy Garton Ash, *The Magic Lantern: The Revolutions of '89 Witnessed in Warsaw, Budapest, Berlin, and Prague* (New York: Vintage Books, 1993).
10 See Vladimir Tismaneanu, *Fantasies of Salvation: Nationalism, Democracy and Myth in Postcommunist Europe* (Princeton, NJ: Princeton University Press, 1998).
11 Readers interested in detailed and thoughtful analyses of the postrevolutionary dynamics in these countries should consult such journals at *Transitions, East European Constitutional Review, East European Politics and Societies*, and *Problems of Postcommunism*.
12 For the impact of 1989 on the rethinking of liberalism's agenda, see Jerzy Szacki, *Liberalism After Communism* (Budapest and London: Central European University Press, 1995); Ira Katznelson, *Liberalism's Crooked Circle: Letters to Adam Michnik* (Princeton, NJ: Princeton University Press, 1997).
13 See Ivo Banac, ed. *Eastern Europe in Revolution* (Ithaca, NY and London: Cornell University Press, 1992).
14 See Claus Offe, *Varieties of Transition: The East European and East German Experience* (Cambridge, MA: MIT Press, 1997), especially pp. 29–105.
15 See Ferenc Fehér, Agnes Heller, György Márkus, *Dictatorship Over Needs* (New York: St. Martin's Press, 1983).
16 See Ernest Gellner, *Conditions of Liberty: Civil Society and Its Rivals* (New York: Allen Lane/The Penguin Press, 1994).
17 Daniel Chirot, op. cit.
18 See Karen Dawisha, *Eastern Europe, Gorbachev, and Reform: The Great Challenge* (Cambridge and New York: Cambridge University Press, 1990).
19 See "The Strange Death of Soviet Communism: An Autopsy." Special issue of *The National Interest*, 31 (Spring 1993), especially the articles by Francis Fukuyama, Myron Rush, Charles Fairbanks, Peter Reddaway, and Stephen Sestanovich.
20 For the dilemmas of decommunization, see Tina Rosenberg, *The Haunted Land: Facing Europe's Ghosts After Communism* (New York: Random House, 1995).
21 For an excellent historical exploration of the breakdown of communism in East Central Europe and the post-1989 struggle for democracy in the region, see Gale Stokes, *The Walls Came Tumbling Down: The Collapse of Communism in Eastern Europe* (New York: Oxford University Press, 1993).

15

22 See Vladimir Tismaneanu, "Romanian Exceptionalism? Democracy, Ethnoc-
   racy, and Uncertain Pluralism in Post-Ceauşescu Romania," in Karen Dawisha
   and Bruce Parrott, eds., *Politics, Power, and the Struggle for Democracy in South-
   East Europe* (Cambridge: Cambridge University Press, 1997), pp. 403–51.
23 Václav Havel, *Disturbing the Peace: A Conversation with Karel Hvizdala* (New
   York: Knopf, 1990); George Konrad, *Antipolitics* (New York and London:
   Harcourt Brace Jovanovich, 1984).
24 Václav Havel, *Summer Meditations* (New York: Vintage Books, 1993).

Part I

CAUSES

1

WHAT HAPPENED IN EASTERN EUROPE IN 1989?

Daniel Chirot

American sociologist Daniel Chirot is well known for his writings on social change, modern revolutions and tyrannies. In this essay he offers a comprehensive interpretation of the main causes of the revolutions of 1989. While acknowledging the paramount importance of the economic decline of Leninist regimes, he identifies the major causes of the breakdown in the political and moral crises of these societies. Communist elites derived their spurious legitimacy from their self-designated role as exponents of historical progress. In other words, they were in power because they claimed to represent the interests of the working class, and therefore of humanity as a whole. Chirot correctly points out that the disintegration of elite self-confidence and the rise of anti-systemic movements from below led to the moral dissolution of the old Leninist order.

This essay proposes a useful discussion of the novelty of the revolutions of 1989 compared to traditional revolutions. Based on a profound analysis of these major historical convulsions, Chirot reaches an important conclusion regarding the nature of revolutions in the next century. Admitting that political and economic factors will continue to beget social turbulence, Chirot predicts that the "fundamental causes of revolutionary instability will be moral." In this respect, his interpretation is convergent with other essays in this volume (S. N. Eisenstadt, Jeffrey Isaac, Ken Jowitt) and captures the long-term significance of the revolutions of 1989.

*   *   *

The world knows that in Eastern Europe communism collapsed in 1989, and that the USSR set out on a path that not only promises the end of socialism but threatens its very territorial integrity. But knowing this does not explain why it all happened. Nor are the implications of all these revolutionary events as clear as the immediate, short-run strategic effects that follow from the dissolution of the Warsaw Pact and the Council for Mutual Economic Assistance.

There are many ways of looking at the "Revolution of 1989." As with other great revolutionary events – the French Revolution of 1789, the European revolutions of 1848, the Bolshevik Revolution of 1917, or the Chinese Revolution of 1949 – economic, political, cultural, and social analyses offer only partial insights. Everything was interconnected, yet no single analysis can entirely absorb all aspects of such cataclysmic events. Even after two hundred years, the French Revolution is still a subject for debate, and novel interpretations remain possible; and if the political controversy generated by that revolution two centuries ago has cooled somewhat, for well over a century and a half it remained a burning issue at the center of European and world politics.[1]

We should not be surprised, then, if over the next several decades the events of 1989 form the basis of much passionate political and scholarly debate. Having said this, I should add that for those of us interested in social change, revolutionary periods offer the most important fields of observation. We cannot, of course, conduct controlled laboratory experiments that suit the needs of our research. But, in fact, revolutions are large-scale social experiments. Although they are not tailored to scholarly ends, or by any stretch of the imagination controllable, they are the closest thing we have to those major scientific experiments that have shaped our understanding of the physical world. Great revolutions, then, are better windows into how societies operate in the long run than almost any other type of historical event. Therefore, aside from being immediately and keenly interested in the events that took place in Eastern Europe in 1989 because they are reshaping the international political order, we also have a fascinating, unexpected, revealing glimpse into how seemingly stable, enduring social systems fail and collapse.

The underling causes

Economic problems

There is no question that the most visible, though certainly not the only reason for the collapse of East European communism has been economic. It is not that these systems failed in an absolute sense. No East European country, not even Romania, was an Ethiopia or a Burma, with famine and a reversion to primitive, local subsistence economies. Perhaps several of these economies, particularly Romania's, and to a more limited extent Poland's, were headed in that direction, but they had very far to fall before reaching such low levels. Other economies – in Hungary, but even more so in Czechoslovakia and East Germany – were failures only by the

20

standards of the most advanced capitalist economies. On a world scale these were rich, well-developed economies, not poor ones. The Soviet Union, too, was still a world economic and technological power, despite deep pockets of regional poverty and a standard of living much lower than its per capita production figures would indicate.[2]

There is no need to go over the defects of socialist economies in detail. These have been explained by the many excellent economists from those countries, particularly the Poles and Hungarians – the two most famous of whom are Wlodzimierz Brus and János Kornai.[3]

The main problem is that investment and production decisions were based largely, though not entirely, on political will rather than domestic or international market pressures. To overcome the force of the domestic market, which ultimately meant consumer and producer wishes and decisions, the quantities and prices of goods and services were fixed by administrative order. And to exclude external market forces, which might have weakened domestic guidance of the economy, foreign trade with the advanced capitalist world was curtailed and strictly controlled, partly by fiat but also by maintaining nonconvertible currencies. The aim of curtailing the power of market forces was achieved, but an inevitable side effect was that under these conditions it became impossible to measure what firms were profitable and what production processes were more or less efficient. There were no real prices.

As the inefficiencies of socialist economies became evident, it proved impossible to reform them, largely because the managers were so closely tied to the ruling political machinery. They were able to lobby effectively to steer investments in their direction, regardless of the efficiency of their enterprises. Success as a manager was measured by the ability to produce more, maintain high employment, and attract politically directed investment, not by producing marketable goods more efficiently. Equally important, the very concept of profit as a measure of efficiency was foreign to these managers.[4]

Such systems developed inevitable shortages of desired goods. This was partly because production was so inefficient that it kept the final output of consumer goods lower than it should have been at such high levels of industrialization. And the very crude ways of measuring success, in terms of gross output, slighted essential services and spare parts, so that the very production process was damaged by shortages of key producer goods and services.

But whereas in some cases it was possible to carry out reform, most notably in agriculture and some services (the outstanding successes were the Chinese decollectivization of agriculture after 1976 and the Hungarians' ability to privatize some services and small-scale agricultural production), in industries the power of the communist party and its managers was simply too strong to carry out real change. Furthermore, the sincere commitment

21

to full employment and the maintenance of low food prices further damaged efficiency.[5]

But none of this would have made the slightest sense without the ideological base of communism. Some critics of communist economic arrangements have argued that the system was simply irrational. In strict economic terms, it may have been, but that hardly explains its long life. The key is that political will was ultimately the primary determinant of economic action, and this will was based on a very coherent world view developed by Lenin, Stalin, and the other Bolshevik leaders. This view then spread to other communist leaders, and was imposed on about one-third of the world's population.

Lenin was born in 1870, and Stalin in 1878 or 1879. They matured as political beings in their teens and early twenties when the most advanced areas of the world were in the industrial heartland of Western Europe and the United States: in the Ruhr, or in the emerging miracles of modern technology being constructed in the American Middle West, from Pittsburgh and Buffalo to Chicago. It is not mere coincidence that these areas, and others like them (including the major steel and shipbuilding centers of Britain, or the coal and steel centers of northern France and Belgium), became, one hundred years later, giant rust belts with antiquated industries, overly powerful trade unions, and unimaginative, conservative, and bureaucratic managers. It has been in such areas, too, that industrial pollution has most ravaged the environment, and where political pressures resistant to free trade and the imposition of external market forces were the fiercest in the advanced countries. But in 1900 these areas were progressive, and for ambitious leaders from a relatively backward country like Russia, they were viable models.

Lenin, Stalin, and all the other Bolshevik intellectuals and leaders – Trotsky, Kamenev, Zinoviev, Bukharin, and so many others – knew that this was what they ultimately had to emulate. They felt, however, that they would make it all happen more quickly and more efficiently by socialist planning than by the random and cruel play of market forces. Despite the inherent inefficiencies of socialism, these astonishing, visionary men – particularly Stalin – actually succeeded. The tragedy of communism was not its failure, but its success. Stalin built the institutional framework that, against all logic, forced the Soviet Union into success.[6] By the 1970s the USSR had the world's most advanced late nineteenth-century economy, the world's biggest and best, most inflexible rust belt. It is as if Andrew Carnegie had taken over the entire United States, forced it into becoming a giant copy of U.S. Steel, and the executives of the same U.S. Steel had continued to run the country into the 1970s and 1980s!

To understand the absurdity of this situation, it is necessary to go back and take a historical look at the development of capitalism. There have been five industrial ages so far. Each was dominated by a small set of "high technology" industries located in the most advanced parts of the industrial world. Each has been characterized by rapid, extraordinary growth and innovation in the leading sectors, followed by slower growth, and finally relative stagnation, overproduction, increasing competition, declining profits, and crisis in the now aging leading sectors. It was precisely on his observations about the rise and fall of the first industrial age that Karl Marx based his conclusions about the eventual collapse of capitalism. But each age has been followed by another, as unexpected new technologies have negated all the predictions about the inevitable fall of profits and the polarization of capitalist societies into a tiny number of rich owners and masses of impoverished producers.

The ages, with their approximate dates, have been: (1) the cotton-textile age dominated by Great Britain, which lasted from about the 1780s into the 1830s; (2) the rail and iron age, also dominated by Britain, which went from the 1840s into the early 1870s; (3) the steel and organic-chemistry age, one that also saw the development of new industries based on the production and utilization of electrical machinery, which ran from the 1870s to World War I, and in which the American and German economies became dominant; (4) the age of automobiles and petrochemicals, from the 1910s to the 1970s, in which the United States became the over-whelmingly hegemonic economy; and (5) the age of electronics, infor-mation, and biotechnology, which began in the 1970s and which will certainly run well into the first half of the next century. In this last age, it is not yet certain which economies will dominate, though certainly the Japanese and West Europeans are well on their way to replacing the Americans.[7]

Transitions have been difficult. Depressions and political turmoil from the 1820 to the 1840s, in the 1870s and 1880s, and in the 1920s and 1930s can be explained, in good part, by the complications of passing from one age to another. World War I – or more particularly the mad race for colonies in the late nineteenth century and the European arms race, especially the naval one between Germany and Britain – was certainly a function of the shifting economic balance in Europe. World War II resulted from the unsatisfactory outcome of World War I, and from the Great Depression of the 1930s. The shocks from the latest transition to the fifth industrial age have been mild by comparison, but the difficulties that attended past transitions produced many predictions about the imminent collapse of capitalism that seemed reasonable at the time.[8] This brief bit of economic history has to be connected to the events of 1989.

The Soviet model – the Leninist-Stalinist model – was based on the third industrial age, the one whose gleaming promises of mighty, smoke-filled concentrations of chemical and steel mills, huge electric generating plants, and hordes of peasants migrating into new factory boomtowns mesmerized the Bolshevik leadership. The Communist Party of the Soviet

Union found out that creating such a world was not easy, especially in the face of stubborn peasant and worker refusal to accept present hardships as the price for eventual industrial utopia. But Stalin persuaded the CPSU that the vision was so correct that it was worth paying a very high price to attain it. The price was paid, and the model turned into reality.[9]

Later, the same model was imposed on Eastern Europe. Aside from the sheer force used to ensure that the East European complied, it must also be said that the local communists, many of whom were only a generation younger than Stalin, accepted the model. Those who came from more backward countries particularly shared Stalin's vision. In Romania, Nicolae Ceauşescu held on to it until his last day in power. It was based on his interpretation of his country's partial, uneven, and highly unsatisfactory drive for industrialization in the 1930s, when he was a young man just becoming an active communist.[10] To a degree we usually do not realize, because China remained so heavily agricultural, this was Mao's vision too.[11] Today its last practitioner is Ceauşescu's contemporary and close ideological ally, Kim Il Sung.

In the Soviet Union, in the more backward areas of Eastern Europe, in the already partly industrial areas of China (especially on the coast and in Manchuria), and in North Korea, the model worked because there were a lot of peasants to bring into the labor force, because this type of economy required massive concentrations of investments into huge, centralized firms, and because, after all, the technology for all this was pretty well worked out. Also, producer goods were more important than consumer goods at this stage. (It is worth remembering, too, that these were all areas where industrialization had begun *before* communism, either because of local initiatives, as in Russia or most of Eastern Europe, or because of Japanese colonial investments, as in North Korea and Manchuria.)

I should note, in passing, that the model is particularly disastrous for very backward economies that have no industrial base to begin with. Thus, whatever successes it may have had in East Asia and Europe, it has produced nothing but disaster when tried in Africa or Indochina.

But if the Stalinist model may be said to have had some success in creating "third age" industrial economies, it never adapted well to the fourth age of automobiles, consumer electrical goods, and the growth of services to pamper a large proportion of the general population. This is why we were able to make fun of the Soviet model, even in the 1950s and 1960s, because it offered so few luxuries and services. But the Soviets and those who believed in the Stalinist-Leninist model could reply that, yes, they did not cater to spoiled consumers, but the basic sinews of industrial and military power, the giant steel mills and power generating plants, had been built well enough to create an economy almost as powerful as that of the United States.

Alas for the Soviet model, the fifth age turned out to be even more different. Small firms, very rapid change, extreme attention to consumer needs, reliance on innovative thinking – all were exactly what the Stalinist model lacked. Of course, so did much of America's and Western Europe's "rust belt" industry – chemicals, steel, autos. But even as they fought rearguard actions to protect themselves against growing foreign competition and technological change, these sectors had to adapt because market pressures were too intense to resist. Their political power was great, but in capitalist societies open to international trade it was not sufficient to overcome the world market. In the Soviet case, such industries, protected by the party and viewed as the very foundation of everything that communism had built, were able to resist change, at least for another twenty years. That was what the Brezhnev years were – a determined effort to hold on to the late nineteenth-century model the Bolsheviks had worked so hard to emulate. So, from being just amusing, their relative backwardness in the 1970s and 1980s became dangerous. The Soviets and East Europeans (including the Czechs and East Germans) found themselves in the 1980s with the most advanced industries of the late nineteenth and early twentieth centuries – polluting, wasteful, energy intensive, massive, inflexible – in short, with giant rust belts.[12]

Of course, it was worse than this. It was not just the adherence to an outdated, inflexible model that prevented adequate progress, but all of the well-known failures of socialism. The point is that the struggle to keep out the world market, to exclude knowledge about what was going on in the more successful capitalist world, became more and more difficult. It also became more dangerous because it threatened to deepen backwardness. Finally, what had been possible in the early stages of communism, when the leadership was fresh and idealistic about creating a more perfect world, no longer succeeded in the face of the growing awareness and cynicism about the model's failure.

But the Soviet and East European leaders in the Brezhnev years were very aware of their growing problems. Much of their time was spent trying to come up with solutions that would nevertheless preserve the key elements of party rule, Soviet power, and the new ruling class's power and privilege. The Soviets urged their East European dependencies to overcome their problems by plunging into Western markets. That was the aim of détente. China, of course, followed the same path after 1978. This meant borrowing to buy advanced technology, and then trying to sell to the West to repay the debts. But as we now know, the plan did not work. The Stalinist systems were too rigid. Managers resisted change. They used their political clout to force ever greater investments in obsolete firms and production processes. Also, in some cases, most notably in Poland and Hungary, foreign loans started to be used simply to purchase consumer goods to make

25

people happier, to shore up the crumbling legitimacy of regimes that had lost what youthful vigor they had once possessed and were now viewed simply as tools of a backward occupying power. This worked until the bills came due, and prices had to be raised. Societies with little or no experience with free markets responded to price increases with political instability. This was especially true in Poland, but it became a potential problem in Hungary (and China) because it created growing and very visible social inequities between the small class of new petty entrepreneurs and the large portion of the urban population still dependent on the socialist sector.[13] (Kornai and others have explained why the partial freeing of the market in economies of shortage create quasi-monopolistic situations favoring the rapid accumulation of profits by those entrepreneurs able to satisfying long repressed, immense demand.)[14]

What had seemed at first to be a series of sensible reforms proved to be the last gasp of European communism. The reforms did not eliminate the rigidities of Stalinism, but they spread further cynicism and disillusionment, exacerbated corruption, and opened the communist world to a vastly increased flow of Western capitalist ideas and standards of consumerism. They also created a major debt problem. In this situation, the only East European leader who responded with perfect consistency was Ceauşescu. He reimposed strict Stalinism. But neither Romania's principled Stalinism, Hungarian semireformism, nor Polish inconsistency and hesitation worked.[15]

Political and moral causes of change

If understanding economic problems is fundamental, it is nevertheless the changing moral and political climate of Eastern Europe that really destroyed communism there. There is no better way to approach this topic than by using the old concept of legitimacy. Revolutions occur only when elites and some significant portion of the general population – particularly intellectuals, but also ordinary people – have lost confidence in the moral validity of their social and political system.

There have never been advanced industrial countries, except at the end of major, catastrophic wars, in which the basic legitimacy of the system collapsed. And if some serious questions were raised in Germany after World War I, France in 1940, or Germany and Japan in 1945, there were no successful revolutions there. It would be laughable to claim that Eastern Europe's economic problems in the 1980s approached such levels of massive crisis as those brought about by utter defeat in international war. To have had such revolutionary situations developing in times of peace and relative stability, in societies with a strong sense of their nationhood, with functioning infrastructures, police forces, armies, and governments, in the absence of foreign invaders or international crises, without precipitating civil wars, famines, or even depressions, is unprecedented. No mere recitation of economic problems can provide sufficient explanation.

To see how this loss of legitimacy occurred, it is necessary to go back to the beginning. In the mid to late 1940s, at least among cadres and a substantial number of young idealists, communism had a considerable degree of legitimacy, even where it had been imposed by force, as in all of Eastern Europe. After all, capitalism seemed to have performed poorly in the 1930s, the liberal European democracies had done little to stop Hitler until it was too late, and Stalin appeared to be a leader who had saved the Soviet Union. The claim that Marxism-Leninism was the "progressive," inevitable wave of the future was not so farfetched. In fact, many intellectuals throughout Europe, East and West, were seduced by these promises.[16]

In the Soviet Union itself, as in China after 1949, communism benefited from the substantial nationalist accomplishments it had to its credit. Foreigners had been defeated and national greatness reasserted. For all of the problems faced by these regimes, there was clear economic growth and extraordinary progress.[17]

The repressions, terror, and misery of life in the early 1950s soured some believers, but after Stalin's death, reform seemed possible. And after all, the claims made about rapid urbanization, industrialization, and the spread of modern health and educational benefits to the population were true. Not 1956, when the Hungarian revolution was crushed, but 1968 was the decisive turning point. That was when the implications of the Brezhnev policy became clear. Fundamental political reform was not going to be allowed. It must be said in Brezhnev's defense that what happened in 1989, in both Eastern Europe and China, has proved that in a sense his policy of freezing reform was perfectly correct. To have done otherwise would have brought about an earlier demise of communism. Economic liberalization gives new hope for political liberalization to the growing professional and bureaucratic middle classes and to the intelligentsia. It further increases the appeal of liberal economic ideas as well as of democracy. The demand for less rigid central control obviously threatens the party's monopoly of power.

Whatever potential communist liberalism may have had in the Prague Spring of 1968, the way in which it was crushed, and the subsequent gradual disillusion with strictly economic reform in Hungary and Poland in the 1970s, brought to an end the period in which intellectuals could continue to hope about the future of communism.

But this was not all. The very inflexibility of communist economies, the unending shortages, and the overwhelming bureaucratization of every aspect of life created a general malaise. The only way to survive in such systems was through corruption, the formal violation of the rules. That, in turn, left many, perhaps almost all of the managerial and professional class, open to the possibility of blackmail, and to a pervasive sense that they were living a perpetual lie.[18]

Then, too, there was the fact that the original imposition of the Stalinist model had created tyranny, the arbitrary rule of the few. One of the characteristics of all tyranny, whether ideological and visionary, as in this case, or merely self-serving and corrupt, is that it creates the possibility for the dissemination and reproduction of petty tyranny. With tyrants at the top, entire bureaucracies become filled with tyrants at every level, behaving arbitrarily and out of narrow self-interest. The tyrants at the top cannot hope to enforce their will unless they have subservient officials, and to buy that subservience they have to allow their underlings to enjoy the fruits of arbitrary power. In any case, arbitrary, petty tyranny becomes the only model of proper, authoritative behavior.

This is one of the explanations given in recent attempts to explain the almost uncontrolled spread of purges in the USSR in the 1930s, and of course the ravages of the Chinese Cultural Revolution from 1966 to 1976. Once the model is set from the top, imitating that behavior becomes a way of ensuring survival for officials. But even beyond that, a tyrannical system gives opportunities for abuse that do not otherwise exist, and lower level officials use this to further their own narrow ends. (This is not meant to suggest that in some way the tyrants who ruled such systems, and their immediate followers, can be absolved of responsibility for the abuses; it does imply that the way tyrannies exercise power is necessarily deeply corrupt.)[19]

Daily exposure to petty tyranny, which at the local level rarely maintains the ideological high ground that may have inspired a Lenin, Stalin, Mao, or even a Ceauşescu, also breeds gradual disgust with corruption and the dishonesty of the whole system. In the past, peasants subjected to such petty tyranny may have borne it more or less stoically (unless it went too far), but educated urbanites living in a highly politicized atmosphere where there are constant pronouncements about the guiding ideological vision of fairness, equality, and progress could not help but react with growing disgust.[20]

In that sense, the very success of communism in creating a more urban, more educated, more aware population also created the potential for disintegration. The endless corruption, the lies, the collapse of elementary social trust, the petty tyranny at every level – these were aspects of life less easily tolerated by the new working and professional classes than they might have been by peasants. (This remains, of course, the advantage of the Chinese communists; they can still rely on a vast reservoir of peasant indifference and respect for authority as long as agriculture is not resocialized.)[21]

The whole movement to create alternate social institutions, free of the corruption and dishonesty of the official structures, was the great ideological innovation that began to emerge in Poland in the 1970s and 1980s in the efforts to establish a "civil society." Traditional revolutionary resistance, taking to the streets, covert military actions, and assassinations were all generally fruitless because they provoked heavy military intervention by the Soviets. But by simply beginning to turn away from the state, by refusing to take it seriously, Polish and then other Central European intellectuals exposed the shallowness of communism's claims, and broke what little legitimacy communist regimes still had. Because of his early understanding of this fact, and his excellent descriptions of how this new ideology grew in Central Europe, Timothy Garton Ash has earned his justly deserved fame.[22]

Certainly, in the Soviet Union all these forces were at work, too, but the patriotism engendered by superpower status (though it has turned out that this was largely Russian, not "Soviet" pride and patriotism), the sheer size of the military, and the long history of successful police terror and repression kept the situation under better control than in much of Central Europe. Yet, combined with the slow erosion of legitimacy was the fundamental economic problem of failure to keep up with the rapidly emerging fifth industrial age in Western Europe, in the United States, and – most astonishingly for the Soviets – in East Asia.[23]

There is no doubt that in the mid-1980s, after Solidarity had apparently been crushed in Poland, with the Soviets massacring Afghan resistance fighters, with Cuban troops successfully defending Angola, and with Vietnam controlling all of Indochina, it seemed to the rest of the world that Soviet military might was insurmountable in countries where the Soviet system had been imposed. But underneath, the rot was spreading. So the question is not "What was wrong with Eastern Europe" or "Why was communism so weak?" Every specialist and many casual observers knew perfectly well what was wrong. But almost none guessed that what had been a slowly developing situation for several decades might take such a sudden turn for the worse. After all, the flaws of socialist economic planning had been known for a long time. Endemic corruption, tyranny, arbitrary brutality, and the use of sheer police force to maintain communist parties in power were hardly new occurrences. None of them answer the question, "Why 1989?" Almost all analysts thought the Soviet system would remain more or less intact in the USSR and in Eastern Europe for decades.

To understand why this did not happen requires a shift in analysis from a discussion of general trends to a review of some specific events in the 1980s.

The events of the 1980s

If there was a central, key series of developments that began to unravel the entire system, it has to be in the interaction between events in Poland in

29

the early 1980s and a growing perception by the Soviet leadership that their own problems were becoming very serious.

As late as 1987, and throughout most of 1988, most specialists felt that the Soviet elite did not understand the severity of their economic situation. Gorbachev almost certainly did, as did many of the Moscow intellectuals. But there was some question about the lesser cadres, and even many of the top people of the government. But as Gorbachev's mild reforms failed to have a beneficial impact, as the original impact of his policy of openness, encouragement, and antialcoholism ran into sharply diminishing returns, the Soviet economy began to slip back into the stagnation of the late Brezhnev years.[24]

Serious as rising discontent in the Soviet Union might have seemed to Gorbachev, of more immediate concern was the direct military threat of the Soviet's inability to keep up with the developments of the fifth industrial age. While the Soviet nuclear deterrent was unquestionably safe and effective in preventing a frontal attack by the United States, the growing gap between Western and Soviet computer and electronic technology threatened to give NATO (and ultimately Japan) a striking advantage in conventional weapons. This is almost certainly why the Soviets were so worried about "Star Wars," not simply because the illusion of an effective antiballistic missile defense was likely to unbalance the nuclear arms race. Pouring billions into this kind of research was likely to yield important new advantages in lesser types of electronic warfare that could be applied to conventional air and tank battles. This would nullify the Soviet's numerical advantage in men and machines, and threaten Soviet military investments throughout the world.[25]

Given the long-standing recognition by the major powers that nuclear war was out of the question, a growing advantage by the capitalist powers in electronic warfare threatened to turn any future local confrontation between Western and Soviet allies into a repetition of the Syrian–Israeli air war of 1982. From the Soviet point of view, the unbelievable totality of Israel's success was a warning of future catastrophes, even if Israel's land war in Lebanon turned out to be a major failure.[26]

There was one other, chance event that precipitated change in the Soviet Union by revealing to the leadership the extent of the country's industrial ineptitude. This was the Chernobyl catastrophe. But unlucky as it may have been, it served more to confirm what was already suspected than to initiate any changes. The fact is that many such massive industrial and environmental accidents have happened in the Soviet Union. When they occurred in the past, they had little effect, though throughout the 1970s and 1980s there was a growing environmental movement. But on top of everything else, the 1986 nuclear plant accident seemed to galvanize Gorbachev and his advisers.[27]

Meanwhile, in Eastern Europe, the communist orthodoxy imposed under Brezhnev was seriously threatened in Poland. Rising discontent there had made Poland ungovernable by the mid-1980s. It seemed that Hungary was going to follow soon. Economic reforms were not working, the population was increasingly alienated, and while there was no outward sign of immediate revolt, the Jaruzelski regime had no idea how to bring the situation under sufficient control to carry out any measures that might reverse the economic decline and help regain the trust (rather than the mere grudging and cynical acceptance) of the population.[28]

In retrospect, then, the events in Poland in the late 1970s, from the election of a Polish pope, which galvanized the Poles and created the massive popular demonstrations that led to the creation of Solidarity, to the military coup that seemed to destroy Solidarity, had set the stage for what was to happen. But the slow degeneration of the situation in Poland, or in all of Eastern Europe, would not have been enough to produce the events of 1989 had it not been for the Soviet crisis. On the other hand, had there been no breakdown of authority in Poland, and a looming, frightening sense of economic crisis and popular discontent in Hungary, and probably in the other East European countries as well, the Soviets would certainly have tried to carry out some reforms without giving up their European empire. The two aspects of the crisis came together, and this is why everything unraveled so quickly in the late 1980s.[29]

Gorbachev must have realized that it was only a matter of time until there was an explosion – a bread riot leading to a revolution in Poland, or a major strike in Hungary – which would oblige the government to call out the army. The problem was that neither the Polish nor the Hungarian army was particularly reliable. The special police could always be counted on, but if they were overwhelmed, it would be necessary to call in Soviet troops. This the Soviet economy could not bear if it was also to reform itself enough to begin to meet the challenges of the fifth industrial age, especially if this involved increased trade and other contacts with the advanced capitalist countries.

I believe that sometime in 1988 Gorbachev decided he must head off the danger before it was too late to prevent a catastrophic crisis.[30] I cannot prove this, because the documentation is not available, but I am almost certain that because of this decision, in discussions with the Poles there emerged the plan to allow partly free elections and the reopening of talks with Solidarity. The aim would be to relegitimize the regime, and give it enough breathing room to carry out economic reforms without risking strikes and massive civil disobedience. The idea of "roundtable" talks between Solidarity and the regime was proposed in a televised debate between Lech Wałęsa and a regime representative on November 30, 1988. The talks themselves began February 6, 1989.[31]

It did not work. The reason is that everyone – Gorbachev, the communist parties of Eastern Europe, foreign specialists, and intelligence services in NATO and the Warsaw Pact – vastly underestimated the degree to which the moral bankruptcy of communism had destroyed any possibility of relegitimizing it.

There was something else, too – an event whose import was not fully appreciated in the West, and which remains almost unmentioned. In January 1989, Gorbachev tried an experiment. He pulled almost all of the Soviet army out of Afghanistan. The United States and the Pakistani army expected this to result in the rapid demise of the communist regime there. To everyone's surprise, it did not. I think this might have been an important card for Gorbachev. He could point to Afghanistan when his conservative opponents, and especially his military, questioned his judgment. Afghanistan was proof that the Soviets could partly disengage without suffering catastrophe, and that in some cases it might even be better to let local communists handle their own problems. I suspect that a rapid victory by the anticommunist guerrillas in Afghanistan would have slowed progress in Eastern Europe, if not ending it entirely.[32]

We know how rapidly event followed event. Despite the patently unfair arrangements for the Polish election designed to keep the communist party in power, the electorate refused, and party rule collapsed. Since the Soviets had agreed to the process, and wanted to avoid, at almost any cost, a war of invasion, they let Poland go. Once it became obvious that this was happening, the Hungarians set out on the same path.[33]

Then, partly out of a well-timed sense of public relations, just before George Bush's visit, the Hungarians officially opened their border with Austria. In fact, the border had no longer been part of any "iron curtain" for a long time, but this move gave thousands of vacationing East Germans the idea that they could escape to the West. We know that this set off a mass hysteria among East Germans, who had given up hope of reform, and whose demoralization and disgust with their system led hundreds of thousands to want to flee. They rushed to West German embassies in Budapest and Prague, and began demonstrating in East Germany, particularly in Leipzig and Dresden.[34]

The failure of communism in East Germany in many ways represents the ultimate failure. Here was a country that was not poor, where there were two hundred automobiles for every thousand inhabitants, and where for years Western, particularly West German, sympathizers had said that communism was working by producing a more communal, more kindly Germany than the harsh, market-driven, materialistic West German Federal Republic. It was another misconception born of wishful thinking.[35]

It is known that Honecker ordered repressive measures. Earlier, during the summer, Chinese officials had visited East Berlin to brief the East Germans on how to crush prodemocracy movements. But during his early October visit to East Germany, Gorbachev had publicly called for change and let it be known that the Soviets would not intervene to stop reform.[36]

Now, in October, ambulances were readied to cart away the thousands of dead and injured bodies in Leipzig and perhaps Dresden that were sure to be produced by the crackdown. This was prevented. Most accounts credit a local initiative in Leipzig led by the conductor Kurt Masur, although the central party machinery, taken in hand by Egon Krenz, also played a pacifying role. It is likely that an appeal was made to the Soviets, and that the local Soviet military commander said he would not intervene. Knowing this, the East German Communist Party simply overthrew Honecker rather than risk physical annihilation.[37]

East Germany was no China, despite Honecker's claim that it would be. It had no reserve of ignorant, barely literate peasant boys to bring into the breach; and its economy was far too dependent on the West German connection to risk a break. So, once repression was abandoned, the system collapsed in a few weeks. With East Germany crumbling, the whole edifice of communist rule in Eastern Europe simply collapsed. On November 9 the Berlin Wall was opened. It was no longer possible to maintain it when the government of East Germany was losing control over its population, and the rate of flight was increasing at such a rapid rate.

East Germany was always the key Soviet position in Europe.[38] It was on the internal German border that the cold war began, and it was there that the military might of the two superpowers was concentrated. When the Soviets abandoned the East German hard-liners, there was no hope anywhere else in Eastern Europe. The Bulgarians followed in order to preserve what they could of the party, and Todor Zhivkov resigned after thirty-five years in power on the day after the Berlin Wall was opened (November 10). This was surely no coincidence. A week later demonstrations began in Prague, and within ten days it was over. Only Ceauşescu of Romania resisted.[39]

Enough is now known about Ceauşescu's Romania that it is unnecessary to give much background. Only three points must be made.

First, Ceauşescu himself still held on to the Stalinist vision. Aside from the possible exception of Albania (which began to change in the spring of 1990),[40] there was only one other communist country where the model was so unquestioned – North Korea. In fact, Ceauşescu and Kim Il Sung long considered themselves close allies and friends, and their style of rule had many similarities. Yet in Romania, and probably in North Korea, this model turned sour about two decades ago, and pursuing it meant economic stagnation, a growing gap between reality and ideology, and the progressive alienation of even the most loyal cadres.[41]

Second, Romania was the most independent of the Warsaw Pact European countries, and so felt itself less dependent on Soviet support.

33

But though this brought considerable legitimacy to the Romanian regime in the 1970s, when partial independence was thought to be grounds for hope, by the late 1980s that hope had failed, and the intellectuals, as well as a growing number of ordinary urban people, had noticed that the Soviet Union had become more progressive than Romania.[42] In southern Romania they listened to Bulgarian television and radio, and when they heard that even there (for the Romanians Bulgaria has always been a butt of jokes as a backward, thick-headed, peasant nation) there were reforms, it must have had a considerable impact. In the north and west, Romanians could pick up the Hungarian and Yugoslav media, and so be informed about what was going on elsewhere. In the east, of course, they had the example of the Soviet Union, and of Romanian-speaking Soviet Moldavia, where, for the first time since the 1940s, people were freer to demonstrate than in Romania itself. I should add that aside from broadcasts from these neighboring countries, Radio Free Europe also played a major role in educating Romanians about what was going on elsewhere in Eastern Europe. The point is that, again unlike China, it proved impossible to keep news about the world out of the reach of the interior.

Finally, and this is much less known than other aspects of Romania's recent history, even at its height the Ceauşescu regime relied heavily on the fear of Soviet invasion to legitimize itself. There was always the underlying assumption that if there was too much trouble, Soviet tanks would come in. Was it not better to suffer a patriotic Romanian tyrant than another episode of Soviet occupation? Once it became clear, in 1989, that the Soviets were not going to march, the end was in sight. It was only because Ceauşescu himself was so out of touch with reality, and because he had so successfully destroyed his communist party by packing it with relatives and sycophants (like Kim Il Sung), that no one told him the truth, and he was thus unable to manage the more peaceful, gradual, and dignified exit of his Bulgarian colleague Todor Zhivkov.[43]

So, in the end, communism collapsed. The ramifications are far from clear, and there is no way of knowing how things will develop in the Soviet Union. But come what may in the USSR, it is certain that the Soviet empire in Eastern Europe is dead, and that there are almost no foreseeable circumstances that would make the Soviet army invade any of its former dependencies. We cannot be sure what directions the various revolutions of Eastern Europe will take, though it is safe to predict that there will be important differences from country to country. On the whole, it is also possible to be somewhat optimistic about the future of Eastern Europe, or at least its northern "Central European" parts, if not necessarily the Balkans and the Soviet Union. Why this is so I shall leave to my concluding remarks, in which I will try to draw together some of the lessons Eastern Europe has taught us about revolution and social change in general.

The causes of revolution in advanced societies

Eastern Europe and the traditional causes

Most widely accepted sociological models of revolution are of limited help in explaining what happened in Eastern Europe in 1989. There was no sudden fall in well-being after a long period of improvement. If the Polish, Hungarian, and Romanian economies were deteriorating (at very different rates), those of East Germany and Czechoslovakia were not causing immediate problems. People felt deprived when they compared themselves with West Europeans, but this had been true for well over three decades. In Poland, as a matter of fact, the sharpest period of economic deterioration was in the early 1980s, and though the situation had not improved much since then, it could be assumed that people were getting used to it.[44]

In Poland, a prolonged period of protest was marked by open explosions in 1956, 1968, 1970, 1976, and of course 1980–81. As time advanced, Poles learned to organize better and more effectively. But this gradual mobilization and organization seemed to have been decisively broken by the military seizure of power. In fact, there is good evidence that the party and police had learned even more from the long series of protests than the protesters themselves, and had become adept at handling trouble with just the right level of violence. Certainly, in the early 1980s the Jaruzelski regime was able to impose peacefully a whole series of price increases that in the past had provoked massive, violent uprisings.[45]

Only in Hungary was there much open mobilization of protest in the late 1980s, and that only in the last couple of years. Much of it was over ecological and nationalist issues that did not take the form of direct antiregime activity. In fact, the communists even supported some of this activity.[46]

None of the other countries had much open dissent. At most, in Czechoslovakia a few, seemingly isolated intellectuals had organized themselves, but they had no followers. In East Germany the Protestant churches had supported some limited draft protests and a small peace movement, but the regime had never been directly threatened. In Bulgaria only a handful of intellectuals ever made any claims to protest. In Romania, there had been some isolated outbreaks of strikes in the late 1970s, and a major riot in Brasov, in 1987, but there even intellectual protest was muted, rarely going beyond very limited literary activities.[47]

Nor was the international position of the East European countries at stake. Whereas in the Soviet Union, key elites, particularly in the KGB, saw the impending danger to the USSR's international strength, in Eastern Europe no one cared about this kind of issue. None of the East European elites saw their countries as potentially powerful nations, nor was their national existence threatened by any outsiders except the Soviets. And that threat, present since 1945, was now so highly attenuated as to be almost absent. That the Soviets were unpopular in Eastern Europe was a given, and a very old one, but there was no new risk of further intervention or damage because of these countries' weakness.[48]

Perhaps, however, the debt crisis in Poland and Hungary (and in Romania, because it had provoked such harsh and damaging counter-measures by Ceauşescu) was the equivalent of visible international failure that exposed the incapacity of the regimes. But though this remained severe in Polant and Hungary in the late 1980s, elsewhere the problem was not acute.[49]

Nor can a very strong case be made for the rise of an economically power-ful new class fighting for political power. Political and economic power was firmly in the hands of what Djilas had called the New Class. But that class, the professional party cadres, had been in charge for four decades, and it seemed neither highly dissatisfied nor in any way revolutionary. The leadership of the revolutions, if there was any, was in the hands of a few intellectuals who represented no particular class.[50]

Poland, of course, was different. There, an alliance between the Catholic Church, the unionized working class, and dissident intellectuals was very well organized, and it had almost taken power in 1980. But the days of Solidarity seemed to have passed, and the regime reasserted visible control. Virtually none of the Polish opposition thought there was much chance of success in an open, violent confrontation. So even in Poland, this was not a traditional revolution. The opportunity for that had passed with the successful imposition of martial law.[51]

What happened was that the moral base of communism had vanished. The elites had lost confidence in their legitimacy. The intellectuals, power-less as they seemed to be, disseminated this sense of moral despair and cor-ruption to the public by their occasional protests and veiled commentaries, and the urban public was sufficiently well educated and aware to under-stand what was going on. The cumulative effect of such a situation, over decades, cannot be underestimated. Those who had had hope, during the 1940s and 1950s, were replaced by those who had never had hope and who had grown up knowing that everything was a lie. Educated youths, not just university students but high school students as well, knew enough about the rest of the world to realize that they had been lied to, that they had been cheated, and that their own leaders did not believe the lies.[52]

What took everyone by surprise was the discovery that the situation was not all that different in the Soviet Union. Nor could anyone foresee the kind of panicked realism, combined with astounding flexibility and willingness to compromise, shown by Gorbachev. In the end, this was the reason revo-lution came in 1989 rather than in the 1990s, But, sooner or later, it would have happened.

Eastern Europe and other modern revolutions

This brings up a serious issue. It has long been assumed that modern methods of communication and the awesome power of tanks, artillery, and air power would prevent the kind of classical revolution that has shaken the world so many times since 1789.

Even relatively inefficient regimes, such as the Russian autocracy, or the Kuomintang (KMT) in China, fought successfully against revolution until their armies were decisively weakened by outside invaders. In China's case, it took the communists two decades to build the strong army that finally won power for them, and they probably would have failed had it not been for the Japanese invasion.[53]

Many utterly corrupt, weak African, Asian, and Latin American regimes have held on to power for a long time with little more than mercenary armies whose loyalties were purchased by allowing them to loot their own countries. This is what goes on, for example, in Myanmar (formerly Burma), Guatemala, and Zaire. Cases where such regimes were overthrown show that it takes long years of guerrilla organization and warfare to carry out revolutions, and then the chances of success are slim. If revolutions occurred in Batista's Cuba and Somoza's Nicaragua, in Uganda Idi Amin held on until he foolishly provoked Tanzania into attacking him. If Baby Doc Duvalier was frightened into leaving office in Haiti, it is not clear, even today, that the Duvalier system has been removed fully.[54]

Finally even anticolonial wars, in which the overwhelming majority of populations have sympathized with revolutionary movements, have been long, bloody events when the colonizers have chosen to fight back, as the Dutch did in Indonesia, the French in Indochina and Algeria, and the British in Kenya and Malaya (where, however, the Malay population rallied to the British side against the Chinese revolutionaries). A particularly startling case was the Bangladesh war, when massive popular opposition to Pakistani rule still needed help from an Indian military invasion to get rid of the Pakistani army.[55]

Only internal military coups, as when the Ethiopian or – much earlier the Egyptian monarchies were removed, seem to make for relatively easy revolutions.[56]

But none of these types of revolutions fit what happened in Eastern Europe. There, even if the Romanian case is included, the total level of bloodshed was minuscule compared with other revolutions. There were no military coups. In Romania there was almost certainly cooperation between the army and the population, but no direct coup, and that was the only case where the army was involved at all. But compared with any African, Latin American, or almost any noncommunist Asian dictatorship, the East European communist regimes were overwhelmingly strong. They had large, effective, loyal secret police forces, an abundance of tanks and soldiers led by well-trained (though not necessarily enthusiastic) officers, excellent internal communications, and no threat of external, hostile invasion. Only in Romania was the army thoroughly alienated.

Again, we are left with the same explanation: utter moral rot.

Few observers have noticed a startling parallel between events in Eastern Europe in 1989 and in Iran in 1979. There, too, the shah should have been stronger. But even though there were a lot of deaths in the final days, and months of rioting before the shah's departure in January, many were taken by surprise by the overwhelming lack of legitimacy of the regime. Even the newly prosperous middle classes and the young professionals, who had much to lose if the shah was overthrown, failed to back him.[57]

While this is not a suitable place to discuss Iranian society and politics in the 1960s and 1970s, it is evident that the rapid modernization and urbanization of the society helped its intellectuals disseminate their feelings of disgust about the shah's regime, with its empty posturing, its lies, its torturers, its corruption, and its lack of redeeming moral values.

We can wonder, of course, to what extent the rising intellectual and professional classes in urban France in 1787 to 1789 felt the same way about the French monarchy, church, and aristocracy, and the extent to which such feelings played a decisive role in unleashing that revolution. We know that in Petrograd and Moscow from 1915 to 1917, whatever the level of popular misery, the professional and middle classes felt a good bit of disgust at the corruption and lack of morality at the imperial court.

The lesson may be that in fact we need to combine some Marxist notions of class with an understanding of John Rawls's theory of justice as fairness to understand what happened in Eastern Europe.[58] Economic modernization did, indeed, produce a larger middle class (not in the sense of bourgeois ownership, of course, but in the cultural and educational sense, as well as in its style of life). That class was in some ways quite favored in communist regimes. But because of the flaws of the socialist system of economic management, it remained poorer than its West European counterpart, and even seemed to be falling further behind by the 1980s. That is the Marxist, or class and material, basis of what happened.

But more important, the educated middle classes in a modern society are well informed, and can base their judgments about morality on a wider set of observations than those with very limited educations. The artistic and literary intellectuals who addressed their work to these middle classes helped them understand and interpret the immorality of the system, and so played a major role. They needed receptive audiences, but it was their work that undid East European communism.

Without the social changes associated with the economic transformations that took place in Eastern Europe from 1948 to 1988, these revolutions would not have taken place. But it was not so much that new classes were striving for power as that a growing number saw through the lies on which the whole system was based. That is what utterly destroyed the will of those in power to resist.

Once these conditions were set, the massive popular discontent with material conditions, particularly on the part of the working classes in the giant but stagnating industries that dominated communist economies, could come out into the streets and push these regimes over.

Models and morals

That raises three final points. First, the fundamental reason for the failure of communism was that the utopian model it proposed was obviously not going to come into being. Almost everything else could have been tolerated if the essential promise was on its way to fulfilment. But once it was clear that the model was out of date, and its promise increasingly based on lies, its immorality became unbearable. Perhaps, in the past, when other ideologically based models failed to deliver their promises, systems could still survive because the middle classes and intellectuals were present in smaller numbers. But in an advanced society the absurdity of basing a whole social system on an outdated industrial age was more than economic mistake. It undermined the whole claim to scientific validity which lay at the heart of Marxism-Leninism.

Second, much of the standard of morality that created such a revolutionary situation in Eastern Europe was based on the middle classes' interpretation of what was going on in other countries, namely in Western Europe. This is one reason why, despite all the economic and political troubles that are sure to accumulate in the near feature in Eastern Europe, there is some reason for optimism. Western Europe is no longer the warlike set of competing imperialistic powers it was when the East Europeans first began to look to the West as their model in the nineteenth century, and through 1939. All of Western Europe is democratic, its various countries cooperate very well with each other, and on the whole have abandoned their imperialistic pretensions. This means that, as a model, Western Europe is a far healthier place than it was in the past.

This does not mean that all future revolutionary intellectuals and scandalized middle classes will look to Western Europe, or the United States, as their model. After all, the Iranians looked to Islam, and it is only because Eastern Europe has long been so close to Western Europe that it automatically looks in that direction.

Third, we must come to realize that in the twenty-first century there will still be economic problems, political instability, and revolutions. But more than ever, the fundamental causes of revolutionary instability will be moral. The urban middle and professional classes, the intellectuals and those to whom they most directly appeal, will set the tone of political change. Regimes to which they do not accord legitimacy because these regimes are seen as unfair and dishonest will be shaky. When these classes can be persuaded to defend their own narrow material interests, when they accept immoral and unfair behavior, then regimes, no matter how corrupt, will be safe. But it would be foolish for regimes that are defending essentially unjust social systems to rely too much on the continued acquiescence of their middle classes and intellectuals.

But many of us who study social change must be reminded that we barely know how to study moral perceptions and legitimacy. We have been so busy studying material changes, which are, after all, more easily measured and perceived, that we do not know where to look to sense the moral pulse of key classes and intellectuals. In some ways, the lesson of Eastern Europe has this to offer too. Sometimes literature written for what seems to be a handful of people is a better measure of the true state of mind of a society than public opinion polls, economic statistics, or overt political behavior.

An alternative "civil society" – places where people could interact freely and without government interference, where they could turn their backs on the party-state's corruption – was in creation in Eastern Europe before 1989. This alternative civil society was the creation of intellectuals, novelists, playwrights, poets, historians, and philosophers like Václav Havel, Miklós Haraszti, Adam Michnik, George Konrád, and hundreds of other, less famous ones. In a sense, in their literature and pamphlets, in their small discussion circles, they imagined a future that most of their people could only dimly perceive, and which hardly anyone believed possible.

Vladimir Tismaneanu, in an article entitled "Eastern Europe: The Story the Media Missed," correctly pointed out that most Western observers never grasped the significance of this creation of an alternative "civil society."[59] That is, almost correctly, because even before 1989 those most closely following the intellectual life of East Central Europe were aware of what was going on, and were writing about it. Timothy Garton Ash was the best known, but a few other scholars saw it too.[60] On the whole, however, most of the specialists on communism were too hard-headed, too realistic, and even too dependent on social-science models to take such highly intellectualized discussions seriously.

After the fact, it is easy for us to say this. Before the fact, almost none of us saw it.

Notes

Source Reprinted by permission of the publisher from *The Crisis of Leninism and the Decline of the Left*, ed. Daniel Chirot (Seattle, WA: University of Washington Press, 1991), pp. 3–32. Copyright © 1991 University of Washington Press.

Acknowledgment I would like to thank Tim McDaniel for his helpful comments on this paper.

1 Because of the second centennial anniversary in 1989, this has been a particularly busy period for the publication of new works on the French Revolution. That the event still generates considerable excitement is shown by the controversies about Simon Schama's hostile critique of the Revolution, *Citizens: A Chronicle of the French Revolution* (New York: Knopf, 1988). A more positive evaluation is Eric J. Hobsbawm's *Echoes of the Marseillaise: Two Centuries Look Back on the French Revolution* (New Brunswick: Rutgers University Press, 1990). A lively review essay about recent books on the Revolution is Benjamin R. Barber's "The Most Sublime Event," *The Nation*, March 12, 1990, pp. 351–60.

2 A review of the condition and prospects for the East European economies can be found in *East European Politics and Societies* 2:3 (Fall 1988), "Special Issue on Economic Reform," ed. John R. Lampe. Although the articles in this issue emphasize the region's economic problems, not all are pessimistic, and none predicted the astounding political changes that were to begin within months of publication. The same is true of a slightly older, but still recent, review of Eastern Europe's economies, with some comparative chapters on other socialist economies in Ellen Comisso and Laura Tyson, eds., *Power, Purpose, and Collective Choice: Economic Strategy in the Socialist States* (Ithaca, NY: Cornell University Press, 1986). A surprisingly positive account of the Soviet economy published a few years ago by Ed A. Hewett also seemed to soften the nature of the crisis, even though Hewett gave an excellent account of the many problems facing the Soviets. See his *Reforming the Soviet Economy: Equality Versus Efficiency* (Washington D.C.: Brookings Institution, 1988).

3 János Kornai, *Economics of Shortage*, 2 vols. (Amsterdam: North Holland, 1980), and Wlodzimierz Brus, *Socialist Ownership and Political Systems* (London: Allen and Unwin, 1977).

4 The popular resistance to accepting capitalist profits should not, after all, be surprising. Karl Polanyi's seminal work, *The Great Transformation* (Boston, MA: Beacon, 1957), showed how difficult it was for the English to accept the notion that market forces should regulate the economy in the early nineteenth century. By now, the capitalist West has had almost two centuries to get used to this dramatic change in the organizing principles of society, but only in the last few decades has resistance to the market waned in Western Europe. That Eastern Europeans, and even more the Russians, should view markets with suspicion is understandable. Among the many discussions of this, Geoffrey Hosking's book, *The Awakening of the Soviet Union* (Cambridge, MA: Harvard University Press, 1990), is particularly good. He writes: "How many times over the last year or two have I heard Soviet citizens use the word 'speculator' to disparage private traders or co operatives providing at high prices goods and services seldom available at all in the state sector? This sullen egalitarianism dovetails neatly with the interest of the party-state apparatus in retaining their network of controls and hence their grip on the economy" (p. 132).

5 On China, see Nicholas Lardy, *Agriculture in China's Modern Economic Development* (Cambridge: Cambridge University Press, 1983), pp. 190–221. On Hungary see Tamás Bauer, "The Hungarian Alternative to Soviet-Type Planning," *Journal of Comparative Economics* 7:3 (1983), pp. 304–16. See also Ellen Comisso and Paul Marer, "The Economics and Politics of Reform in Hungary," in Comisso and Tyson, eds., *Power, Purpose, and Collective Choice*, pp. 245–78.

6 Although the story is now well known, it is worth reviewing the nightmarish quality of this success. For a good account, see the essays in Moshe Lewin, *The Making of the Soviet System* (New York: Pantheon, 1985).

7 The attempt to fit the industrial era into such simple stages oversimplifies its economic history. Walt W. Rostow identifies nine "trend periods" in *The World Economy: History and Prospect* (Austin, TX: University of Texas Press, 1978), pp. 298–348. My industrial ages group together his first and second periods (1790–1848), take his third period (1848–73) as a distinct age, group together his fourth and fifth periods (1873–1920), his sixth, seventh, and eighth periods (1920–72), and consider his ninth (starting in 1972) as the beginning of a new industrial age. I rely more on the history of technology provided by David S. Landes in *The Unbound Prometheus: Technological Change and Industrial Development in Western Europe from 1750 to the Present* (Cambridge: Cambridge University Press, 1969) and by the various authors in Carlo M. Cipolla's edited series, *The Fontana Economic History of Europe* (Glasgow: Fontana/Collins, vols. 4–6, 1973–76), than on price data and business cycles. I explain my reasoning more fully in Daniel Chirot, *Social Change in the Modern Era* (San Diego, CA: Harcourt Brace Jovanovich, 1986), pp. 223–30. The point, however, is not to argue about precise periodization, but to recognize that there are different technologies, different types of social organization, and different models of behavior at different stages of the industrial era. The forceful maintenance of an outdated model is one of the main reasons for the backwardness of Soviet-type economies.

8 Karl Polanyi's *The Great Transformation* was one such prediction. So was Lenin's in *Imperialism: The Highest Stage of Capitalism* (New York: International Publishers, 1939). For an account of the ideological effects of the Great Depression of the 1930s on Eastern Europe, see Daniel Chirot, "Ideology, Reality, and Competing Models of Development in Eastern Europe Between the Two World Wars," *East European Politics and Societies* 3:3 (1989), pp. 378–411.

9 Alexander Erlich, *The Soviet Industrialization Debate* (Cambridge, MA: Harvard University Press, 1960). Whether or not this strategy was necessary remains a subject of debate in the Soviet Union, where Stephen F. Cohen's book on Bukharin has been greatly appreciated by the Gorbachev reformers, because Bukharin was the most important ideological opponent of the Stalin line. See Cohen's *Bukharin and the Bolshevik Revolution: A Political Biography, 1888–1938* (Oxford: Oxford University Press, 1980). For Eastern Europe, however, the issue is moot.

10 Vladimir Tismaneanu, "The Tragicomedy of Romanian Communism," *East European Politics and Societies* 3:2 (1989), pp. 329–76, gives the most recent and best short account of the origins and development of the Romanian Communist Party from the prewar period until 1989, and explains Ceaușescu's role in determining its fate.

11 Lardy, *Agriculture in China's Modern Economic Development*, pp. 130, 155, 158, 165.

12 Geoffrey Hosking quotes the Soviet reform economist Otto Latsis, who put it this way: "They build irrigation channels which bring no increase in agricultural production. They produce machine tools for which there are no operators, tractors for which there are no drivers, and threshing machines which they know will not work. Further millions of people supply these superfluous products with electricity, ore, oil, and coal. In return they receive their wages like everyone else, and take them to the shops. There, however, they find no goods to buy, because their work has not produced any." And Hosking also quotes

Soviet Premier Ryzhkov: "We produce more tractors in this country than all the capitalist countries put together. And yet we don't have enough tractors." *The Awakening of the Soviet Union*, p. 134.

13 Kazimierz Poznanski ascribes the failure of the Polish reforms in the second half of the 1970s to political pressure rather than to economic mismanagement, but it would be fruitless to argue about which came first. See his "Economic Adjustment and Political Forces: Poland since 1970," in Comisso and Tyson, eds., *Power, Purpose, and Collective Choice*, pp. 279–312.

14 Comisso and Marer, in their article "The Economics and Politics of Reform in Hungary," cover this and the other major contradictions in the Hungarian economic reforms, pp. 267–78.

15 On the debt crisis and Eastern Europe, see Laura D'Andrea Tyson, "The Debt Crisis and Adjustment Responses in Eastern Europe: A Comparative Perspective," in Comisso and Tyson, eds., *Power, Purpose, and Collective Choice*, pp. 63–110. On Romania, see Ronald H. Linden, "Socialist Patrimonialism and the Global Economy: The Case of Romania," in the same volume pp. 171–204.

16 Jan Gross stresses this in "Social Consequences of War: Preliminaries to the Study of Imposition of Communist Regimes in East Central Europe," *East European Politics and Societies* 3:2 (1989), pp. 213–14. There is no way of quantifying the extent to which youthful enthusiasm helped communist cadres take power and effectively transform their societies in the late 1940s and early 1950s, but the phenomenon is attested to by numerous literary sources describing the period. Even such bitter anticommunists as Milan Kundera, in *The Joke* (New York: Harper and Row, 1982), verify this. Had there never been a substantial body of energized believers, it is unlikely that the sheer force of Soviet military might could have held all of Eastern Europe in its grip. On the other hand, as Gross and others, for example Elemér Hankiss in "Demobilization, Self-Mobilization, and Quasi-Mobilization in Hungary, 1948–1987," *East European Politics and Societies* 3:1 (1989), pp. 105–51, have pointed out, communist regimes worked hard to destroy social cohesion and any type of genuine solidarity, so that in the long run it was inevitable that the enthusiasm of the early intellectual believers would be curbed and debased. As for Western – particularly French – Marxism, Tony Judt believes that it also contributed to the legitimacy of East European communist regimes. See his *Marxism and the French Left* (Oxford: Oxford University Press, 1986), pp. 236–8. Thus the rise and demise of Marxism in Eastern and Western Europe are not wholly separate phenomena, but fed on each other.

17 The best known explanation of communism as nationalism is Chalmers Johnson, *Peasant Nationalism and Communist Power: The Emergence of Revolutionary China, 1937–1945* (Stanford, CA: Stanford University Press, 1962), especially pp. 176–87. Johnson explicitly compares Yugoslavia with China. To varying degrees, but most strongly in Poland, Czechoslovakia, and Albania, the communists were able to make similar claims as national saviors after 1945 elsewhere in Eastern Europe. In East Germany, Hungary, Bulgaria, and Romania, they could at least claim to represent the substantial leftist nationalist sentiments that had been silenced during the period of nazism or the German alliance.

18 Again, it is difficult to quantify feelings of moral revulsion. But the sense of all-pervasive corruption and self-disgust can be grasped in most literature of Eastern Europe, starting in the 1950s and becoming ever more obvious with time. A particularly somber view is given by Petru Dumitriu's *Incognito* (New York: Macmillan, 1964).

19 Although he certainly exaggerates the role of local officials, this is a central theme in J. Arch Getty's revisionist view of the Stalinist purges in *Origins of the Great Purges: The Soviet Communist Party Reconsidered, 1933–1938* (Cambridge: Cambridge University Press, 1985). On the Chinese Cultural Revolution, see Hong Yung Lee, *The Politics of the Chinese Cultural Revolution* (Berkeley and Los Angeles, CA: University of California Press, 1976). While such events could not have begun without central direction, they could not have been carried out without local officials trying to ingratiate themselves by imitating the top. But this very process led to widespread cynicism and corruption, and so had to undermine the long-term legitimacy of communism.

20 James C. Scott's argument about how the violation of a "moral economy's" sense of justice leads to revolts is based on observations of peasants, but it applies even more to urban intellectuals and professionals. It is now evident that they also have a "moral economy," though one tied to their own sense of self-worth rather than to their subsistence. See *The Moral Economy of the Peasant: Rebellion and Subsistence in Southeast Asia* (New Haven, CT: Yale University Press, 1976), particularly pp. 157–92.

21 Yet it is difficult to believe that China will not follow the same course as Eastern Europe in future years. The crisis of the Democracy Movement in the spring of 1989 was caused by all the same conditions that led to the collapse of communism in Eastern Europe: the contradictions of economic reform in a system still run by communist officials, growing corruption, loss of faith in the official ideology, and increasing disgust with the endless hypocrisy of those in power. The main difference, of course, was that China in 1989 was much less developed, much less urbanized than the East European countries, and also much more insulated from the effects of the economic and political crisis in the Soviet Union. For a brief review of the events in China and their causes, see Jonathan D. Spence's new book, *The Search for Modern China* (New York: Norton, 1990), pp. 712–47.

22 His major essays from the late 1980s have been collected in Timothy Garton Ash, *The Uses of Adversity* (New York: Random House, 1989).

23 Kazimierz Poznanski, *Technology, Competition and the Soviet Bloc in the World Market* (Berkeley, CA: Institute of International Studies, University of California, 1987).

24 Each new report from the Soviet Union makes the Brezhnev years and the prognosis for the future seem bleaker. For years the CIA reports painted a more pessimistic economic picture than the official Soviet reports, but recently Soviet economists have said that even the CIA reports were too optimistic. As an example of what is now known about the state of the Soviet economy, and how it got to its present crisis, see Bill Keller, "Gorbachev's Need: To Still Matter," *New York Times*, May 27, 1990, pp. 1, 6. None of this is new to the academic specialists; see, for example, Marshall Goldman, *USSR in Crisis: The Failure of an Economic System* (New York: Norton, 1983).

25 That scientists did not believe the extravagant claims made by the proponents of the Strategic Defense Initiative is clear. See, for example, Franklin A. Long, Donald Hafner, and Jeffrey Boutwell, eds., *Weapons in Space* (New York: Norton, 1986), particularly the essay by Hans Bethe, Jeffrey Boutwell, and Richard Garwin, "BMD Technologies and Concepts in the 1980s," pp. 53–71. Yet the Soviets were very troubled by it, and it was Gorbachev's political genius that figured out that American funding for military research could be reduced only in the context of a general move toward disarmament, and this necessitated a reversal of traditional Soviet foreign policy that would reassure

the West. For an appreciation of Gorbachev's policy in an otherwise harshly critical article, see Elena Bonner, "On Gorbachev," *New York Review of Books*, May 17, 1990, p. 14. In general, it seems to me that the Soviets' fear that their conventional warfare capabilities would be undermined by the West's technological superiority has been relatively neglected in most of the discussion about arms control. It has, however, been noted by experts. See Alan B. Sherr, *The Other Side of Arms Control: Soviet Objectives in the Gorbachev Era* (Boston, MA: Unwin Hyman, 1988), pp. 38, 63.

26 Chaim Herzog, *The Arab–Israeli Wars* (New York: Random House, 1982), pp. 347–48. That the Soviets remained very concerned by this is shown by statements in Alexei Arbatov, Oleg Amirov, and Nikolai Kishilov, "Assessing the NATO–WTO Military Balance in Europe," in Robert D. Blackwell and F. Stephen Larrabee, eds., *Conventional Arms Control and East-West Security* (Durham, NC: Duke University Press, 1989), pp. 78–79.

27 Hosking, *The Awakening of the Soviet Union*, pp. 56–60.

28 The desperate, almost comical attempts made by the Jaruzelski regime to create new organizations and institutions that would reimpose some sort of political and social coherence, and bring society back into the system, are explored very well by George Kolankiewicz in "Poland and the Politics of Permissible Pluralism," *East European Politics and Societies* 2:1 (1988), pp. 152–83. But even Kolankiewicz thought that the attempt to include broader segments of the population, particularly the intellectuals, in officially defined institutions might meet with partial success. In the event, it turned out that these desperate inclusionary policies also failed.

29 Timothy Garton Ash, "Eastern Europe: The Year of Truth," *New York Review of Books*, February 15, 1990, pp. 17–22 (also appears as Chapter 5 in this volume). A collection of Garton Ash's new essays on 1989 appears in *We the People: The Revolution of '89. Witnessed in Warsaw, Budapest, Berlin and Prague* (Cambridge: Granta/Penguin, 1990).

30 The summer of 1988 was certainly a time when it became obvious that the forces of political and social disintegration in the Soviet Union were starting to get out of hand, too, and this no doubt influenced Gorbachev greatly. See the essays of Boris Kagarlitsky in *Farewell Perestroika. A Soviet Chronicle* (London: Verso, 1990), particularly "The Hot Summer of 1988," pp. 1–29.

31 The whole process is well documented by Polish publications, particularly issues of *Rzeczpospolita, Polityka*, and *Trybuna Ludu*. I thank Dieter Bingen of Cologne's Bundesinstitut für ostwissenschaftliche und internationale Studien for helping me understand the sequence of events in Poland during this period.

32 Bill Keller, "Getting Out with Honor" (February 2, 1989), in Bernard Gwertzman and Michael T. Kaufman, eds., *The Collapse of Communism* (New York: New York Times, 1990), pp. 10–12. This book is a collection of relevant articles published in the *New York Times* during 1989.

33 John Tagliabue, "Solidarity May Win 40 Percent of Parliament" (February 19, 1989), *The Collapse of Communism*, pp. 20–1, "Stunning Vote Casts Poles into Unchartered Waters" (June 5, 1989), p. 121; "Warsaw Accepts Solidarity Sweep and Humiliating Losses by Party" (June 8, 1989), pp. 121–3; "Jaruzelski, Moved by 'Needs and Aspirations' of Poland Names Walesa Aide Premier" (August 19, 1989), pp. 130–2. To this must be added the August 17, 1989, article from Moscow by Bill Keller, "In Moscow, Tone is Studied Calm," pp. 132–3.

34 Henry Kamm, "East Germans Put Hungary in a Bind" (September 1, 1989), *The Collapse of Communism*, pp. 154–6; and Serge Schmemann, "East Germans

Line Émigré Routes, Some in Hope of Their Own Exit" (October 4, 1989), p. 158, and "Security Forces Storm Protesters in East Germany" (sent from Dresden, October 8, 1989), p. 159.

35 Thomas A. Baylis, "Explaining the GDR's Economic Strategy," in Comisso and Tyson, eds., *Power, Purpose, and Collective Choice*, especially the optimistic conclusion, pp. 242–4. A conventionally favorable summary of how East German communist labor relations worked is found in Marilyn Rueschemeyer and C. Bradley Scharf, "Labor Unions in the German Democratic Republic," in Alex Pravda and Blair A. Ruble, eds., *Trade Unions in Communist States* (Boston, MA: Allen and Unwin, 1986). Judging by the comments from these and similar studies, East Germans should not have behaved the way they did in 1989.

36 In a speech on October 7 in the GDR, Gorbachev said, "life itself punishes those who delay." Timothy Garton Ash, "The German Revolution," *New York Review of Books*, December 21, 1989, p. 14. Then, on October 25 in Helsinki, he said that the Soviet Union did not have the moral or political right to intervene in the affairs of Eastern Europe. This was interpreted by his spokesman, Gennadi I. Gerasimov, as the replacement of the Brezhnev Doctrine by the "Sinatra Doctrine" (after the song "I Did It My Way"). Bill Keller, "Gorbachev in Finland, Disavows Any Right of Regional Intervention," in *The Collapse of Communism* (October 25, 1989), pp. 163–6.

37 Garton Ash, "The German Revolution," p. 16.

38 Christopher Jones, "Gorbachev and the Warsaw Pact," *East European Politics and Societies* 3:2 (1989), pp. 215–34.

39 Serge Schmemann, "East Germany Opens Frontier to the West for Migration or Travel: Thousands Cross," *New York Times*, November 10, 1989, p. 1. Clyde Haberman, "Bulgarian Chief Quits After 35 Years of Rigid Rule," same issue of the *Times*, p. 1. Timothy Garton Ash, "The Revolution of the Magic Lantern," *New York Review of Books*, January 18, 1990, pp. 42–51. The Czech communist regime fell on November 24.

40 Louis Zanga, "Albania Decides to End Its Isolation," *Soviet/East European Report*, Radio Free Europe/Radio Liberty, May 1, 1990, p. 4; Zanga, "Even in Albania Economic Reforms and a Multiparty System," *Soviet/East European Report*, RFE/RL, January 10, 1991, pp. 1, 4.

41 The Ceauşescu regime began to move in this direction in the early 1970s, though the full ramifications of the return to autarkic Stalinism did not become entirely obvious until the early 1980s. For an explanation of the changes in the early 1970s, see Ken Jowitt, "Political Innovation in Rumania," *Survey* 4 (Autumn 1974), pp. 132–51, and Daniel Chirot, "Social Change in Communist Romania," *Social Forces* 57:2 (1978), pp. 495–7. Jowitt noted Ceauşescu's references to his "beloved friend" Kim Il Sung and to the fact that a young reform communist who had built up well-educated, technocratic cadres, and who was expected to become increasingly important, was suddenly demoted. That was Ion Iliescu, the man who was to become the first post-communist president of Romania! Jowitt again emphasized the similarity of the North Korean and Romanian regimes in "Moscow 'Centre,'" *East European Politics and Societies* 1:3 (Fall 1987), p. 320. For a brief description of what Romania was like by 1988, see Daniel Chirot, "Ceauşescu's Last Folly," *Dissent*, Summer 1988, pp. 271–5. In North Korea, despite the many similarities with Romania, decay was not as advanced in the late 1980s, perhaps because, as Bruce Cumings has suggested, Kim's autarkic Marxist patrimonialism was more in tune with Korean historical and cultural tradition than Ceauşescu's

was with Romania's past. See Bruce Cumings, "Corporatism in North Korea," *Journal of Korean Studies* 4 (1982–83), particularly p. 277, where he quotes Ken Jowitt's quip about Romania and North Korea being examples of "socialism in one family." Since then, that quote has been widely repeated without being attributed.

42 One of the best accounts of what was going on in Romania was written by the Romanian dissident Pavel Campeanu: "Birth and Death in Romania," *New York Review of Books*, October 23, 1986. That article was written anonymously. His "The Revolt of the Romanians," *New York Review of Books*, February 1, 1990, was signed. See also Daniel N. Nelson, *Romanian Politics in the Ceaușescu Era* (New York: Gordon and Beach, 1988), pp. 213–17.

43 There could hardly be a better demonstration of how removed Ceaușescu had become from reality than the way in which he was overthrown. The shock on his face as the crowd he was addressing began to jeer him, December 21, 1989, was captured on television. More than this was the unbelievable ineptitude of his attempt to escape, even though, in fact, his security forces had the capacity to resist. Some highly placed Romanians have told me that Ceaușescu realized in the last few days that changes had to be made, and that he was hoping to reassert his full control before starting to reform. But it is quite clear that despite the years of growing misery and the alienation of all Romanians outside the Ceaușescu family, he still believed he had enough legitimacy to carry on. His surprise may have been due to the fact that the demonstration against him was probably instigated by elements in the army and from with the Securitate itself. The reports in the *New York Times* on Romania from December 22 to December 25, 1989, give the essence of the story without, however, clarifying what still remains, much later, a murky sequence of events.

44 The famous J-Curve theory of James Davies predicted that a growing gap between rewards and expectations would lead to revolutions; see his article, "Toward a Theory of Revolution," *American Sociological Review* 27:1 (1962), pp. 5–19. Ted Gurr expanded on this and other "psychological explanations" of revolution in *Why Men Rebel* (Princeton, NJ: Princeton University Press, 1970). These would be, at best, weak explanations of what happened, except for the obvious point that many people must have been dissatisfied for regimes that were essentially intact to fall so quickly. There is no obvious reason why discontent should have been any higher in 1989 than five, ten, or twenty years earlier.

45 Michael Bernhard has shown that in fact the party-state machine in Poland learned from the events of the 1970s and of 1980, and that Jaruzelski was able to impose martial law, raise prices repeatedly, and avoid the political turmoil that had occurred earlier. "The Strikes of June 1976 in Poland," *East European Politics and Societies* 1:3 (1987), pp. 390–1. Both the opposition and the regime became more sophisticated with time, but by the mid-1980s, the regime had won. The prevailing political attitude, according to many, and on the whole fairly reliable surveys done in Poland, was growing apathy toward all political issues. See Jane I. Curry, "The Psychological Barriers to Reform in Poland," *East European Politics and Societies* 2:3 (1988), particularly p. 494. David S. Mason's *Public Opinion and Political Change in Poland, 1980–1982* (Cambridge: Cambridge University Press, 1984) consistently shows this, but also that the turn in the "J," that is, the growing gap between a deteriorating reality and high expectations created by the growth of the early 1970s, took place in the late 1970s and in 1980. As the 1980s unfolded, people's expectations fell into line with reality as the excitement of 1980–81 was

replaced by the apathy and hopelessness of martial law. See particularly pp. 42–53 and 222–32.

46 Elemér Hankiss in "Demobilization, Self-Mobilization, and Quasi-Mobilization in Hungary, 1948–1987," pp. 131–9.

47 Vladimir Tismaneanu, quoting Václav Havel, points out that the dissidents in these countries made up a "minuscule and rather singular enclave." *The Crisis of Marxist Ideology in Eastern Europe: The Poverty of Utopia* (London: Routledge, 1988), p. 166. In his chapter on intellectual dissidents (pp. 160–82), however, Tismaneanu is prophetic in noting that the refusal of the intellectuals to accept the lies of communism can destroy these systems precisely because they are ultimately based on ideas. This, in fact, was the entire premise of the dissident intellectuals, particularly in Poland, Czechoslovakia, and Hungary.

48 The analysis of conflicts between states trying to reform, in order to keep up their power in the international arena, and obstructionist traditional elites makes up an important part of Theda Skocpol's theory of revolution in *States and Social Revolutions* (Cambridge: Cambridge University Press, 1979). Classes more committed to reform, then, play an important role in conducting revolutions. But however much merit this argument has in explaining the classical French, Russian, and Chinese revolutions, it seems to have little bearing on what happened in Eastern Europe in 1989. It may, however, have considerable bearing on the future of politics in Russia.

49 Przemyslaw T. Gajdeczka of the World Bank claimed in 1988 that the debt problem was more or less under control, and that international lenders rated only three countries poorly: Poland, Romania, and Yugoslavia. "International Market Perceptions and Economic Performance: Lending to Eastern Europe," *East European Politics and Societies* 2:3 (1988), pp. 558–76.

50 That rising classes cause revolutions is at the heart of the Marxist theory of revolution. An interesting twist to this was suggested by George Konrád and Iván Szelényi in *The Intellectuals on the Road to Class Power* (Brighton: Harvester Press, 1979). Intellectuals were identified as the rising class that helped put the communists into power and were becoming the ruling class. But intellectual dissidents in Eastern Europe represented no class, were not numerically large, and were held together by a common moral position, not their position in the economic structure. Zygmunt Bauman identified their role more correctly by pointing out that they were more the carriers of national consciousness and morality than a class as such. "Intellectuals in East-Central Europe: Continuity and Change," *East European Politics and Societies* 1:2 (1987), pp. 162–86.

51 Only in Poland could it be said that Charles Tilly's theory about revolutions – that it is organization of the revolutionary groups that counts most – works at all. But even in Poland, the height of organizational coherence in Solidarity was reached in 1980. To the limited extent that Poland fits Tilly's theories about mobilization, this cannot explain the loss of nerve and collapse in the other communist regimes. See Tilly's *From Mobilization to Revolution* (Reading: Addison-Wesley, 1978).

52 Thus the first step of what Jack A. Goldstone has called the "natural history" approach to the study of revolutions, based largely on the 1938 work of Crane Brinton, turns out to describe some of what happened in Eastern Europe too: "Prior to a great revolution, the bulk of the 'intellectuals' – journalists, poets, playwrights, essayists, teachers, members of the clergy, lawyers, and trained members of the bureaucracy – cease to support the regime, writing condem-

nations and demanding major reforms." Goldstone, "The Comparative and Historical Study of Revolutions," *Annual Review of Sociology* 8 (1982), pp. 189–90. See also Crane Brinton, *The Anatomy of Revolution* (New York: Vintage, 1965). But most recent theorists of revolution have not taken this observation as anything more than a symptom of deeper class and structural conflicts, and none seem to have believed it could be the prime cause of revolutions. Goldstone's own theory that rapidly rising demographic pressures explain revolutions has much validity in premodern history (pp. 204–5); it has no bearing on Eastern Europe.

53 See Johnson, *Peasant Nationalism*, pp. 31–70.

54 It would be pointless to extend the number of examples, because there are so many. For some African cases, see Robert H. Jackson and Carl G. Rosberg, *Personal Rule in Black Africa: Prince, Autocrat, Prophet, Tyrant* (Berkeley and Los Angeles, CA: University of California Press, 1982), particularly Chapter 6, "Tyrants and Abusive Rule" (about the incredible misrule of Idi Amin of Uganda and Macias Nguema of Equatorial Guinea). For Haiti, Robert I. Rotberg's classic study, *Haiti: The Politics of Squalor* (Boston, MA: Houghton Mifflin, 1971), remains excellent. The tyranny in Burma and the revolution of 1988 (whose ultimate effects are still pending, despite the effective repression that took place during that year) are discussed by Bertil Lintner in *Outrage: Burma's Struggle for Democracy* (Hong Kong: Review Publishing, 1989).

55 Leo Kuper, in *Genocide* (New Haven, CT: Yale University Press, 1981), estimates that up to three million Bengalis were killed as the Pakistani Army tried to reverse the overwhelming electoral victory of the independence-minded Awami League (pp. 78–80). Of course, it was not just the army, but a general collapse into anarchy and interethnic warfare, that contributed to the high death toll. The point is that despite all this, as in Cambodia in 1979, or Uganda, also in 1979, the nightmare perpetrated by the government in control against the wishes of the large majority of the population could be overthrown only by outside military intervention (p. 173). By these standards, the European colonial powers, however brutal they may have been, seem to have been more prone to give in to a combination of moral arguments against what they were doing and simple calculations of the costs and benefits of their colonial wars. None of these cases shed much light on what happened in Eastern Europe, either internally or because of any Soviet actions. After all, the last case of large-scale killing by the Soviets in Eastern Europe was in Hungary in 1956.

56 Ryszard Kapuscinski's *The Emperor* (London: Picador/Pan, 1984), about the fall of Haile Selassie, makes that emperor seem very much of a Ceauşescu-like figure – out of touch with his population and with his own elite. But some have pointed out that Kapuscinski's book may have been as much about his native Poland under Gierek as about Ethiopia. The violence that followed the first, peaceful stage of the Ethiopian Revolution, however, is unlikely to be repeated in Eastern Europe, though it is a chilling reminder of what happens when a disintegrating multiethnic empire tries to hold itself together at any cost.

57 Tim McDaniel has pointed out the extraordinary analogy between the Russian Revolution of 1917 and the Iranian one of 1978–79. In both cases, autocratic modernizing regimes, despite some real successes, managed to alienate almost all elements in the society. In the case of Iran, this was even more startling because, as in Eastern Europe, there was no major defeat, just a

collapse. *A Modern Mirror for Princes: Autocratic Modernization and Revolution in Russia and Iran* (Princeton, NJ: Princeton University Press, 1991).

58 John Rawls, *A Theory of Justice* (Cambridge, MA: Harvard University Press, 1971).

59 *Bulletin of the Atomic Scientists*, March 1990, pp. 17–21.

60 For example, Tony R. Judt in a paper delivered at the Woodrow Wilson Center in Washington during the summer of 1987 and published as "The Dilemmas of Dissidence: The Politics of Opposition in East-Central Europe," *East European Politics and Societies* 2:2 (1988) pp. 185–240. The journals *Telos* and *Cross Currents*, run by scholars from Central Europe, were aware of what was going on, as were some other equally specialized publications in Europe. But before the events of 1989, very few scholars or intellectuals paid much attention to such publications, and even most specialists, especially those in the policy-related fields, hardly took them seriously.

2

AMIDST MOVING RUINS

Leszek Kolakowski

Leszek Kolakowski is one of the most influential Polish intellectuals whose writings played an enormous role in the awakening and development of the anti-totalitarian opposition in East Central Europe. Involved for many years in the saga of the neo-Marxist, "revisionist" struggle for a "socialism with a human face," Kolakowski reached the conclusion that the system was inherently corrupt and that there was no real way to improve it via gradual reforms from above. This essay discusses a number of fascinating topics directly related to the events of 1989: the inner self-destructive logic of Sovietism; the limits of predictive power of what used to be called "Sovietology"; the role of Poland and Solidarity in the destruction of the myth of communist infallibility; and the crucial role played by Mikhail Gorbachev in catalyzing and galvanizing the system's collapse.

Compared to other contributions in this volume, Kolakowski's essay informs the reader about the pre-history of 1989, emphasizing the critical significance of the crises of 1956 and 1968, as well as the meaning of the struggle for national independence and dignity in the coalescence of anticommunist movements. His predictions about the forthcoming debates on the past and the attempts to obtain "certificates of national innocence" are intimately consonant with Tony Judt's contribution to this volume.

* * *

Euphoria is always brief, whatever causes it. The "post-communist" euphoria is over and the premonitions of imminent dangers are mounting. The monster is dying in its own monstrous way. Shall we see another monster take its place, a series of bloody struggles between its various remnants? How many new countries will emerge from the chaos and what will they be: democratic, dictatorial, national-fascist, clerical, civilized, barbaric? Will millions of refugees, escaping from famine and war, stampede into Europe? Every day newspapers provide gloomy warnings; many are written by knowledgeable people. The only thing we know for certain: nothing is certain; nothing is impossible.

LESZEK KOLAKOWSKI

Predicting the unpredictable

And when we say "nothing is certain" we mean a modest, humanly accessible certainty ("moral assurance," as Descartes would have it) and not the perfect certainty that is beyond human reach. We are now told by scientists that in various natural processes some minuscule events may trigger, unpredictably, large-scale catastrophic changes and "unpredictable" results. To foresee them, one needs not just a better, more detailed knowledge of initial conditions but the absolute knowledge that only the divine mind can possibly possess.

Historical processes are like that. "Laws of history" and "historical inevitability" are Hegelian-Marxist fakes. There was no historical necessity in that relatively weak Athenian infantry defeating the powerful Persian army at Marathon. Had the Greeks lost – as any outside observer must have rationally expected – there would have been no history of Europe as we now know it. No historical laws prevented Mohammed from being killed before his escape from Mecca; none ordered Martin Luther, an obscure monk from a provincial town, to initiate the debate about who is entitled to forgive sins. There was no inevitability in the success of the Bolshevik revolution – indeed an unpredictable coincidence of many accidents assured its victory – or the Red Army's defeat by the Poles in 1920 and failure to conquer Europe, or Hitler's establishment of dictatorship in Germany. These momentous historical events were produced by chance, or if one prefers, by miraculous interventions of Providence.

With the benefit of hindsight, it is possible to explain how such miracles were prepared by the course of events that preceded them; such explanations are easy; it is reasonable to say that none of these events was miraculous to such an extent that it might have happened at any time, in any place, in any circumstance. The circumstances, however, made them possible, but by no means necessary. We often discern certain "trends" that we expect will one day culminate in a catastrophe (in the original sense of "upturn," sometimes destructive, sometimes beneficial), when the trajectory of a movement is suddenly broken. But we are never able – except, occasionally on a very short time scale – of predicting the character, pace, or timetable of break. Of course, in most of our actions, consciously or otherwise, we make predictions; and most often we are not disappointed. We naturally assume that tomorrow will be very much like today; this in fact is the safest way of moving through life. Most frequently tomorrow is indeed very much like today – the sun rises; there is no snow in summer.

While many people did in fact predict the collapse of the Soviet empire, and proved to be right, were they really especially wise or more abundantly endowed with the gift of prophecy than those who expected its indefinite duration? The present author, having made such predictions on many occasions, in very general terms, but never on timing and pace, in asking such questions may not be thought to wish to justify himself. He would rather boast of being among the credible prophets. The predictions have indeed been borne out, but on what basis were they originally made? To say simply that all earlier empires eventually fell is unhelpful, meaningless, as some survived in good health for centuries. Certainly, one could (and did) notice a number of serious tensions – insoluble problems – enfeebling and corroding the multinational Soviet tyranny: glaring economic inefficiency; persistent poverty in the population; nationalist passions; the crisis of legitimacy once the ruling ideology had lost the last remnants of its vitality; the growing technological gap between the territories of "real socialism" and democratic countries; various symptoms of cultural and religious revival.

Still, none of those observable facts or tendencies – or all of them jointly – could justify predictions about the immediate future. Where there is decay, one may expect death one day, but no one can be really sure about the forces of resilience remaining in the aging body before it turns into a corpse. As the ancient saying goes, nobody is so old that he could not survive for one more year. People have lived in misery for decades; why not decades more? National passions have always been present, but Russification was able to progress as well. Communist ideology was dying, but might it not be feasible to maintain the despotic power without ideology? The technological gap was growing, but the army and police seemed to be intact, technically skilled. The "dissident" movement existed but did not extend beyond a few dozen individuals; it was nearly destroyed by persecution. Many people reasoned in this way; the course of events made fools of them. Why were "we" right and "they" wrong? Because they bet on the safest way of predicting, tomorrow will be very much like today; "we" had good reasons to make an apparently riskier wager, and we won. Why?

A brief history of communism

After Stalin's death the totalitarian *will* to power survived, but its effectiveness and skill in enforcing slavery grew weaker and weaker, all the regressions and U-turns notwithstanding. A tyrannical regime, suddenly made ashamed of mass slaughter, that seeks to replace it with selective terror is doomed. Genocidal measures were no longer practicable – as they had been under Iosif Vissarionovich [Stalin]'s rule – where all layers of the ruling apparatus, even the highest and the most privileged, were affected. The safety of the rulers allowed for a more relative and more fragile control of the ruled, on the condition that they agreed to be obedient, passive, and ignorant, and made no attempt to revolt. In addition to a measure of physical safety, a minimum of moral safety was also instituted.

A small example will illustrate the change. When I visited Moscow in October 1990, a Russian friend called my attention to a simple fact, the significance of which I had failed to notice. It was known that under Khrushchev a relatively large-scale housing construction program had been developed in the cities; people in great numbers secured their family dwellings. However small and inferior in standard, they gave people space for privacy, little nooks to breathe in. My Russian friend told me that without these modest but individual flats no opposition movement would have been possible. How foolish of Khrushchev! People crammed like sardines in miserable workers' barracks or in small flats shared by several families, hating each other and spying on each other, jostling all the time, and deprived of all moments of privacy, were unlikely to think about anything but sheer survival. The improvement of living conditions turned out to be politically dangerous. Far from appeasing people, making them more docile, as certain Sovietologists expected, such measures slowly opened up a space for critical thinking, ultimately for rebellion. A slightly reduced misery made misery more painful; it operated to release the energy of revolt. Many observers (apart from a number of experts) have known this from a study of history.

The most active and fearless Soviet rebels of the 1960s were dispatched to concentration camps and psychiatric prisons or forced to emigrate; some were murdered. Many experts heaved a sigh of relief: we told you so; a handful of madmen tomorrow will be like today. It was not to be; the Soviet intelligentsia was never to lose what it had gained (or to regain what it had lost): the ridiculous emptiness of the Marxist–Leninist ideology was denounced and spectacularly displayed for all to see.

And what about the repeated revolts and uprisings on the peripheries of the empire? Again, they were shrugged off by many experts: such agitation was pointless; do you know how many tanks the Soviet army has, and how many Poland and Hungary can command? And troops, and airplanes? How many days do you imagine the supply of fuel will last in Poland? Experts read newspapers with occasional reports on CIA assessments of Soviet bloc military performance. Indeed, given the absence of fuel, tanks, and airplanes, was there any point to revolt? Keep silent, you silly Poles, Czechs, Hungarians; the Yalta agreement holds; nobody will help you; the curtain is everlasting; tomorrow will be like today; keep silent and you may make your life better; revolt, and you will be crushed. The experts have spoken.

It must be stressed that most often the revolts, when they occurred and had an ideological articulation, were ostensibly socialist. Apart from a few individuals with the reputation of being eccentric, who, before the late 1980s, would have thought to demand the reprivatization of industry? What did the Poles in 1956 and the Czechs in 1968 want but a better, economically efficient socialism, tolerant in cultural matters, neither oppressive nor mendacious? The Hungarian revolution of 1956 was triggered by the second funeral of Lászlo Rajk; Rajk was a Stalinist hangman tortured to death by other Stalinist hangmen. The last stage of the Polish opposition movement started at the end of 1975 with protests against amendments to the constitution that were intended practically to inscribe into law Poland's membership in the Soviet bloc and the permanence of the Party dictatorship; ostensibly, the protesters defended the integrity of the Stalinist constitution of 1952.

But the Soviets knew better; they were not easily fooled. And they were right. They knew that "socialism with a human face" was, for all practical purposes, no socialism, at least no socialism in the sense they conceived it: a socialism defined by the arbitrary dictatorship of the Party, the lack of civil liberties, and the overall nationalization of everything, including people's minds, historical knowledge, every means of communication, all human relationships. That they were right has been glaringly borne out by recent events: an attempt to produce a "communism with a human face" in the Soviet Union resulted in no communism at all, no face to look at. Is the crocodile with a human face possible, Soviet skeptics asked, after the pathetic Czechoslovak experience?

Even when we accept that unexpected events do often occur, and that the life routine is disturbed (the refrigerator breaks down, a friend suddenly dies of a heart attack, there is a civil war in a "far away country of which we know very little"), the principle that "tomorrow will be very much like today" is not only the easiest and mentally the safest to adopt, but also the most rational as well. We could not survive without having it embedded in our minds. Having lived for many years in peace, we admit that a war may happen, but we do not really believe it. The Soviet super-power was indeed a dangerous animal, but its behavior was known; the Western powers were generally aware of what to expect. Still, surprises did happen, such as the Soviet invasion of Afghanistan. To anyone familiar with the history of the empire, with the possible exception of President Carter, there was nothing in that event at all out of keeping with the prin cipal patterns of Soviet policy. The world was a place full of hazard; but once the machine became deregulated, we felt that the perils increased, though at first glance, the opposite seemed to be the case, particularly when imperialism fell to pieces. The little certainty we habitually enjoyed was lost; our routine reactions did not fit into an unfamiliar environment; our sight was clouded and instead of rejoicing, various sinister future scenarios were imagined, none of which was entirely impossible. The continuity has been broken; until a new kind of fragile stability appears, there will be more panic than peace of mind.

There were many energies at work that contributed to the final demise of the empire. One, however modest, was the presence of individuals who obstinately predicted its disintegration. Those who foresaw its indefinite vitality contributed – willingly or not – to its perpetuation. It is known, of course, that in political and economic affairs predictions are never wholly innocent. We are not like meteorologists and we influence the object spoken of. Those who predicted the sorry end of the empire in the not-too-distant future almost invariably wished it to happen. Those who believed in its perpetuity were more differentiated: some were fellow-travelers; some simply accepted and approved the permanence of the exist-ing division of the world and cheerfully (scientifically, to be sure) pointed out all the symptoms of the oncoming "convergence"; some, while hostile to the communist system, believed it to be so immensely strong that short of global war nothing would crush it.

It is perhaps more accurate to say that the perpetuity-mongers were more mistaken than to say that the death-prophets (or death-wishers) were clairvoyant. The latter were unable to pack together into one equation the heterogeneous factors that corroded the seemingly immovable, card-board palace of communism and correctly calculated the date on which it would crumble; for that, they can hardly be blamed. The former simply refused to see and to discern what was perfectly visible; they may be blamed for that self-inflicted blindness.

What did Mikhail Sergeevich do?

Since the causes of the catastrophe were many and disparate, both internal and external, it is vain to seek for the "main cause," the "weightiest factor"; the same needs to be said about all historical earthquakes.

Among the many factors, the personal contribution of Mikhail Sergeevich Gorbachev cannot be omitted, though it is evident that he both shaped events and was shaped by them. He did not come to power in order to dismantle the empire and communist institutions. Repeatedly – and incredibly up to the moment when he ordered the dissolution of the Communist Party – he declared his allegiance to communism. What this meant, nobody, including himself, could say, but it was probably not just an attempt to placate "conservatives," "hardliners," "Stalinists," "reactionaries," "hawks," – no word is quite accurate; he clearly meant something, however vague his formulations. Inevitably, he was seen by some as a cunning Soviet strategist seeking to deceive the West, to throw it off its guard so as better to grip it by the throat later; others perceived him to be a bold reformer who wished only to lead his country onto the path of civilization, decency, and the rule of law. In fact, it became increas-ingly clear that he had no precise (or even imprecise) plan, that *perestroika* was an empty word (*glasnost* was not), that he reacted to events generally unprepared, in haste. Still, by repeatedly insisting that fundamental though ill-defined changes were urgently needed, he revealed the empire's lack of self-confidence. Once it is recognized that the rulers of an empire doubt its legitimacy, one may safely assume that the end is in sight. Gorbachev was aware – he is not stupid – that his appeals would set into motion various forces that might go beyond what he intended, but he failed to foresee the social energies he would unintentionally release. He hoped to keep the reforms (whatever this meant) within the limits he himself set – at the outset this, it seems, was his concept of democracy – but he showed himself incapable of containing the mounting waves; like so many other reformers in history, he fell prey to his own reformist zeal, destroying what in his mind was to be put straight and perfected.

What did Poland do?

One of the things most derided and mocked by twentieth-century Polish writers and thinkers was the idea of Polish messianism; emerging in poetry and philosophy after the defeat of the 1830 anti-Russian uprising, it depicted Poland as the "Christ of nations," whose suffering and cruci-fixion would redeem mankind. This seemed a ridiculous, self-comforting, and self-compensating fantasy, but on closer inspection there may have been some truth in it. Poland, the first country to defeat the Red Army shortly after the Revolution, prevented Europe from falling victim to communism, and perhaps confirmed the Hegelian notion that in every historical form the seeds of its future demise can be discerned from the outset. Poland was the only country invaded by the allied armies of Hitler and Stalin; this invasion triggered the Second World War. It was the first country to fight the Third Reich and one of two occupied (with Yugoslavia) that continued armed resistance against the German invaders. After the war, under communist rule, it was the first country to develop a mass movement of criticism, ideologically articulated, which culminated in 1956 in the change of leadership and the first appointment of a Communist Party leader without investure by Moscow, indeed in defiance of the Kremlin. The disillusionment was not slow in coming. It was the first country in which the communist ideology clearly and irreversibly died away. And the first in which a mass civic movement "Solidarność" (Solidarity) emerged and swept like fire over the land in 1980, nearly destroying the communist state machinery. Poland was the first (and only) country where overt military dictatorship was imposed in 1981 when it became obvious that the Communist Party was falling apart. The democratic opposition movement survived, however, despite mass repres-sions; it was determined to challenge the regime again. Poland was the only country in which communist authorities felt compelled to call a referendum, lost it, and then, miracle of miracles, said aloud that they had done so. It was the first country which forced the communist rulers to organize partially a free election of which the results were so devastating as to cause the Party to collapse and the first noncommunist government in a communist country to be formed. It is fair to add, however, that, as a price of its early success, Poland soon came to be outstripped by other latecomers; it had its own fully free election very much later, in October 1991.

A Messiah? Perhaps. This is not to say that the history of Poland, after or before the war, was an uninterrupted pageant of virtue and bravery; far from it. Still, its pioneering role in the slow decomposition of Sovietism cannot be denied.

Nationalism, communism, and the left

A wave of nationalist passions and hatred is today flooding post-communist Europe: this was predictable, predicted, and anticipated with alarm. The standard and often repeated explanation for this phenomenon is that nationalist ideologies stepped into a "vacuum" left by communism; that they had been "frozen" for decades, thawed by sudden political changes. The reality is less simple. There was no ideological "vacuum" suddenly opened up by the destruction of the old regime; the communist ideology had ceased to exist as a viable idea years earlier. And nationalist passions were not exactly "frozen"; they had been asserting themselves for a long time, parallel to the gradual enfeeblement of the totalitarian machinery. The process had been going on for over thirty years before the glorious year 1989! This memorable year, at least in certain communist countries, was not an explosion blowing up a sound, well-settled building; rather, it was like the breaking up of an egg, from inside the shell, in which an embryo chicken had been maturing for some time. The event, though making the transition to a quite new life possible, was less catastrophic and considerably less noisy than an explosion. Still, the chicken was frail at the beginning.

In doctrinal terms, communism was the anticipation of a world in which all mediating devices between the individual and the species as a whole – including the nation – would be made redundant and would therefore vanish; the cosmopolitan character of capital and the internationalism of the working class were expected to prepare the demise of nation, recognized to be a historical anachronism. The Leninist movement, however, while accepting this philosophy, promoted also the anti-Marxist idea of national self-determination as a purely destructive tactical device that would – and did – contribute to the decomposition of the czarist empire and of the entire century-old post-Viennese European order.

Communism in power was intended to eradicate the very reality of nation as a focus of people's separate loyalty (the only all-embracing loyalty was to be to the Soviet state and the Party). However, the Communisty Party from the very beginning and almost to the end stirred up and exploited nationalist movements elsewhere to help undermine the hostile "capitalist" powers. This policy, while justified by the Leninist concept of imperialism, soon became indistinguishable from the imperial czarist policy of old. Inside the Soviet state, nationalism as an ideology and an expression of national feelings was in principle forbidden, but Russian nationalism (not Ukrainian or Georgian, of course) stealthily came onto the stage in the 1930s, and was stimulated by every means during the war and in the post-Stalinist era, especially in the 1960s and later. It was, not without its inconsistencies, tolerated or encouraged; anti-yellow racism and anti-Semitism were its natural ingredients. In the "satellite" countries, the ruling party felt compelled, in proportion to the decay of the communist idea, to employ nationalism increasingly as a tool of self-legitimacy. They desperately sought to depict themselves as the best possible embodiment of national tradition; official language was more and more larded with patriotic slogans. In fact, a contradiction between the image of communism as a splendid edifice built from scratch, on a cultural desert, and communism as the continuation of everything good in the national tradition could be detected from almost the beginning.

In Poland, this was perhaps more spectacular than elsewhere. There were limits, of course. Still, beating the drum of national megalomania was usually rewarded; public anti-German and anti-Semitic hatred were sometimes encouraged, sometimes silenced, depending on political needs. The only thing strictly forbidden was mention of the issue of national independence; people were supposed to act as fervent patriots but never to allude to one detail – the sovereignty of their own state.

And so, nationalisms did not suddenly jump out of a freezer; they were simply allowed more room to expand. Tribal or national feelings and loyalties have always been a natural part of human life; "tribe" or "nation" equates with experience; "mankind," or "humankind" does not. Preferential solidarity with one's own cultural, historical, and linguistic niche is something people need, not something to be forbidden or deplored. Why should we expect or demand that people become perfectly cosmopolite, so that a Frenchman would be indifferent to whether something was happening in Guatemala or in France? To be sure, national feelings carry an ugly potential; they may, in unfavorable circumstances, produce jingoistic, hate-filled bellicosity. This, however, is not always and everywhere inevitable. Passionate love often leads to homicide, but it would be wrong to say that love is homicidal by nature. Patriots and chauvinists may be distinguished from one another; both breeds are found in every European nation. National hostilities generally have to do with territories and minorities. After centuries of European history, populations are mixed all over the continent; there are no clear ethnic borders; many linguistic islands exist. The hatred and mistrust generated by these conditions are not likely to evaporate in the near future. It is a fact that racist and chauvinist movements are dangerously increasing in many parts of Western Europe, quite independently of events in the East; the idea of the nation-state seems to gain in popularity in the very period of European unification.

Will the funeral of communism in Europe bring significant changes to the political maps of Western countries, especially on the left, if that word retains any meaning at all? The answer: probably not. Social democratic parties with good antitotalitarian credentials can proceed with their social agendas – reasonable or unreasonable – and need not worry much about the demise of Leninism, though their left wings may indeed lose strength. As to communist parties of Muscovite rite, the greatest number in Europe managed to change their names and ideology relatively early, or just happily passed away. One may be suspicious about the social democratic butterflies flowing out of ugly communist pupas; but having lost their ideological armor, they cannot be what they once were. The Italian party, having abandoned – rather late – the sickle and hammer, will probably continue to struggle for admission to the "democratic spectrum" from its previous seat among the supporters of tyranny; it may weaken, but it may survive, vying for space with social democrats.

The other communist party of significance, the French, is in a different position. Its incorrigible Stalinism was until recently reasonable and well devised. After all, these people were Communists not because they expected certain specific political conditions to give them again two junior posts in a socialist government. What they wanted was total power and nothing less. The only way to secure such power would be for the Red Army to occupy France and appoint local Communists as their reliable satraps. In such a scenario, the strength of the party in numbers would not matter very much; only discipline and obedience would count. There would always be a sufficient number to run concentration camps efficiently and to organize chaotically the distribution of coupons for bread. But the dream of Soviet occupation is over. And, if the communist leader, Marchais, were suddenly to say that he had converted to democracy, was going to reform himself, this would be a really dangerous move because France would die of laughter. Still, the Party may survive ambiguously for some time, vying with the National Front, and feeding itself on anti-European resentments, together with an emphasis on the perennial issue of unemployment.

As to the various leftist sects of Trotskyite or Maoist persuasion, they may survive because their virtue, unlike that of the Stalinist parties, has been to remain completely and happily immune from all reality. Though they claimed to be ideologically independent of Sovietism, they lived under the umbrella of Soviet "socialism"; their pathetic sobbing at the sight of crumbling tyrannies can now be heard. But they will possibly survive (perhaps except for strictly terrorist organizations directly or indirectly supported by the KGB) because, not unlike adventist or millenarian sects, they have voluntarily decided to live permanently in the immutable reality of the past. They may survive for centuries, excommunicating each other as agents of imperialism, scientifically predicting each year that the next year will bring the cataclysmic and irreversible world crisis of capitalism, as a result of which "the masses" will grant them the dictatorial power they deserve, given the correctness of their scientific theory. A friend told me that he once met in America, long ago, the basilissa of Byzantium, who kept her dynastic legitimacy intact. Five centuries cannot abrogate the legitimacy, since the pagans had no right to destroy the empire. So, there is no reason that the legitimate heirs of Lenin and Trotsky should not continue to make their claims for the next half millennium.

This is not to say that the political arrangements of Western Europe and its party systems are going to last indefinitely. Those arrangements may well fall apart in the next decade or so, paving the way to new ones, reflecting shifting priorities in public life. It is not the decline of communism that makes such a redistribution of political forces conceivable. The victory of democracy is by no means assured; there are various noncommunist forms of tyranny.

Looking for the radiant past

Predictably, all nations trying to construct something new on the rubble of communism are now searching for their blessed innocence. People want to depict themselves as heroes of the resistance; they wish to appear indignant and pure, on the lookout for real communist culprits. One sometimes has the impression that through the decades of communism the population consisted of a handful of miserable traitors and a mass of noble rebels. The real history was very different. To be sure, there are, among the remnants of the old regime, real murderers, people who directly ordered and carried out the most hideous tasks – the secret police thugs, arrogant and bumptious party *apparatchiks*, confident in the eternity of their power; they are deservedly held in contempt; some should be punished. But the simple truth is that in most of those countries – Poland in the late 1970s and 1980s was again the exception – the antitotalitarian opposition movement embraced only a tiny minority. Those people saved the soul of these nations; until recently, most of the others preferred to cross the street at their sight. An enormous majority sought to survive by adapting themselves to the seemingly perennial "system," not because of an enthusiastic commitment to the communist idea but because of the sheer need to carry on life in relative safety. The mass opposition movement started when it was patent to all (except perhaps to certain American Sovietologists) that the tiger was on its deathbed.

There were true believers (fewer and fewer, no doubt) and there were others whose minds were molded and reduced to permanent apathy, passivity, and hopelessness. Totalitarianism was never satisfied with a simple avoidance of opposition; it did everything to make everyone serve as active accomplices. And, to a large extent, it succeeded: the great majority voted in the sham elections to avoid unpleasant consequences, though not very serious ones; they took part in the obligatory marches on the occasion of major political festivities. The police informers were easily recruited, won over by miserable privileges, often agreeing to serve as the result of very mild pressure. It was normal to canvass the support of all Party functionaries for every kind of need. There was never a great problem in finding non-Party people to serve in "parliaments," or in various decorative bodies having no power, built to glorify the true power-holders. There were, of course, differences between the countries, between the historical phases of the development (and decline) of the various regimes. Historians will be kept busy for generations seeking to represent the undistorted picture of those years. The established popular image will, as usual, be a figment of the imagination, a certificate of national innocence. We may as well expect in due course something analogous to the German *Historikerstreit*, especially in Russia.

It is not easy to convince oneself that those communist decades were a kind of unnatural hole in the historical process, an empty time, a total break in continuity, a sheer waste; but it is difficult and unpleasant to include communism in the continuous course of the national past because then the nation as a whole must carry the burden of responsibility. There is such a thing as national guilt; otherwise, there would be no reason that people would need to whitewash their own nation from culpability for past crimes in which they personally had no part. Could half of Europe and half of Asia have been raped by a handful of bloodthirsty madmen, by Lenin and Stalin? Such things do not happen; it is nice to believe that they do, and to live with the innocent conscience of the rape victim.

And since communism was awful (as it indeed was), it will be normal to believe that the precommunist past, czarist Russia in particular, was an unceasing festival of hilarity. On both counts, popular historical perception will scarcely deal with reality. There is no point in deploring this. Self-deception is a necessary part of life, both in the individual and in the nation; it provides us all with moral safety.

Source Reprinted by permission of the publisher from *Daedalus* (journal of the American Academy of Arts and Sciences), from the issue entitled "The Exit from Communism," 121:2 (Spring 1992): 43–56.

3

WHAT WAS SOCIALISM, AND WHY DID IT FALL?

Katherine Verdery

American anthropologist Katherine Verdery's refreshing interpretation of "what was socialism" bears upon the nature of the Leninist legacies and offers a useful counterpart to political scientist Ken Jowitt's contribution to this volume. She discusses the state socialist experiments in East Central Europe focusing on the economic and social underpinnings of those systems. Particularly significant is her examination of the uses of surveillance and redistribution as the two faces ("negative" and "positive") of regime legitimization. Pointing out the interplay between domestic and international constraints and disruptions, Verdery provides a framework for understanding both "how" and "why" the collapse of communism took place. She shows how capitalism (market relations) emerged in some countries before the official political demise of Leninism occurred. Indeed, time mattered tremendously in the competition between the capitalist and socialist systems. Verdery presents the failure of state socialism "to catch up" with its Western rival as eventually resulting in mass disaffection, elite desperation, and ideological prostration. In accord with Jowitt's analysis of the "Leninist Extinction," she concludes that the revolutions of 1989 have challenged all established norms, identities, and certainties, both East and West.

* * *

The startling disintegration of Communist Party rule in Eastern Europe in 1989, and its somewhat lengthier unraveling in the Soviet Union between 1985 and 1991, rank among the century's most momentous occurrences. Especially because neither policy-makers nor area specialists predicted them, these events will yield much analysis after the fact, as scholars develop the hindsight necessary for understanding what they failed to grasp before. In this chapter, I aim to stimulate discussion about why Soviet-style socialism fell. Because I believe answers to the question require understanding how socialism "worked," I begin with an analysis of this and then suggest how it intersected fatefully with certain features of its world-system context.

What was socialism?

The socialist societies of Eastern Europe and the Soviet Union differed from one another in significant respects – for instance, in the intensity, span, and effectiveness of central control, in the extent of popular support or resistance, and in the degree and timing of efforts at reform. Notwithstanding these differences within "formerly existing socialism,"[1] I follow theorists such as Kornai in opting for a single analytical model of it.[2] The family resemblances among socialist countries were more important than their variety, for analytic purposes, much as we can best comprehend French, Japanese, West German, and North American societies as variants of a single capitalist system. Acknowledging, then, that my description applies more fully to certain countries and time periods than to others, I treat them all under one umbrella.

For several decades, the analysis of socialism has been an international industry, employing both Western political scientists and Eastern dissidents. Since 1989 this industry has received a massive infusion of new raw materials, as once-secret files are opened and translations appear of research by local scholars (especially Polish and Hungarian) into their own declining socialist systems.[3] My taste in such theories is "indigenist": I have found most useful the analyses of East Europeans concerning the world in which they lived. The following summary owes much to that work, and it is subject to refinement and revision as new research appears.[4] Given temporal and spatial constraints, I will compress elements of a longer discussion, emphasizing how production was organized and the consequences of this for consumption and for markets.[5] I believe these themes afford the best entry into why Party rule crumbled much faster than anyone expected.

Production

From the earliest days of the "totalitarian" model, Americans' image of "Communism" was of an autocratic, all-powerful state inexorably imposing its harsh will on its subjects. Even after most area specialists ceased to use the term "totalitarian" in their writing, the image of totalitarian autocracy persisted with both the broader public and many politicians; indeed, it underpinned Ronald Reagan's view of the "evil empire" as late as the 1980s. Yet the image was by and large wrong. Communist Party states were not all-powerful: they were comparatively weak. Because socialism's leaders managed only partially and fitfully to win a positive and supporting attitude from their citizens – that is, to be seen as legitimate – the regimes were constantly undermined by internal resistance and hidden forms of sabotage *at all system levels*.[6] This contributed much to their final collapse. I will describe briefly some of the elements of socialist nontotalitarianism and signal a few places where resistance lay.[7]

Socialism's fragility begins with the system of "centralized planning," which the center neither adequately planned nor controlled. Central planners would draw up a plan with quantities of everything they wanted to see produced, known as targets. They would disaggregate the plan into pieces appropriate for execution and estimate how much investment and how many raw materials were needed if managers of firms were to fill their targets. Managers learned early on, however, that not only did the targets increase annually but the materials required often did not arrive on time or in the right amounts. So they would respond by bargaining their plan: demanding more investments and raw materials than the amounts actually necessary for their targets. Every manager, and every level of the bureaucracy, padded budgets and requests in hopes of having enough in the actual moment of production. (A result of the bargaining process, of course, was that central planners always had faulty information about what was really required for production, and this impeded their ability to plan.) Then, if managers somehow ended up with more of some material than they needed, they hoarded it. Hoarded material had two uses: it could be kept for the next production cycle, or it could be exchanged with some other firm for something one's own firm lacked. These exchanges or barters of material were a crucial component of behavior within centralized planning.

A result of all the padding of budgets and hoarding of materials was widespread shortages, for which reason socialist economies are called economies of shortage.[8] Shortages were sometimes relative, as when sufficient quantities of materials and labor for a given level of output actually existed, but not where and when they were needed. Sometimes shortages were absolute, since relative shortage often resulted in lowered production, or – as in Romania – since items required for production or consumption were being exported. The causes of shortage were primarily that people lower down in the planning process were asking for more materials than they required and then hoarding whatever they got. Underlying their behavior was what economists call soft budget constraints – that is, if a firm was losing money, the center would bail it out. In the U.S. economy, with certain exceptions (such as Chrysler and the savings-and-loan industry), budget constraints are hard: if you cannot make ends meet, you go under. But in socialist economies, it did not matter if firms asked for extra investment or hoarded raw materials; they paid no penalty for it.

A fictitious example will help to illustrate – say, a shoe factory that makes women's shoes and boots. Central planners set the factory's targets for the year at one hundred thousand pairs of shoes and twenty thousand pairs of boots, for which they think management will need ten tons of leather, a half-ton of nails, and one thousand pounds of glue. The managers calculates what he (or she) would need under ideal conditions, if his workers worked consistently during three eight-hour shifts. He adds some for wastage, knowing the workers are lazy and the machines cut badly; some for theft, since workers are always stealing nails and glue; some to trade with other firms in case he comes up short on a crucial material at a crucial moment; and some more for the fact that the tannery always delivers less than requested. The manager thus refuses the plan assigned him, saying he cannot produce that number of shoes and boots unless he gets thirteen rather than ten tons of leather, a ton rather than a half-ton of nails, and two thousand rather than one thousand pounds of glue. Moreover, he says he needs two new power stitchers from Germany, without which he can produce nothing. In short, he has bargained his plan. Then when he gets some part of these goods, he stockpiles them or trades excess glue to the manager of a coat factory in exchange for some extra pigskin. If leather supplies still prove insufficient, he will make fewer boots and more shoes, or more footwear of small size, so as to use less leather; never mind if women's feet get cold in winter, or women with big feet can find nothing to wear.

With all this padding and hoarding, it is clear why shortage was endemic to social systems, and why the main problem for firms was not whether they could meet (or generate) demand but whether they could procure adequate supplies. So, whereas the chief problem of economic actors in Western economies is to get profits by selling things, the chief problem for socialism's economic actors was to procure things. Capitalist firms compete with each other for markets in which they will make a profit; socialist firms competed to maximize their bargaining power with suppliers higher up. In our society, the problem is other sellers, and to outcompete them you have to befriend the buyer. Thus our clerks and shop owners smile and give the customer friendly service because they want business; customers can be grouchy, but it will only make the clerk try harder. In socialism, the locus of competition was elsewhere: your competitor was other buyers, other procurers, and to outcompete them you needed to befriend those higher up who supplied you. Thus in socialism it was not the clerk – the provider, or "seller" – who was friendly (they were usually grouchy) but the procurers, the customers, who sought to ingratiate themselves with smiles, bribes, or favors. The work of procuring generated whole networks of cozy relations among economic managers and their bureaucrats, clerks and their customers. We would call this corruption, but that is because getting supplies is not a problem for capitalists: the problem is getting sales. In a word, for capitalists salesmanship is at a premium; for socialist managers, the premium was on acquisitionsmanship, or procurement.

So far I have been describing the clientelism and bargaining that under-cut the Party center's effective control. A similar weakness in vertical power relations emerges from the way socialist production and shortage bred workers' oppositional consciousness and resistance. Among the many things in short supply in socialist systems was labor. Managers hoarded labor, just like any other raw material, because they never knew how many workers they would need. Fifty workers working three eight-hour shifts six days a week might be enough to meet a firm's targets – *if* all the materials were on hand all month long. But this never happened. Many of those workers would stand idle for part of the month, and in the last ten days when most of the materials were finally on hand the firm would need 75 workers working overtime to complete the plan. The manager therefore kept 75 workers on the books, even though most of the time he needed fewer; and since all other managers were doing the same, labor was scarce. This provided a convenient if unplanned support for the regime's guaranteed employment.

An important result of labor's scarcity was that managers of firms had relatively little leverage over their workers. Furthermore, because supply shortages caused so much uncertainty in the production process, managers had to turn over to workers much control over this process, lest work come to a standstill.[9] That is, structurally speaking, workers under socialism had a somewhat more powerful position relative to management than do workers in capitalism. Just as managers' bargaining with bureaucrats undercut cen-tral power, so labor's position in production undercut that of management.

More than this, the very organization of the workplace bred opposition to Party rule. Through the Party-controlled trade union and the frequent merger of Party and management functions, Party directives were continu-ally felt in the production process – and, from workers' viewpoint, they were felt as unnecessary and disruptive. Union officials either meddled unhelpfully or contributed nothing, only to claim credit for production results that workers knew were their own. Workers participated disdain-fully – as sociologist Michael Burawoy found in his studies of Hungarian factories – in Party-organized production rituals, such as work-unit com-petitions, voluntary workdays, and production campaigns; they resented these coerced expressions of their supposed commitment to a wonderful socialism.[10] Thus, instead of securing workers' consent, workplace rituals sharpened their consciousness and resistance. Against an official "cult of work" used to motivate cadres and workers toward fulfilling the plan, many workers developed an oppositional cult of nonwork, imitating the Party bosses and trying to do as little as possible for their paycheck. Cadres often found no way around this internal sabotage, which by reducing productivity deepened the problems of socialist economies to the point of crisis.

The very forms of Party rule in the workplace, then, tended to focus, politicize, and turn against it the popular discontent that capitalist societies more successfully disperse, depoliticize, and deflect. In this way, socialism produced a split between "us" and "them," workers and Party leaders, founded on a lively consciousness that "they" are exploiting "us." This consciousness was yet another thing that undermined socialist regimes. To phrase it in Gramscian terms, the lived experience of people in socialism precluded its utopian discourse from becoming hegemonic – precluded, that is, the softening of coercion with consent.[11]

Ruling Communist Parties developed a variety of mechanisms to try to obscure this fact of their nature from their subjects, mechanisms designed to produce docile subject dispositions and to ensure that discontent did not become outright opposition. I will briefly discuss two of these mechanisms: the apparatus of surveillance, and redistribution of the social product.

Surveillance and paternalistic redistribution

In each country, some equivalent of the KGB was instrumental in maintaining surveillance, with varying degrees of intensity and success. Particularly effective were the Secret Police in the Soviet Union, East Germany, and Romania, but networks of informers and collaborators operated to some extent in all. These formed a highly elaborate "production" system parallel to the system for producing goods – a system producing paper, which contained real and falsified histories of the people over whom the Party ruled. Let us call the immediate product "dossiers," or "files," though the ultimate product was political subjects and subject dispositions useful to the regime. This parallel production system was at least as important as the system for producing goods, for producers of files were much better paid than producers of goods. My image of this parallel production system comes from the memoirs of Romanian political prisoner Herbert Zilber:

> The first great socialist industry was that of the production of files. . . . This new industry has an army of workers: the informers. It works with ultramodern electronic equipment (microphones, tape recorders, etc.), plus an army of typists with their typewriters. Without all this, socialism could not have survived. . . . In the socialist bloc, people and things exist only through their files. All our existence is in the hands of him who possesses files and is constituted by him who constructs them. Real people are but the reflection of their files.[12]

The work of producing files (and thereby political subjects) created an atmosphere of distrust and suspicion dividing people from one another. One never knew whom one could trust, who might be informing on one to the police about one's attitudes toward the regime or one's having an American to dinner. Declarations might also be false. Informers with a denunciation against someone else were never asked what might be their motive for informing; their perhaps-envious words entered directly into constituting another person's file – thus another person's sociopolitical being. Moreover, like all other parts of the bureaucracy, the police too padded their "production" figures, for the fact of an entry into the file was often more important than its veracity.[13] The existence of this shadowy system of production could have grave effects on the people "processed" through it, and the assumption that it was omnipresent contributed much to its success, in some countries, in suppressing unwanted opposition.

If surveillance was the negative face of these regimes' problematic legitimation, its positive face was their promises of social redistribution and welfare. At the center of both the Party's official ideology and its efforts to secure popular support was "socialist paternalism," which justified Party rule with the claim that the Party would take care of everyone's needs by collecting the total social product and then making available whatever people needed – cheap food, jobs, medical care, affordable housing, education, and so on. Party authorities claimed, as well, that they were better able to assess and fill these needs than were individuals or families, who would always tend to want more than their share. Herein lay the Party's paternalism: it acted like a father who gives handouts to the children as he sees fit. The Benevolent Father Party educated people to express needs it would then fill, and discouraged them from taking the initiative that would enable them to fill these needs on their own. The promises – socialism's basic social contract – did not go unnoticed, and as long as economic conditions permitted their partial fulfillment, certain socialist regimes gained legitimacy as a result. But this proved impossible to sustain.

Beyond its effects on people's attitudes, paternalism had important consequences for the entire system of production discussed previously and for consumption; here I shift to the question of why consumption was so central in the resistance to socialism. A Party that pretends to meet its citizens' needs through redistribution and that insists on doing so exclusively – that is, without enlisting their independent efforts – must control a tremendous fund of resources to redistribute. Nationalizing the means of production helped provide this, and so did a relentlessly "productionist" orientation, with ever-increased production plans and exhortations to greater effort.

The promise of redistribution was an additional reason, besides my earlier argument about shortages, why socialism worked differently from capitalism. Socialism's inner drive was to accumulate not profits, like capitalist ones, but distributable resources. This is more than simply a drive for autarchy, reducing dependency on the outside: it aims to increase dependency of those within. Striving to accumulate resources for redistribution involves things for which profit is totally irrelevant. In capitalism, those who run lemonade stands endeavor to serve thirsty customers in ways that make a profit and outcompete other lemonade-stand owners. In socialism, the point was not profit but the relationship between thirsty people and the one with the lemonade – the Party center, which appropriated from producers the various ingredients (lemons, sugar, water) and then mixed the lemonade to reward them with, as it saw fit. Whether someone made a profit was irrelevant: the transaction underscored the center's paternalistic superiority over its citizens – that is, its capacity to decide who got more lemonade and who got less.

Controlling the ingredients fortified the center's capacity to redistribute things. But this capacity would be even greater if the center controlled not only the lemons, sugar, and water but the things they come from: the lemon trees, the ground for growing sugar beet and the factories that process them, the wells and the well-digging machinery. That is, most valuable of all to the socialist bureaucracy was to get its hands not just on resources but on resources that generated *other* usable resources, resources that were themselves further productive. Socialist regimes wanted not just eggs but the goose that lays them. Thus if capitalism's inner logic rests on accumulating surplus value, the inner logic of socialism was to accumulate means of production.[14]

The emphasis on keeping resources at the center for redistribution is one reason why items produced in socialist countries so often proved uncompetitive on the world market. Basically, most of these goods were not being made to be sold competitively: they were being either centrally accumulated or redistributed at low prices – effectively given away. Thus, whether a dress was pretty and well made or ugly and missewn was irrelevant, since profit was not at issue: the dress would be "given away" at a subsidized price, not sold. In fact, the whole point was *not* to sell things: the center wanted to keep as much as possible under its control, because that was how it had redistributive power; and it wanted to give away the rest, because that was how it confirmed its legitimacy with the public. Selling things competitively was therefore beside the point. So too were ideas of "efficient" production, which for a capitalist would enhance profits by wasting less material or reducing wages. But whatever goes into calculating a profit – costs of material or labor inputs, or sales of goods – was unimportant in socialism until very late in the game. Instead, "efficiency" was understood to mean "the full use of existing resources," "the maximization of given capacities" rather than of results, all so as to redirect resources to a goal greater than satisfying the population's needs.[15] In other words, what was rational in socialism differed from capitalist rationality. Both are stupid in their own way, but differently so.

Consumption

Socialism's redistributive emphasis leads to one of the great paradoxes of a paternalist regime claiming to satisfy needs. Having constantly to amass means of production so as to enhance redistributive power caused Party leaders to prefer heavy industry (steel mills, machine construction) at the expense of consumer industry (processed foods or shoes). After all, once a consumer got hold of something, the center no longer controlled it; central power was less served by giving things away than by producing things it could continue to control. The central fund derived more from setting up a factory to make construction equipment than from a shoe factory or a chocolate works. In short, these systems had a basic tension between what was necessary to legitimate them – redistributing things to the masses – and what was necessary to their power – accumulating things at the center. The tension was mitigated where people took pride in their economy's development (that is, building heavy industry might also bring legitimacy), but my experience is that the legitimating effects of redistribution were more important by far.

Each country addressed this tension in its own way. For example, Hungary after 1968 and Poland in the 1970s gave things away more, while Romania and Czechoslovakia accumulated things more; but the basic tension existed everywhere. The socialist social contract guaranteed people food and clothing but did not promise (as capitalist systems do) quality, ready availability, and choice. Thus the system's mode of operation tended to sacrifice consumption in favor of production and controlling the products. This paradoxical neglect of consumption contributed to the long lines about which we heard so much (and we heard about them, of course, because we live in a system to which consumption is crucial).

In emphasizing this neglect of consumption as against building up the central resource base, I have so far been speaking of the *formally* organized economy of socialism – some call it the "first" or "official" economy. But this is not the whole story. Since the center would not supply what people needed, they struggled to do so themselves, developing in the process a huge repertoire of strategies for obtaining consumer goods and services. These strategies, called the "second" or "informal" economy, spanned a wide range from the quasi-legal to the definitely illegal.[16] In most socialist countries it was not illegal to moonlight for extra pay – by doing carpentry, say but people doing so often stole materials or illegally used tools from their workplace; or they might manipulate state goods to sell on the side. Clerks in stores might earn favors or extra money, for example, by saving scarce goods to sell to special customers, who tipped them or did some important favor in return. Also part of the second economy was the so-called "private plot" of collective-farm peasants, who each held their individual plot legally and in theory could do what they wanted with it: grow food for their own table or to sell in the market at state-controlled prices. But although the plot itself was legal, people obtained high outputs from it not just by virtue of hard work but also by stealing from the collective farm: fertilizer and herbicides, fodder for their pigs or cows, work time for their own weeding or harvesting, tractor time and fuel for plowing their plot, and so on. The second economy, then, which provisioned a large part of consumer needs, was parasitic upon the state economy and inseparable from it. It developed precisely because the state economy tended to ignore consumption. To grasp the interconnection of the two economies is crucial, lest one think that simply dismantling the state sector will automatically enable entrepreneurship – already present in embryo – to flourish. On the contrary: parts of the second economy will wither and die if deprived of the support of the official, state economy.

It is clear from what I have said that whereas consumption in our own society is considered primarily a socioeconomic question, the relative neglect of consumer interests in socialism made consumption deeply political. In Romania in the 1980s (an extreme case), to kill and eat your own calf was a political act, because the government prohibited killing calves: you were supposed to sell them cheap to the state farm, for export. Romanian villagers who fed me veal (having assured themselves of my complicity) did so with special satisfaction. It was also illegal for urbanites to go and buy forty kilograms of potatoes directly from the villagers who grew potatoes on their private plot, because the authorities suspected that villagers would charge more than the state-set price, thus enriching themselves. So Romanian policemen routinely stopped cars riding low on the chassis and confiscated produce they found inside.

Consumption became politicized in yet another way: the very definition of "needs" became a matter for resistance and dispute. "Needs," as we should know from our own experience, are not given: they are created, developed, expanded – the work especially of the advertising business. It is advertising's job to convince us that we need things we didn't know we needed, or that if we feel unhappy, it's because we need something (a shrink, or a beer, or a Marlboro, or a man). Our need requires only a name, and it can be satisfied with a product or service. Naming troubled states, labeling them as needs, and finding commodities to fill them is at the heart of our economy. Socialism, by contrast, which rested not on devising infinite kinds of things to sell people but on claiming to satisfy people's *basic* needs, had a very unadorned definition of them – in keeping with socialist egalitarianism. Indeed, some Hungarian dissidents wrote of socialism's relationship to needs as a "dictatorship."[17] As long as the food offered was edible or the clothes available covered you and kept you warm, that should be sufficient. If you had trouble finding even these, that just meant you were not looking hard enough. No planner presumed to investigate what kinds of goods people wanted, or worked to name new needs for newly created products and newly developed markets.

At the same time, however, regime policies paradoxically made consumption a problem. Even as the regimes prevented people from consuming by not making goods available, they insisted that, under socialism, the standard of living would constantly improve. This stimulated consumer appetites, perhaps with an eye to fostering increased effort and tying people into the system. Moreover, socialist ideology presented consumption as a "right." The system's organization exacerbated consumer desire further by frustrating it and thereby making it the focus of effort, resistance, and discontent. Anthropologist John Borneman sees in the relation between desire and goods a major contrast between capitalism and socialism. Capitalism, he says, repeatedly renders desire concrete and specific, and offers specific – if ever-changing – goods to satisfy it. Socialism, in contrast, aroused desire *without* focalizing it, and kept it alive by deprivation.[18]

As people became increasingly alienated from socialism and critical of its achievements, then the politicization of consumption also made them challenge official definitions of their needs. They did so not just by creating a second economy to grow food or make clothes or work after hours but also, sometimes, by public protest. Poland's Communist leaders fell to such protest at least twice, in 1970 and in 1980, when Polish workers insisted on having more food than government price increases would permit them. Less immediately disruptive were forms of protest in which people used consumption styles to forge resistant social identities. The black markets in Western goods that sprang up everywhere enabled alienated consumers to express their contempt for their governments through the kinds of things they chose to buy. You would spend an entire month's salary on a pair of blue jeans, for instance, but it was worth it: wearing them signified that you could get something the system said you didn't need and shouldn't have. Thus consumption goods and objects conferred an identity that set you off from socialism, enabling you to differentiate yourself as an individual in the face of relentless pressures to homogenize everyone's capacities and tastes into an undifferentiated collectivity. Acquiring objects became a way of constituting your selfhood against a deeply unpopular regime.

Bureaucratic factionalism and markets

Before turning to why these systems fell, I wish to address one more issue: politicking in the Party bureaucracy. Although this took different and specific forms in the different countries, it is important to mention the issue, for socialism's collapse owed much to shifts in the balance among factions that emerged within the Party apparatus. Even before 1989, researchers were pointing to several forms of intra-Party division. Polish sociologist Jadwiga Staniszkis, writing specifically of the moment of transition, speaks of three factions – the globalists, the populists, and the middle-level bureaucracy; others, writing more generally, distinguish between "strategic" and "operative" elites, the state bureaucracy and the "global monopoly," the bureaucracy and the Party elite, "in-house" and "out-of-house" Party workers, and so forth.[19] One way of thinking about these various divisions is that they distinguish ownership from management, or the people who oversaw the paperwork of administration from those "out in the field," intervening in actual social life.[20] We might then look for conflicting tendencies based in the different interests of these groups – such as conflicts between the central "owners" or paperworkers, on one hand, who might persist in policies that accumulated means of production without concern for things like productivity and output, and the bureaucratic managers of the allocative process or its fieldworkers, on the other, who *had* to be concerned with such things. Although the power of the system itself rested on continued accumulation, such tendencies if unchecked could obstruct the work of those who had actually to deliver resources or redistribute them. Without actual investments and hard material resources, lower-level units could not produce the means of production upon which both bureaucracy and center relied. If productive activity were so stifled by "overadministration" that nothing was produced, this would jeopardize the redistributive bureaucracy's power and prestige.

Thus, when central accumulation of means of production began to threaten the capacity of lower-level units to produce; when persistent imbalances between investment in heavy industry and in light industry, between allocations for investment and for consumption, and so on, diminished the stock of distributable goods; and when the center's attempts to keep enterprises from meddling with surplus appropriation obstructed the process of production itself – this is when pressure arose for a shift of emphasis. The pressure was partly from those in the wider society to whom not enough was being allocated and partly from bureaucrats themselves whose prestige and, increasingly, prospects of retaining power depended on having more goods to allocate. One then heard of decentralization, of the rate of growth, of productivity – in a word, of matters of output, rather than the inputs that lay at the core of bureaucratic performance. This is generally referred to as the language of "reform."

For those groups who became concerned with questions of output and productivity, the solutions almost always involved introducing mechanisms such as profitability criteria and freer markets. This meant, however, introducing a subordinate rationality discrepant with the system's inner logic and thereby threatening continued Party rule. Market forces create problems for socialism in part for reasons treated implicitly or explicitly above in contrasting capitalism's demand-constrained economies with socialism's economy of shortage (its lack of interest, for example, in the salability of its products). But more broadly, markets create problems because they move goods horizontally rather than vertically toward the center, as all redistributive systems require. Markets also presuppose that individual interest and the "invisible hand," rather than the guiding hand of the Party, secure the common good.[21] Because these horizontal movements and individualizing premises subverted socialism's hierarchical organization, market mechanisms had been suppressed. Reformers introducing them were opening a Pandora's box.

Why did it fall?

My discussion of socialism's workings already points to several reasons for its collapse; I might now address the question more comprehensively. To do this requires, in my view, linking the properties of its internal organization (discussed above) with properties of its external environment, as well as with shorter-term "event history." This means examining the specific conjuncture of two systems – "capitalist" and "socialist," to use ideal types – one encompassing the other.[22]

In event-history terms, the proximate cause of the fall of East European and Soviet socialism was an act of the Hungarian government: its dismantling of the barbed wire between Hungary and Austria, on the eve of a visit by President George Bush, and its later renouncing the treaty with the GDR that would have prevented East German emigration through Hungary. This culmination of Hungary's long-term strategy of opening up to the West gave an unexpected opportunity for some East German tourists to extend their Hungarian vacations into West Germany; the end result, given that Gorbachev refused to bolster the East German government with Soviet troops in this crisis, was to bring down the Berlin Wall. To understand the conjuncture in which Hungary could open its borders and Gorbachev could refuse Honecker his troops requires setting in motion the static model I have given above and placing it in its international context. This includes asking how socialism's encounter with a changing world capitalism produced or aggravated factional divisions within Communist Parties.

International solutions to internal problems

My discussion of socialism indicated several points of tension in its workings that affected the system's capacity for extended reproduction. Throughout their existence, these regimes sought to manage such tensions in different ways, ranging from Hungary's major market reforms in the 1960s to Romania's rejection of reform and its heightened coercive extraction. In all cases, managing these tensions involved decisions that to a greater or lesser degree opened socialist political economies to Western

75

capital. The impetus for this opening – critical to socialism's demise – came chiefly from within, as Party leaders attempted to solve their structural problems without major structural reform. Their attitude in doing so was reminiscent of a "plunder mentality" that sees the external environment as a source of booty to be used as needed in maintaining one's own system, without thought for the cost. This attitude was visible in the tendency of socialist governments to treat foreign trade as a residual sector, used to supplement budgets without being made an integral part of them.[23] Because of how this opportunistic recourse to the external environment brought socialism into tighter relationship with capitalism, it had fateful consequences.

The critical intersection occurred not in 1989 or 1987 but in the late 1960s and early 1970s, when global capitalism entered the cyclical crisis from which it is still struggling to extricate itself. Among capitalists' possible responses to the crisis (devaluation, structural reorganization, etc.), an early one was to lend abroad: facilitating this option were the massive quantities of petrodollars that were invested in Western banks, following changes in OPEC policy in 1973. By lending, Western countries enabled the recipients to purchase capital equipment or to build long-term infrastructure, thereby expanding the overseas markets for Western products.[24]

The loans became available just at the moment when all across the socialist bloc, the first significant round of structural reforms had been proposed, halfheartedly implemented, and, because profitability and market criteria fit so poorly with the rationale of socialism, largely abandoned. Reluctance to proceed with reforms owed much, as well, to Czechoslovakia's Prague Spring, from which the Party apparatus all across the region had been able to see the dangers that reform posed for its monopoly on power. Instead of reforming the system from within, then, most Party leaderships opted to meet their problems by a greater articulation with the surrounding economy: importing Western capital and using it to buy advanced technology (or, as in Poland, to subsidize consumption), in hopes of improving economic performance. Borrowing thus became a substitute for extensive internal changes that would have jeopardized the Party's monopoly over society and subverted the inner mechanisms of socialism. In this way, the internal cycles of two contrasting systems suddenly meshed.

The intent, as with all the international borrowing of the period, was to pay off the loans by exporting manufactured goods into the world market. By the mid-1970s it was clear, however, that the world market could not absorb sufficient amounts of socialism's products to enable repayment and, at the same time, rising interest rates added staggeringly to the debt service. With the 1979–80 decision of the Western banking establishment not to lend more money to socialist countries, the latter were thrown into complete disarray. I have already mentioned several features that made socialist economies inept competitors in the international export market. The "plunder" stance toward external economics, the system's fundamental organization against notions of salability of its products, the shortage economy's premium on acquisitionsmanship rather than on salesmanship, the neglect of consumption and of producing to satisfy consumer needs with diverse high-quality products – all this meant that an adequate response to the hard-currency crisis would have catastrophic effects on socialism's inner mechanisms. To this was added the fact that socialist economies were "outdated"; as Jowitt put it, "After 70 years of murderous effort, the Soviet Union had created a German industry of the 1880s in the 1980s."[25]

In these circumstances, the balance of power tilted toward the faction within the Communist Party of the Soviet Union that had long argued for structural reforms, the introduction of market mechanisms, and profit incentives, even at the cost of the Party's "leading role." The choice, as Gorbachev and his faction saw it, was to try to preserve either the Soviet Union and its empire (by reforms that would increase its economic performance and political legitimacy) or collective property and the Party monopoly. Gorbachev was ready to sacrifice the latter to save the former but ended by losing both.

While Western attention was riveted on the speeches of policy-makers in the Kremlin, the more significant aspects of reform, however, were in the often-unauthorized behavior of bureaucrats who were busily creating new property forms on their own. Staniszkis describes the growth of what she calls "political capitalism," as bureaucrats spontaneously created their own profit-based companies from within the state economic bureaucracy. Significantly for my argument that socialism's articulation with world capitalism was crucial to its fall, the examples she singles out to illustrate these trends are all at the interface of socialist economies with the outside world – in particular, new companies mediating the export trade and state procurement of Western computers.[26] In fact, she sees as critical the factional split between the groups who managed socialism's interface with the outside world (such as those in foreign policy, counterintelligence, and foreign trade) and those who managed it internally (such as the Party's middle-level executive apparatus and the KGB).[27] Forms of privatization already taking place as early as 1987 in Poland and similar processes as early as 1984 in Hungary[28] show the emerging contours of what Staniszkis sees as the reformists' goal: a dual economy. One part of this economy was to be centrally administered, as before, and the other part was to be reformed through market/profit mechanisms and selective privatization of state property. The two were to coexist symbiotically.[29]

These forms of "political capitalism" arose in part by economic managers' exploiting the shortages endemic to socialism – shortages now aggravated to crisis proportions. In the new hope of making a profit, "political capitalists" (I call them "entrepratchiks") were willing to put into circulation reserves known only to them – which they would otherwise have hoarded – thus alleviating shortages, to their own gain. As a result, even antireformist Soviet and Polish bureaucrats found themselves acquiescing in entrepratchiks' activities, without which, in Staniszkis's words, "the official structure of the economic administration was absolutely unsteerable."[30] Contributing to their tolerance was rampant bureaucratic anarchy, a loss of control by those higher up, rooted in the "inability of superiors to supply their subordinates (managers of lower level) with the means to construct a strategy of survival."[31] Because superiors could no longer guarantee deliveries and investments, they were forced to accept whatever solutions enterprising subordinates could devise – even at the cost of illicit profits from state reserves. Entrepratchiks soon began to regard the state's accumulations much as Preobrazhensky had once urged Soviet leaders to regard agriculture; as a source of primitive accumulation. They came to find increasingly attractive the idea of further "privatization," so important to Western lenders.

It is possible (though unlikely) that socialist regimes would not have collapsed if their hard-currency crisis and the consequent intersection with capitalism had occurred at a different point in capitalism's cyclicity. The specifics of capitalism's own crisis management, however, proved unmanageable for socialist systems. Without wanting to present recent capitalism's "flexible specialization" as either unitary or fully dominant (its forms differ from place to place, and it coexists with other socio-economic forms), I find in the literature about it a number of characteristics even more inimical to socialism than was the earlier "Fordist" variant, which Soviet production partly imitated. These characteristics include: small-batch production; just-in-time inventory; an accelerated pace of innovation; tremendous reductions in the turnover time of capital via automation and electronics; a much-increased turnover time in consumption, as well, with a concomitant rise in techniques of need-creation and an increased emphasis on the production of events rather than goods; coordination of the economy by finance capital; instantaneous access to accurate information and analysis; and an overall decentralization that increases managerial control (at the expense of higher-level bodies) over labor.[32]

How is socialism to mesh with this? – socialism with its emphasis on large-scale heroic production of means of production, its resources frozen by hoarding – no just-in-time here! – its lack of a systemic impetus toward innovation, the irrelevance to it of notions like "turnover time," its neglect of consumption and its flat-footed definition of "needs," its constipated and secretive flows of information (except for rumors!) in which the center could have no confidence, and the perpetual struggle to retain central control over all phases of the production process? Thus, I submit, it is not simply socialism's embrace with capitalism that brought about its fall but the fact that it happened to embrace a capitalism of a newly "flexible" sort. David Harvey's schematic comparison of "Fordist modernity" with "flexible post-modernity" clarifies things further: socialist systems have much more in common with his "Fordist" column than with his "flexible" one.[33]

Let me add one more thought linking the era of flexible specialization with socialism's collapse. Increasing numbers of scholars note that accompanying the change in capitalism is a change in the nature of state power: specifically, a number of the state's functions are being undermined.[34] The international weapons trade has made a mockery of the state's monopoly on the means of violence. The extraordinary mobility of capital means that as it moves from areas of higher to areas of lower taxation, many states lose some of their revenue and industrial base, and this constrains their ability to attract capital or shape its flows. Capital flight can now discipline all nation-state governments.[35] The coordination of global capitalism by finance capital places a premium on capital mobility, to which rigid state boundaries are an obstacle. And the new computerized possibilities for speculative trading have generated strong pressures to release the capital immobilized in state structures and institutions by diminishing their extent.[36]

This has two consequences for the collapse of socialism. First, groups inside socialist countries whose structural situation facilitated their fuller participation in the global economy now had reasons to expand their state's receptivity to capital – that is, to promote reform. Second, the control that socialist states exerted over capital flows into their countries may have made them special targets for international financial interests, eager to increase their opportunities by undermining socialist states. These internal and international groups each found their chance in the interest of the other. It is in any case clear from the politics of international lending agencies that they aim to reduce the power of socialist states, for they insist upon privatization of state property – the basis of these states' power and revenue. Privatization is pushed even in the face of some economists' objections that "too much effort is being invested in privatization, and too little in creating and fostering the development of new private firms" – whose entry privatization may actually impede.[37]

No time for socialism

Rather than explore further how flexible specialization compelled changes in socialism, I wish to summarize my argument by linking it to notions of time. Time, as anthropologists have shown, is a fundamental dimension of human affairs, taking different forms in different kinds of society. The Western notion of a linear, irreversible time consisting of equivalent and divisible units, for instance, is but one possible way of conceptualizing time and living it. A given cultural construction of time ramifies throughout its social order. Its calendars, schedules, and rhythms establish the very grounds of daily life (which is why elites, especially revolutionary ones, often manipulate them), undergird power and inequality, and affect how people make themselves as social beings.

Capitalism exists only as a function of time – and of a specific conception of it. Efforts to increase profits by increasing the velocity of capital circulation are at its very heart. Thus, each major reorganization of capitalism has entailed, in Harvey's terms, "time–space compression": a shrinking of the time horizons of private and public decision-making, whose consequences encompass ever-wider spaces owing to changed communications and transport technology.[38] The basic logic of socialism, by contrast, placed no premium on increasing turnover time and capital circulation. Although the rhetoric of Stalinism emphasized socialism as a highly dynamic system, for the most part Soviet leaders acted as if time were on their side. (When Khrushchev said, "We will bury you," he was not too specific about the date.) Indeed, I have argued that in 1980s Romania, far from being speeded up, time was being gradually slowed down, flattened, immobilized, and rendered nonlinear.[39]

Like the reorganization of capitalism at the end of the nineteenth century, the present reorganization entails a time–space compression, which we all feel as a mammoth speedup. Yet the socialism with which it intersected had no such time-compressing dynamic. In this light, the significance of Gorbachev's perestroika was its recognition that socialism's temporality was unsustainable in a capitalist world. Perestroika reversed Soviet ideas as to whose time-definition and rhythms were dominant and where dynamism lay: no longer within the socialist system but outside it, in the West. Gorbachev's rhetoric from the mid-1980s is full of words about time: the Soviet Union needs to "catch up," to "accelerate" its development, to shed its "sluggishness" and "inertia" and leave behind the "era of stagnation." For him, change has suddenly become an "urgent" necessity.

> [By] the latter half of the seventies . . . the country began to lose momentum. . . . Elements of stagnation . . . began to appear. . . . A kind of "braking mechanism" affect[ed] social and economic development. . . . The inertia of extensive economic development was leading to an economic deadlock and stagnation.[40]

These are the words of a man snatched by the compression of space and time.

Even as he spoke, new time/space-compressing technologies were wreaking havoc on the possible rhythms of his and other leaders' control of politics, as Radio Free Europe made their words at once domestic *and* international. Soviet leaders could no longer create room for themselves by saying one thing for domestic consumption and something else for the outside world: they were now prisoners of simultaneity. The role of Western information technology in undermining socialism was evident in the spread of Solidarity's strikes in 1980, news of which was telephoned out to the West and rebroadcast instantly into Poland via Radio Free Europe and the BBC, mobilizing millions of Poles against their Party. The revolutions of 1989 were mediated similarly.

I am suggesting, then, that the collapse of socialism came in part from the massive rupture produced by its collision with capitalism's speedup. If so, it would be especially useful to know something more about the life-experience of those people who worked at the interface of these two temporal systems and could not help realizing how different was capitalism's time from their own. Bureaucrats under pressure to increase foreign trade and foreign revenues, or importers of computer equipment, would have discovered that failure to adapt to alien notions of increased turnover time could cost them hard currency. They would have directly experienced time-annihilating Western technologies, which effected a banking transaction in milliseconds as opposed to the paper-laden hours and days needed by their own financial system. Did the rise of "profitability" criteria in the command economy owe something to such people's dual place ment? Did they come to experience differently their sense of themselves as agents? My point, in short, is that the fall of socialism lies not simply in the intersection of two systems' temporal cycles but rather in the collision of two differently constituted temporal orders, together with the notions of person and activity proper to them.

If socialist economies had not opened themselves to capital import and to debt servicing, perhaps their collision with capitalist speedup would have been less jarring – or would at least have occurred on more equal terms. But the capitalist definition of time prevailed, as socialist debtors bowed to its dictates (even while postponing them), thereby aggravating factional conflicts within the elite. Because its leaders accepted Western temporal hegemony, socialism's messianic time proved apocalyptic. The irony is that had debtor regimes refused the definitions imposed from without – had they united to default simultaneously on their Western loans (which in 1981 stood at over $90 billion[41]) – they might well have brought down the world financial system and realized Khrushchev's threatening prophecy overnight. That this did not happen shows how vital a thing was capitalists' monopoly on the definition of social reality.

What comes next?

The outcome of the confluence between socialist and capitalist systemic crises is far more complicated than "capitalism triumphant," however.

Ken Jowitt captures this with an unexpected metaphor, that of biological extinction and its attendant erasure of formerly existing boundaries among forms of life. In his brilliant essay "The Leninist Extinction," he pursues the metaphor's implications as follows:

> [One feature] of mass extinctions . . . is that they typically affect more than one species. In this respect, the collapse of European Leninism may be seen more as a political volcano than as an asteroid. A volcano's eruption initially affects a circumscribed area (in this case limited to Leninist regimes), but, depending on its force, the effects gradually but dramatically become global. The Leninist volcano of 1989 will have a comparable effect on liberal and "Third World" biota around the globe.[42]

After describing the new regime "species" that have emerged with changed forms of government in Poland, Hungary, Romania, and elsewhere, as well as other new forms of political life arising out of Yugoslavia and the Soviet Union, he ponders the larger question of the end of the Cold War:

> For half a century we have thought in terms of East and West, and now there is no East as such. The primary axis of international politics has "disappeared." Thermonuclear Russia hasn't, but the Soviet Union/Empire most certainly has. Its "extinction" radically revises the framework within which the West, the United States itself, the Third World, and the countries of Eastern Europe, the former Russian Empire, and many nations in Asia have bounded and defined themselves.
>
> The Leninist Extinction will force the United States [not to mention all those others] to reexamine the meaning of its national identity.[43]

What the Leninist Extinction confronts us with, then, is a conceptual vacuum. Jowitt concludes by invoking the biblical story of Genesis ("the world was without form, and void"), whose theme is bounding and naming new entities, as the "narrative" most appropriate to the immediate future.

In my view, not only is Jowitt absolutely right but one could go even further. It is not just new political identities, including our own, that we will have the task of bounding and naming – a task which, if the example of Bosnia is any indication, is of awesome magnitude. It is also the entire conceptual arsenal through which Western institutions and social science disciplines have been defined in this century. As one reads scholarship on the postsocialist processes of "privatization," the creation of "property rights," the development of "democracy" or "civil society" or "constitutions" – in short, the proposed building of a "liberal state" – profound confusion sets in. One begins to see that these terms do not label useful concepts: they are elements in a massive political and ideological upheaval that is by no means restricted to the "East."

If this is true, then everything we know is up for grabs, and "what comes next" is anyone's guess.

Notes

Source Reprinted by permission of the publisher from Katherine Verdery, *What Was Socialism and What Comes Next* (Princeton, NJ: Princeton University Press, 1996), pp. 19–38. Copyright © 1996 Princeton University Press.

Acknowledgment This chapter was originally entitled "What Was Socialism, and What Comes Next?" and was delivered as a lecture for the Center for Comparative Research in History, Society and Culture, at the University of California, Davis, in January 1993. I am grateful to those – William Hagen, G. William Skinner, and Carol A. Smith – who invited me as well as to members of the Center's seminar, for a very stimulating discussion. I also received helpful advice from Ashraf Ghani. Earlier forms of the argument appeared in "Theorizing Socialism" and in my book, *National Ideology under Socialism: Identity and Cultural Politics in Ceaușescu's Romania* (Berkeley and Los Angeles, CA: University of California Press, 1991). The underlying conceptualization was developed in 1988; after 1989 I added some thoughts on how the model might illuminate the system's collapse. Reprinted from *Contention: Debates in Society, Culture, and Science* 1, no. 3 (1993), by permission of Indiana University Press.

1 Cf. Bahro's "actually existing socialism." Rudolph Bahro, *The Alternative in Eastern Europe* (London: Verso, 1978).
2 János Kornai, *The Socialist System: The Political Economy of Communism* (Princeton, NJ: Princeton University Press, 1992).
3 See especially Elemér Hankiss, *East European Alternatives* (New York: Oxford University Press, 1990); Ágnes Horváth and Árpád Szakolczai, *The Dissolution of Communist Power: The Case of Hungary* (New York: Routledge, 1992); and Jadwiga Staniszkis, *The Dynamics of the Breakthrough in Eastern Europe: The Polish Experience* (Berkeley and Los Angeles, CA: University of California Press, 1991) and *The Ontology of Socialism* (New York: Oxford University Press, 1992).
4 In particular: Pavel Campeanu, *The Origins of Stalinism: From Leninist Revolution to Stalinist Society* (Armonk, NY: M. E. Sharpe, 1986) and *The Genesis of the Stalinist Social Order* (Armonk, NY. M. E. Sharpe, 1988); Ferenc Fehér, Agnes Heller, and György Márkus, *Dictatorship over Needs: An Analysis of Soviet Societies* (New York: Blackwell, 1983); George Konrád and Ivan Szelényi, *The Intellectuals on the Road to Class Power: A Sociological Study of the Role of the Intelligentsia in Socialism* (New York: Harcourt, Brace, Jovanovich, 1979); and János Kornai, *The Socialist System*, and *Economics of Shortage* (Amsterdam: North-Holland, 1980).
5 See also my "Theorizing Socialism: A Prologue to the 'Transition,'" *American Ethnologist* 18 (1991): 419–39.

6 Jan Gross has argued the weakness of socialist states from a somewhat different vantage point. See his discussion of the "spoiler state" in *Revolution from Abroad: The Soviet Conquest of Poland's Western Ukraine and Western Belorussia* (Princeton, NJ: Princeton University Press, 1988). See also my "Theorizing Socialism," pp. 426–8.

7 This section draws upon Michael Burawoy's discussion in *The Politics of Production* (London: Verso, 1985), as well as the sources listed in Note 4.

8 See Kornai, *Economies of Shortage* and *The Socialist System*.

9 See Burawoy, *The Politics of Production*, Chapter 4.

10 Michael Burawoy and János Lukács, *The Radiant Past: Ideology and Reality in Hungary's Road to Capitalism* (Chicago, IL: University of Chicago Press, 1992), Chapter 5.

11 Cf. Burawoy, *The Politics of Production*.

12 Andrei Şerbulescu (Belu Zilber), *Monarhia de drept dialectic* (Bucharest: Humanitas, 1991), pp. 136–8.

13 These observations show how fraught is the use of files in assessing fitness for political office (as in the Czech practice of "lustration").

14 Campeanu, *The Genesis of the Stalinist Social Order*, pp. 117–18.

15 Horváth and Szakolczai, *The Dissolution of Communist Power*, pp. 77–8.

16 See, e.g., István Gábor, "The Second (Secondary) Economy," *Acta Oeconomica* 3–4 (1979): 291–311; and Steven Sampson, "The Second Economy in Eastern Europe and the Soviet Union," *Annals of the American Association of Political and Social Science* 493 (1986): 120–36.

17 Fehérr et al., *Dictatorship over Needs*.

18 John Borneman, *After the Wall* (New York: Basic Books, 1990), pp. 17–18.

19 Jadwiga Staniszkis, "Patterns of Change in Eastern Europe," *Eastern European Politics and Societies* 4 (1990): 77–97; Burawoy and Lukács, *The Radiant Past*, pp. 90–92, 96–100; Campeanu, *The Genesis of the Stalinist Social Order*, pp. 143–57; Konrád and Szelényi, *The Intellectuals on the Road to Class Power*, p. 153; Horváth and Szakolczai, *The Dissolution of Communist Power*, pp. 204–5. See also Leslie Benson, "Partynomialism, Bureaucratism, and Economic Reform in the Soviet Power System," *Theory and Society* 19 (1990): 92.

20 Campeanu, *The Genesis of the Stalinist Social Order*, pp. 143–57; and Horváth and Szakolczai, *The Dissolution of Communist Power*, pp. 204–5.

21 Horváth and Szakolczai, *The Dissolution of Communist Power*, pp. 48–9.

22 Analyses that attempt something like this include Terry Boswell and Ralph Peters, "State Socialism and the Industrial Divide in the World Economy," *Critical Sociology* 17 (1990): 3–34; and Valerie Bunce, "The Empire Strikes Back: The Evolution of the Eastern Bloc from a Soviet Asset to a Soviet Liability," *International Organization* 39 (1985): 1–16. See also Daniel Chirot, "After Socialism, What?" *Contention* 1 (1991): 29–49.

23 Paul Hare, "Industrial Development of Hungary since World War II," *East European Politics and Societies* 2 (1988): 115–51.

24 David Harvey, *The Condition of Postmodernity* (Oxford: Blackwell, 1989), p. 184.

25 Ken Jowitt, "The Leninist Extinction," in Daniel Chirot, ed., *The Crisis of Leninism and the Decline of the Left* (Seattle, WA: University of Washington Press, 1991), p. 78.

26 Jadwiga Staniszkis, "'Political Capitalism' in Poland," *Eastern European Politics and Societies* 5 (1991): 129–30.

27 Staniszkis, "Patterns of Change in Eastern Europe," pp. 79–83.

28 David Stark, "Privatization in Hungary: From Plan to Market or from Plant to Clan?" *East European Politics and Societies* 4 (1990): 364–5.

29 Staniszkis, "Patterns of Change in Eastern Europe," pp. 77–8.
30 Staniszkis, "'Political Capitalism' in Poland," p. 131.
31 Staniszkis, *The Dynamics of the Breakthrough in Eastern Europe*, p. 164.
32 See Harvey, *The Condition of Postmodernity*, pp. 156, 164, 340–1.
33 Ibid., pp. 340–1.
34 E.g., Eric Hobsbawm, *Nations and Nationalism since 1780* (Cambridge: Cambridge University Press, 1990), pp. 181–3; and Charles Tilly, "Prisoners of the State," *International Social Science Journal* 44 (1992): 329–42, and *Coercion, Capital, and European States*, A.D. 990–1990 (Oxford: Blackwell, 1990).
35 Harvey, *The Condition of Postmodernity*, pp. 164–5.
36 Thanks to Jane Guyer for this observation.
37 Peter Murrell, "Privatization Complicates the Fresh Start," *Orbis* 36 (1992): 325.
38 Harvey, *The Condition of Postmodernity*, p. 147.
39 Verdery, *What Was Socialism and What Comes Next* (Princeton, NJ: Princeton University Press, 1996), pp. 39–57.
40 Mikhail Gorbachev, *Perestroika: New Thinking for Our Country and the World* (New York: Harper and Row, 1987), pp. 5, 6.
41 Bunce, "The Empire Strikes Back," p. 39.
42 Jowitt, "The Leninist Extinction," pp. 80–1.
43 Ibid., pp. 81–2.

Part II

MEANING

4

THE BREAKDOWN OF COMMUNIST REGIMES

S. N. Eisenstadt

In this theoretically challenging essay, political sociologist S. N. Eisenstadt emphasizes the role of critical intellectuals in the making of the revolutions of 1989. This is an important topic addressed by other contributors (particularly Timothy Garton Ash). While he notices the similarities with previous revolutionary cleavages in history, Eisenstadt insists on what makes the revolutions of 1989 truly new, unprecedented events of radical transformations of societies, economies, and cultures. He lists as major novel features: the absence of class consciousness among the revolutionaries; their commitment to non-violent means of resistance and opposition; the conspicuous absence of charismatic, utopian, and teleological elements. Indeed, the implication of Eisenstadt's argument is that these were new types of revolutions, in which the ideological blueprints were programmatically rejected.

The revolutionaries of 1989 relied on a broad vision of human and civic rights and consistently opposed the attempts to reduce their aspirations to an ideological straitjacket. Thus, Eisenstadt concludes, in agreement with the selections in this volume from Timothy Garton Ash and Jeffrey C. Isaac, that the revolutions of 1989 symbolized the opposite of the Jacobin (or Marxist) ambition to transform the world along the lines of an eschatological (salvationist) project. Compared to classical revolutions, these major events did not sacralize the center of politics and refused to engage in missionary zealotry. Eisenstadt offers an instructive discussion of revolutionary "causes" and "effects" focusing on the major contradictions of modernity. His interpretation of the risks and threats following the revolutionary drama is close to Bruce Ackerman's and Ken Jowitt's contributions elsewhere in this volume.

* * *

I

The breakdown of the communist regimes in Eastern Europe has been one of the more dramatic events in the history of humankind, certainly one of

89

the most dramatic since the end of the Second World War. What is the significance? Are these revolutions like "the great revolutions" – the English civil war, the American, French, Russian, and Chinese revolutions – which in many ways ushered in modernity, creating the modern political order?[1] Are they likely to lead – after a possibly turbulent period of transition – to a relatively stable world of modernity, with liberal constitutionalism heralding some kind of "end of history"? Or do they tell us something of the vicissitudes and fragilities of modernity, even of democratic-constitutional regimes.

II

In one sense, obviously, the breakdown of the communist regimes are revolutions – drastic, dramatic changes of regime. These changes, unlike many of the regime changes in Latin American or South Asian history, were closely connected with crucial ideological and cultural transformations. The revolutionary process itself, the social process that brought about these changes, shows interesting parallels with what happened in the "classical" revolutions. A combination of popular uprisings with struggles at the center – struggles that focused around various attempts at reform, started during Andropov's short regime, especially between "conservatives and reformists" – were very serious indeed. These struggles, combined with wider popular uprisings, together helped topple the communist regime.[2]

Another element common to both these changes and the great revolutions was the crucially important role of intellectuals. They played a vital part in the breakdown of the communist regimes – as the Puritans had in England, as intellectuals did to some degree in America. It is scarcely necessary to emphasize the role played by the different clubs of the Enlightenment in the French Revolution, or the contributions of the Russian intelligentsia.[3] Major intellectual figures like Havel, less well-known Catholic priests in Poland, and a variety of East German Protestant ministers were conspicuous in all these late-twentieth-century processes, so much so that the claim was often made that the breakdown of the communist regimes was indeed the work of intellectuals. While various intellectual groups were important, their mode of activity, as well as their basic orientation, was not that of intellectuals in the classical revolutions.

Their participation in hastening the process of the breakdown of the communist regimes in Eastern Europe did much to intensify the element of principled protest in all these revolutions. The popular protest was not just a protest against wrongdoing by the authorities, a demand for redress, for better behavior. In addition to all such demands, there were highly principled statements made in the name of liberty – what was often called civil society – promulgated essentially by intellectuals. As in the classical revolutions, this principled protest helped bring the regimes

90

down. The combination of political activity by many different groups – with participation by intellectuals – attests to a strong historical and phenomenological relationship with those great revolutions that ushered in modern political life, in which such combinations were central.

Similarly, the processes that brought about the demise of these regimes – the combination of economic decline, together with a deterioration of their international standing, and the growing awareness among large sectors of the population of the sharp contradictions between the bases of their legitimation and their actual performance – were to some extent reminiscent of those common to the classical revolutions.

III

The similarities, where they exist, are striking and by no means accidental. Still, differences are no less obvious – especially those related to new types of technology, particularly in communication – evident in the role television played in all these revolutions. Yet, even in this respect, the differences ought not to be exaggerated. While there was no television or even radio to record or comment on the events of the great revolutions, influencing them, the invention of printing and the use of the presses for political purposes played a crucial role in all the earlier revolutions.

Of greater importance, certainly, is that the repudiated economic structures, developed by the East European regimes, were characterized by a relatively modern, industrialized political economy; the revolutions did not constitute a rebellion or protest against a traditional authoritarian *ancien régime*, a protest in the name of enlightenment and reason against a long-constituted political authority.

Beyond these differences in background and causes, in their respective concrete historical settings, there were far-reaching differences in the revolutionary process itself. First, it would be difficult to say whether these were bourgeois or proletarian revolutions. Even in respect to the classical revolutions, these definitions are not always helpful or enlightening; in respect to the events in Eastern Europe they are meaningless. If there were specific social sectors predominant in bringing down these regimes, they included some intellectuals, certain potential professionals, sometimes abetted by workers, who did not appear to be the bearers of any very strong class consciousness.

Another difference must be noted. With the exception of Romania, the process was relatively bloodless, nonviolent. Where protest and violent demonstrations occurred, they were in comparative perspective very limited. Nor was the violence, when it happened, sanctified or sacralized, as it had been in most of the classical revolutions. There was no such extolling of violence either in Eastern Europe or in the USSR itself. It was the other way around – those who were opposed to the communist regimes accused the incumbents of having recourse to violence, to suppress those who would unseat them.[4]

Although ethnic and national tensions were strong in all these societies, ethnic violence was uncommon – except in the single instance of Yugoslavia– in the process that brought these regimes down. Only later, after their downfall, did such conflicts become much more prominent.

The relatively low level of violence is evident in the fact that the old rulers, except in Romania, were pushed out in a bloodless way. They were rarely punished; few were tried. Even in Germany, where there was talk of bringing Honnecker to court, nothing happened; the Soviets took him away, and only now are East German officials being brought before a general (not East) German court. It is significant that it is mostly in Germany – where the distinct East German state was abolished – that the most widespread legal proceedings are being undertaken. Meanwhile, Zhivkov is now being tried in Bulgaria, and some further developments in this direction will perhaps take place. There will probably be more court cases, there will probably be some witch hunting, but it is very doubtful whether there will be anything like the trials of Charles I or Louis XVI, the "semi trial" of George III in America, or the execution of the czar.

The ruling elites of these regimes (again with the exception of Romania) did not generally fight; they gave up, abdicating relatively easily. Many would certainly have tried to hold on to power had they been able to depend on Soviet tanks to support them. Yet, the relative ease with which the rulers, and not only those at the top, but in the middle echelons of the party and the bureaucracy, gave up, or were prepared, as in Hungary or Bulgaria, to try their fortunes in new open parliamentary elections, is somewhat surprising. Of special interest, certainly, is the fact that the middle echelons of the security forces of the armies no longer protected the rulers or the regimes. They surrendered power quickly, and not because they had lost a war. This is intriguing, especially when one recalls that many of these middle echelons benefited greatly from the regimes: that the security organization and the armies were major avenues of social mobility. Yet, often, the various echelons in these organizations, gave up – willingly or unwillingly – without resistance. Similarly, it is very important to note that almost all the changes of regime were made within the framework of existing political institutions, prevailing constitutions. Even the initial constitutional changes, including the most dramatic – the abolition of the monopoly of the Communist Party – were effected or ratified in the legislative frameworks of the preceding regimes, in the existing parliaments. There was no need to change the whole structure of government to create entirely new constitutional frameworks for this to be done. To no small degree, it was accomplished through processes prescribed by the existing constitutions, or by extra-parliamentary consultants later ratified by the parliaments.

While new constitutions are now being negotiated, and constitutional commissions have been set up to do this work, this is intended to highlight the break with the past. Still, it is impossible to ignore the fact that change was effected relatively peacefully within the framework of existing constitutional institutions. It is much too early to know how stable any of these constitutional arrangements will be.

The same is true of the symbolic changes effected, for instance in Hungary, where the communist symbols were removed everywhere, or in Poland, where some expect the crown to be put back on the Polish eagle, removed by the communist regime. The name of the Czechoslovak Republic, changed to the Republic of the Czechs and Slovaks [before the establishment of two separate states], heralds other important symbolic and radical structural changes that may soon be instituted. Yet, most or all of these changes were effected within existing constitutional frameworks, through existing constitutional procedures and processes – or, at a minimum, ratified by these procedures. Very few changes were made in other ways. These facts emphasize, of course, the far-reaching differences from the way in which the classical revolutions of another age developed.

IV

So, also, the political, social, and cultural programs promulgated by these revolutions are radically different from those of the past. In all these, the earlier charismatic and utopian elements are conspicuously missing.[5] While ideological demands for freedom and a market economy were made – which do indeed contain some vague "utopian" nonrealistic expectations – the market economy was never sanctified in the manner in which the "rights of man" figured in the French Revolution. There was no totalistic, utopian vision rooted in eschatological expectations of a new type of society. The vision or visions promulgated in Central and Eastern Europe, calling for freedom from repressive totalitarian or authoritarian regimes, relied on various pragmatic adjustments. Eschatological visions, the idea of creating a new total cultural and social order according to some utopian prescription, and oriented to some millenial future, were very feeble throughout these last years.[6]

The absence of this utopian or eschatological component was closely related to yet another crucial difference, having to do with the attitude of the revolutionary groups toward the center, toward the construction of a new center. In all the classical revolutions, the utopian and eschatological visions, together with the sanctification of violence, promoted a very strong tendency to charismatize politics. The classical revolutionaries believed that politics could change society; that through the charismatic reconstruction of the political center, a total change of society could be effected. There is very little of such charismatization of the center or of politics in these East European revolutions, though some elements of such belief can be found. Similarly, any tendency to reconstruct the center as a continuous liminal arena remains very weak.[7]

In other words, the Jacobin element – so crucial in all the classical revolutions, certainly in the Puritan (English) one, though milder in America, but very strong in the French and even more in the Russian and Chinese revolutions, which constituted a central core in all the totalitarian communist regimes – is almost entirely missing, though its head reappears here and there from time to time. Indeed, it is "antipolitics" – the flight from central politics as espoused by Györgi Konrád and many others – that seems to be much more in vogue today in Eastern and Central Europe.[8]

Another component of classical revolutions almost wholly missing in Eastern Europe today is that of universalistic visions, emphasizing the missionary role of such visions. While the breakdown of the communist regimes in Eastern Europe was seen by participants and others as having universal significance – a fact continuously emphasized by the media, especially television – these occurrences did not impose revolutionary missions. They were not ideas borne by missionary zealots. While there were continuous contacts between different protest movements and indeed common consultations, no distinctive missionary universalistic utopian vision developed, redolent of the French and Russian revolutions, or of the Puritan revolt. No revolutionary armies walked about from one place to another hoping to reshape their respective societies.[9]

When Havel came to Poland he did not bring an army to revolutionize Poland; he came as head of a friendly neighboring state, to speak before the Polish Sejm. There was no new revolutionary International; only a plethora of discussion groups, seminars, and the like, with a very strong emphasis on common themes, such as civil society, freedom, constitutional democracy, and – to some extent – the free market. There was no strong missionary universalistic push, a core element in many of the great revolutions, especially in France and Russia. Accordingly, the future is much more open. As there is no utopian sanctification of politics, the future is not prescribed by totalistic utopian visions with strong missionary orientations. The weakness of the utopian and missionary elements was closely related to the basic character of intellectuals, the *Kulturträger*, who were active, very often central, but no longer pursuing the roles characteristic of intellectuals in the great revolutions, or in many of the major modern social movements.

The vision they represented had changed from the classical revolutionary one, as indeed had many of their activities. Most of these East European intellectuals grew up and were active – even if frequently suppressed and mostly highly regulated – in the framework of modern academic, professional, or literary institutions recognized to be betraying some of their principal ideals. While often rebelling against the totalistic utopian visions in the name of which the communist regimes legitimized themselves, some were openly pragmatic; others talked in the name of freedom, extolling the ideals of civil society and private morality. They were no longer bearers of the strong Jacobin eschatological visions characteristic of so many of the classical revolutionary intellectuals.

Other actors, wholly secondary in the great revolutions – above all the bearers of national, ethnic, and to some extent religious visions and messages – have become much more important. Primordial and religious themes played a crucial role, not only in Poland, where the church had always been strong, but in other places as well. Certain of the churches in East Germany played a major role in the overthrow of the regime, even if not as dramatically as in Poland.

V

How can one explain these revolutionary changes in Eastern Europe? Are they to be discovered in the "causes" alleged to explain the breakdown of communist regimes? Among the causes commonly given, the stagnation of the economy, the disenchantment among large sectors of the population, the weakening of the legitimation of these regimes, and their diminished international standing are singled out.

While many of the causes of the decline of the Soviet system – the various manifestations of internal stagnation and of weakness in the international arena – are redolent of the decline of many empires, including those which spawned the great classical revolutions, they do not tell enough. Just as such general causes do not distinguish between empires, the Roman, Byzantine, and Abbasid, for example, or the dynastic changes in China (especially the decline of the Ming), or the others which gave rise to the great revolutions, they do not explain the specific reasons for the decline of the communist regimes.[10] Also, they do not suggest the directions these societies may now take.

In order to be able to explain what has happened, it is imperative to look closely at the specific contradictions of these regimes, that were in fact at the very core of their legitimation. On the most general level, these contradictions were rooted in the fact that the Soviet regime, as it developed after its institutionalization in the early 1920s, was characterized by a rather unusual combination of features. It combined "traditional" features – historical, patrimonial, and bureaucratic features characteristic especially, of course, of the czarist empire – with those of a modern regime mobilizing whole populations, rooted in a monolithic revolutionary movement and ideology.[11]

The Soviet regime changed some of the basic parameters of center–periphery relations that had developed under the czarist empire – especially the rather delicate balance between a commitment to the imperial system and the relative political passivity of the periphery. The revolutionary center mobilized and activated the periphery to a very high degree, but at the same time attempted to control it tightly in the name of the communist salvationist vision as borne and promulgated by the ruling elite and its cadres.

Accordingly, the most far-reaching – the most encompassing and crucial – contradictions developed in these regimes were rooted in their bases of legitimation, in the nature of the vision that combined the basic premises of modernity, together with far-reaching strong totalitarian orientations and policies. The most important of these contradictions were between the participatory democratic and the totalitarian, the Jacobin components of the legitimation of these regimes; between the high level of social mobilization effected by these regimes and the attempts to control totally all the mobilized groups.

These contradictions became increasingly apparent after the Stalinist era, but to some extent also after Khrushchev, the time of intensive social mobilization and institution building undertaken in the name of this vision. As Ernest Gellner has pointed out, the exigencies of the routinization of this vision, which became ever more visible after the Khrushchev era, highlighted the contradictions inherent in these communist regimes.[12]

The first arena in which the contradictions became apparent was the economic one – the failure of the planned economy to deliver according to its premises. The growing stagnation of the Brezhnev era constituted the turning point in the articulation of the economic problems of the Soviet regime. The stagnation, brought about by the general inefficiency of central planning in regulating a relatively routinized and diversified modern economy, was exacerbated by the extremely heavy burden of military expenses. Rooted in the strong military orientations of the regime, and in the growth of the military as an autonomous sector of the Soviet society and economy, but also, during the Brezhnev era, in the great military and economic expenses incurred in connection with Soviet international policy in the period of the Cold War, there was a growing tendency of the regime to buy off various sectors of the society through subsidized privileges.

The failure in the economic arena touched on the central nerve of the regime – it was in the economic arena that the salvationist vision of the regime was to be implemented; it was the economic arena that provided the most telling test of the regime's vision.

The contradictions inherent in these policies might have been suppressed by a strong totalitarian regime – but at the same time the consequences of such suppression would have weakened many aspects of the system. Once the totalitarian lid was taken off – as happened under Gorbachev – the contradictions exploded, threatening the very existence of the system.

VI

The contradictions of these regimes explain some of the major characteristics of the civil society that developed within them, and in this context it is essential to examine the processes of economic development and social mobilization that became rooted under communism.[13] The continuous processes of social mobilization, the expansion of education, and the growth of numerous professional groups and organizations created in Soviet Russia a much greater range of nuclei, the kernels of civil society. At the same time, however, civil society was not allowed any autonomy, not even to the extent that it was allowed under the czars.[14] The totalitarian control effected by the Soviet regime almost entirely eroded all the bases of autonomy of civil society that existed.

Still, certain institutional ideological kernels of the civil society could be found in the existence of formal, seemingly legal procedures in many institutions and organizations. Even though these procedures were often only formally acceded to, their existence served as a sort of signal about the proper ways of dealing in the public arena.

The ideological kernels of such civil society were rooted in some of the basic premises of these regimes – especially in their emphasis on freedom, emancipation, and participation in the political arena, which constituted major components of the communist vision. While these emphases were repressed by the Jacobin components of the communist regimes, the latter could never entirely negate or obliterate these themes. These nuclei or kernels of civil society started to develop as some of the basic contradictions of these regimes became more apparent, but also more debilitating.

The growing attempt of the regime to buy off large sectors of the more educated and professional sectors of the society gave rise to one of the major initial directions of the development of civil society in Russia, the Soviet Union, and even more widely in Eastern Europe. Greater spaces were provided in which these sectors were permitted some sort of semi-autonomous activities, but never in the central political arena.

With the continuous weakening of the regimes and the growth, within the ruling sectors, of an awareness of the necessity to reform, more active attempts to impinge on the central political arena started to develop in a great variety of ways. At the same time, it is not clear to what extent orderly constitutional procedures in the central arena would develop or would be adhered to.

Such kernels of civil society were stronger in Eastern Europe, where totalitarian communist rule was of much shorter duration, where certain institutional and ideological traditions of civil society were stronger – even if not especially strong in comparison with those of Western Europe.

Similarly, given the shorter span of communist rule, the stronger traditions of parliamentary regimes and the existence, as in the case of the

Catholic Church in Poland, of a number of autonomous sectors, all these developments were much stronger in the communist regimes in Eastern Europe than in Russia – and it is in these countries that they became central in bringing down the communist regimes.[15]

VII

The specific characteristics of the contradictions of the Soviet and communist regimes provide the starting point for possible explanations of the East European revolutions or regime changes that distinguish them from all the classical revolutions. These revolutions were not oriented against "traditional," premodern, or even modernizing regimes. They were not rebellions or protests against traditional authoritarian regimes, against the divine right of kings, made in the name of modernity or enlightenment. Rather, they constituted a rebellion and protest against what was increasingly perceived by large sectors of the East European societies as a blockage and distortion of modernity, effected by totalitarian regimes. While these regimes blocked and in many ways distorted modernity and development, in some of their basic, symbolic, and institutional aspects, they were very modern societies.

In common with other modern regimes, the legitimation of these regimes was rooted in earlier "classical" types of revolutionary experience (the English, American, and French) – the legitimation of the new center was couched in terms which entailed far-reaching transformations of center–periphery relations. There developed a growing permeation of the center into the periphery, but also the impingement of the periphery on the center, often culminating in the obliteration of at least the symbolic differences between center and periphery, making membership in the collectivity tantamount to participation in the center.[16]

The modernity of these regimes is paradoxically most evident in the fact that all of them promulgated elections. While it is of course true that the elections were a sham, as were the constitutions, one must ask why the czars opposed elections while the Soviet leaders imposed them. They required elections because the regime's legitimacy, couched in modern political terms, accepted the necessity of political participation; appeals to something like the divine right of kings was unthinkable. The "divine" was the voice of the people, a secular eschatological vision borne by the people or an imaginary sector thereof – the proletariat or the like. Accordingly, these regimes promulgated modern constitutions, even if in practice they were as much a sham as the elections themselves. Both the constitutions and the elections attested to the fact that these totalitarian regimes, in their mode of legitimation, in their relations between the center and the periphery, but also in their overall cultural and political program, were modern regimes. Indeed, their cultural and political program was part of the cultural pattern of modernity.

The specific political and cultural policies promulgated by these regimes developed out of tensions inherent in the cultural programs of modernity – especially the tensions between the Jacobin and liberal or pluralistic elements of this program. These Jacobin orientations, with their belief in the transformation of society through totalistic political action, are very modern, even if their historical roots go back to medieval eschatological sources.

The Jacobin element exists in different guises – in many populist, fundamentalist, or fascist movements – and indeed in all modern societies, including those that are democratic-constitutional. It exists also in nationalist movements. As Noberto Bobbio has often emphasized, the Jacobin element is strong in both fascism and in communism, which in a way are mirror images of one another.[17]

In pluralistic, constitutional societies – in the United States, Britain, or France – this Jacobin element is hemmed in; it constitutes only a single component in the overall pluralistic constitutional arrangements. In totalitarian regimes, the pluralistic ideologies and structures were repressed almost totally, but never entirely obliterated. The fact of such repression meant that severe contradictions developed not only in respect to economic performance, but also in respect to basic political premises.

VIII

From the point of view of social and economic conditions or institutions, the communist societies were not traditional or under-developed societies in the sense in which that term is used to designate the so-called Third World – itself a highly heterogeneous entity. Their economic structures were those of a relatively industrialized and urbanized political economy. Moreover, their distinctive mode of industrialization became connected with widespread social mobilization and the expansion of education, conditions that did not always obtain in the Third World. A pretense of equality, even if very shabby, evolved. With respect to the middle and lower groups, it was not only pretense.

These institutional developments – the expansion of education, the controlled but potentially meaningful possibility of political participation, and their connection to industrialization – were created by the regime itself. They were not external to the regime; they generated the major contradictions in the regimes. The Soviet and communist societies were not simply backward and underdeveloped, aspiring to become modern. Rather, they were modern or modernizing societies, which, in seeking to catch up with the more developed, selected and totalized the Jacobin ideological and institutional elements of modernity.

Thus, the revolutions against the communist regimes in Eastern Europe and against the totalitarian regime in Russia need to be seen as rebellions against certain types of modernity which negated in practice other more pluralistic elements of modernity, while officially instituting certain central components of their premises. The rebellions or revolutionary processes, as much as the various attempts at reform, together with the new social and political movements in what had once been the USSR, were rebellions or protests against a misrepresentation of modernity, a flawed interpretation of modernity. They were an unfolding of the dynamics of modern civilization.

IX

It is the specifically modern contradictions of these regimes that provide the beginning of an explanation for why the various ruling groups – and not only the top rulers, but also the middle echelons of the bureaucracy, army, and security forces – gave up so easily. All were highly mobilized and underwent intense processes of political socialization. Politically the most socialized groups of the regime, they were socialized in the name of two quite different components or orientations. One was Jacobin, the eschatological element transformed into a totalitarian setting. They were also socialized in the name of freedom, participation, and democracy – even if these elements were subverted and suppressed. This specific political socialization could easily, under appropriate conditions, intensify their awareness of the contradictions between the premises of the regimes and their performance. It is difficult to know how seriously these groups took their ideals. Once things started to change, however, and the impact of foreign television became greater, the more democratic themes found easy resonance, paradoxically perhaps because of the political socialization received. This may partially explain the strong predisposition of large sectors of these societies to listen to radio and television messages from the West; it may also explain the impact of their messages.

If the downfall of the communist regimes of Eastern Europe must be explained in terms different from those of the "classical" revolutions which ushered in the political program of modernity, there are similarities: the close relations among popular protests, struggles in the center, and the intellectual groups that developed; the place of principled protest; the emphasis on the legitimacy of such protest, central in all of them. All these were characteristic features of the great revolutions; all are characteristic of the modern political process ushered in by these revolutions. From the point of view of the development of such themes, there seems to have developed in the process of breakdown of the communist regimes, a rather interesting parallelism – together with great differences in concrete details – with respect to some developments in the contemporary West, especially with respect to some of those developments which have often been dubbed as "postmodern": the decharismatization of the centers; the weakening of the overall societywide utopian political vision and of the missionary-ideological component. Even when the belief in democracy and the free market sometimes evince such elements, there is a concomitant disposition of many utopian orientations to disperse; "daily" and semi-private spheres of life become central.[18]

X

The fact that the breakdown of these regimes seems to lead to the institutionalization of new and on the face of it democratic-constitutional regimes – more modern societies – does not mean that such institutionalization will be easy. It is now fully recognized that the transition is fragile. Many economic pitfalls, great social turbulence and dislocations attendant on the transition from the communist command economy to some free-market type, the weakness in East European countries of constitutional and democratic traditions, and the continuous threat of the upsurge of primordial, ethnic loyalties, become increasingly apparent. There is always the possibility of economic collapse and general anarchy.

These problems, however, do not simply arise out of the breakdown of "traditional" empires, the transition from some "premodern" to fully modern, democratic society, or from a distorted modernity to a relatively tranquil stage which may well signal some kind of "end of history." The turbulence evident in Eastern Europe today bears witness to some of the problems and tensions inherent in modernity itself, attesting to the potential fragility of the whole project of modernity.

These turbulences highlight tensions inherent in the modern political process, which are indeed characteristic of this process. The most important are tensions between different and often competing conceptions of the "general will," and the relation of these conceptions to the representation of the discrete interests of various sectors of society, i.e., tensions between aggregative policies and politics of the common good, between the articulation and aggregation of different interests and of different conceptions of common good, between – to use Bruce Ackerman's formulation – the routine and "revolutionary" politics.[19]

Contrary to the assumptions of many rational-choice analysts, the mobilization of support around leaders and programs, effected mainly but not only through the medium of parties and of social movements, is not based simply on the aggregation of many discrete interests. Such mobilization also takes place around the articulation of different conceptions of the common good; it plays a central role in the mobilization of political support. Such mobilization will often focus, as Alessandro Pizzorno has shown, around symbols of collective identity – political, social, or ethnic identity –

as well as around the closely related conception of the common good of the whole society, more closely related to the primordial and sacred components of legitimation.[20]

XI

These tensions are inherent in all modern regimes. In authoritarian and totalitarian regimes, they are suppressed but never obliterated. In relatively stable democratic-constitutional regimes, the tensions may be attenuated, but they always simmer, ready, as it were, to erupt in situations of intensive change. The tensions and potential fragility of democratic-constitutional – basically of all modern – regimes, is enhanced by the fact that modern regions develop in highly volatile and continuously changing internal and international settings. The conditions conducive to their institutionalization and continuity are themselves inherently unstable.

In any situation of rapid change, modern societies may develop rather contradictory tendencies in respect to the development of conditions conducive to institutionalization, to the perpetuation and continuity of democratic-constitutional regimes. Such situations generate changes in the definition of the boundaries of the political,[21] in what is seen to be an appropriate range of activities for the state; in the structures of centers of power; in the extent of the access of different sectors of civil society to these centers; in the nature of the linkages among the sectors, and between them and the state; in the types of entitlements extended to different sectors of society.

From the point of view of the construction of civil society and its relations to the state, in such transitional situations, developments could take several directions.[22] One would include the development of new autonomous sectors of civil society; the political activization of such sectors through the activities of multiple elites and counter-elites; the growth of various inter-linking arenas between the state and society, including both the activization of "older" types, such as consultative bodies, and the development of new ones – attuned in different degrees to democratic-constitutional arrangements.

Alternatively, the processes of "transition" may develop in quite other directions. They may work to undermine the conditions favoring the development and continuity of democratic-constitutional regimes. The continuous social and economic transitions may easily change the distribution of power within the major sectors of societing, eroding many autonomous centers of power, creating a power vacuum. Moreover, policies – such as, for instance, those connected with the institutionalization of the welfare state – whose initial aim was to weaken existing semi-monopolistic centers of power, may increase the political and administrative power of the state to such an extent as to obliterate independent bases of power. As attested by de Tocqueville, Marx, and Weber, the specter of the bureaucratization of all major arenas of social and political life has haunted the political discourse of modern societies, with an intensity only reinforced by the development of totalitarian regimes.

Other possibilities exist. Many of the existing sectors of civil society, with their complex interlinking arenas, may become impediments to the restructuring of relations between civil society and the state. The very entrenchment of these sectors may lead them increasingly to represent narrow corporative or ascriptive sectors, and may weaken their initial acceptance of newly emergent common frameworks and centers. Finally, both the older associational structure and the new sectors of civil society may become undermined, giving rise to the development of highly volatile masses. In many such cases these processes have been exacerbated by the emergence of new collective-national and ethnic communities, with ensuing internecine conflicts.

Such developments or transitions – whether from nondemocratic to democratic-constitutional regimes, or within democratic-constitutional regimes – are closely connected with tensions inherent in the modern political process between different and often competing conceptions of the general will, and the relation of such conceptions to the representation of the discrete interests of various sectors of society; i.e., tensions between aggregative policies and politics of the common good, between routine and revolutionary politics.

XII

It is in these situations, as in many involving intensive change in modern regimes, that the confrontation between the different modes of legitimation and the different aspects of the modern political process become especially acute. All such tensions and problems became highly visible in the processes of transition in Eastern Europe. Such periods of change – of transition – are in no way exceptional. They are, as indicated above, exceedingly common, given the continuously changing internal and international settings of the contemporary world. It is in such periods that articulations of protest come forward as a major component of the political process. The most intensive themes and movements of protest are those in which articulation of concrete aggregate interests becomes closely related to the promulgation of different conceptions of the common good.

The ubiquity of these tensions in the modern democratic-constitutional regimes points to one of the most important challenges before these regimes – namely, how to create some common framework in which different views of the common good can compete without undermining the very possibility of the system working. It poses the question of the nature of the common basis or bases of acceptance of a democratic-constitutional regime – beyond adherence to the rules of the game – and the possibility that such common elements may exist in multiple bases of legitimation, so long as no one of them becomes predominant.

The ubiquity of such tensions indicates that one of the major continuous challenges before the modern constitutional regime is not just the assurance that the major political actors will adhere to the existing rules of the game, but also their capacity to incorporate protest, to redefine the boundaries of the political, to transform the bases of legitimation of these regimes. The great crises of these regimes – such as those of the 1930s in many European countries – were usually associated with a failure to achieve such internal transformations.

The constitutional regimes of the West, since the Second World War, though not between the two world wars, evinced, despite continuous fears about the crisis of the state or capitalism, a high degree of capacity for self-transformability. In the West, no democratic regime has broken down since the end of the Second World War. Indeed, the general trend has seemed to go the other way, with the authoritarian regimes – in Spain, Portugal, Greece, and most recently, in some Latin American countries – becoming democratic. Similarly, several non-European countries – India, Japan, and Israel – have been able to maintain democratic-constitutional regimes since the end of the Second World War – as have also Germany and Italy – the two countries in which the breakdown of democracy in the interwar period was most dramatic.

But even within these regimes the possibility of crisis or breakdown cannot be entirely discounted. This is, of course, even more true of the emerging constitutional regimes of Eastern Europe. The initial stages of the breakdown of communist regimes – the relatively peaceful characteristics which distinguished them from the great revolutions – suggested that they might also evince some such capacity for self-transformability. At the same time, however, the turbulences attendant on these transitions cast new doubts about that capacity. Such doubts are due not only to the specific conditions of these transitions, but also to the combination of conditions inherent in modern regimes, especially in democratic-constitutional ones. Thus, the developments in Eastern Europe cast important light on the problematics of modernity, on the inherent fragility of the great historical and cultural project of modernity.

Notes

Source Reprinted by permission of the publisher from *Daedalus* (Journal of the American Academy of Arts and Sciences), from the issue entitled "The Exit from Communism," 121:2 (Spring 1992): 21–41.

1 On the classical modern revolutions, see: S. N. Eisenstadt, *Revolutions and the Transformation of Societies* (New York: Free Press, 1978); idem, "Frameworks of the Great Revolutions: Culture, Social Structure, History and Human Agency," *International Social Science Journal*, 133 (1992): 385–401; M. Lasky, "The Birth of a Metaphor: On the Origins of Utopia and Revolution," *Encounter* 34 (2) (1970): 35–45, and (3) (1970): 30–42; *Utopia and Revolution* (Chicago, IL: University of Chicago Press, 1976). On the Revolutions and modernity, see for instance the special issue "The French Revolution and the Birth of Modernity," *Social Research* (1989).

2 See Eisenstadt, *Revolutions and the Transformation of Societies*.

3 On the role of groups of intellectuals in some of the revolutions, see: A. Cochin, *La Revolution et la Libre Pensée* (Paris: Plon-Nourrit, 1924); idem, *L'esprit du Jacobinisme* (Paris: Universitaires de France, 1979); and J. Baechler, preface in Cochin, *L'esprit du Jacobinisme*, 7–33. See also F. Furet, *French Revolution* (New York: Macmillan, 1970); idem, *Rethinking the French Revolution* (Chicago, IL: University of Chicago Press, 1982) and V. C. Nahirny, *The Russian Intelligentsia: From Torment to Silence* (New Brunswick, NJ: Transaction Books, 1983).

4 On the sanctification of violence in classical revolutions, see: S. N. Eisenstadt, "Frameworks of the Great Revolutions: Culture, Social Structure, History and Human Agency" *International Social Science Journal*, 133 (1992): 385–401.

5 On the utopian elements in the great civilizations and revolutions, see: A. B. Seligman, ed., *Order and Transcendence: The Role of Utopias and the Dynamics of Civilizations* (Leiden: E. J. Brill, 1989); M. Lasky, *Utopia and Revolution*; R. Saage, *Das Ende der Politisches Utopie?* (Frankfurt am Main: Suhrkamp, 1990).

6 On the eschatological elements, see: A. Seligman, *Order and Transcendence*; S. Friedlander, G. Holton, Leo Marx, and E. Skolnikoff, eds., *Visions of Apocalypse: End or Rebirth?* (New York and London: Holmes & Meier, 1985); C. Lefort, *The Political Forms of Modern Society: Bureaucracy, Democracy and Totalitarianism* (Cambridge, MA: MIT Press, 1986); idem, Part II, "On Revolution," in C. Lefort, *Democracy and Political Theory* (Minneapolis, MN: University of Minnesota Press, 1988), 57–163; J. Dunn, "Totalitarian Democracy and the Legacy of Modern Revolutions – Explanation or Indictment?" in J. Dunn, K. D. Bracher, and Sh. Avineri, *Totalitarian and After, International Colloquium in Memory of Jacob L. Talmon*, Jerusalem, 21–24 June 1982, The Israel Academy of Sciences and Humanities (Jerusalem: The Hebrew University Magnes Press, 1984), 37–56; K. D. Bracher, "Turn of the Century and Totalitarian Ideology," in Dunn, Bracher, and Avineri, 70–83; Sh. Avineri, "Different Visions of Political Messianism in the Marxist European Tradition," in Dunn, Bracher, and Avineri, 96–104. On the liminal aspects of the revolutionary process see: S. N. Eisenstadt, "Comparative Liminality: Liminality and Dynamics of Civilization," *Religion* (15) (1985): 315–38.

7 From the vast literature on this subject, see for instance: Pietro Grilli di Corrona, "From Communism to Democracy: Rethinking Regime Change in Hungary and Czechoslovakia," *International Social Science Journal* (128) (May 1991): 315–31.

8 G. Konrád, *Antipolitik – Mitteleuropäische Meditationen* (Frankfurt am Main: Suhrkamp, 1985).

9 On the universalistic and missionary components in the great revolutions, see: C. Lefort in Eisenstadt, *Revolutions*, R. Kosellek, "Historical Criteria of the Modern Concept of Revolutions," in idem, *Futures Past – on the Semantics of Historical Time* (Cambridge, MA: MIT Press, 1985), 39, and S. N. Eisenstadt,

"Frameworks of the Great Revolutions: Culture, Social Structure, History and Human Agency" *International Social Science Journal*, 133 (1992): 385–401.

10 On the analysis of such cases, see: S. N. Eisenstadt, "Frameworks of the Great Revolutions: Culture, Social Structure, History and Human Agency" *International Social Science Journal*, 133 (1992): 385–401. J. A. Goldstone, *Revolution and Rebellion in the Early Modern World* (Berkeley and Los Angeles, CA: University of California Press, 1991).

11 On the specific processes of the breakdown of the communist regime, see for instance from the literature of the West the special issue of *World Politics*, 44 (1) October 1991 ("Liberalization and Democratization in the Soviet Union and Eastern Europe"), also S. N. Eisenstadt, "Center Periphery in Soviet Russia," in A. J. Motyl, ed., *Rethinking Theoretically about Soviet Nationalities* (New York: Columbia University Press, 1992).

12 Remarks made by Ernest Gellner in the seminar on Fundamentalism under the auspices of the American Academy of Arts and Sciences, Chicago, November 1991.

13 See the special issue of *World Politics* mentioned in Note 11 and Eisenstadt, "Center Periphery in Soviet Russia."

14 On civil society in the czarist empire, see for instance E. W. Clowes, S. D. Kassow, and J. L. West, eds, *Between Tsar and People* (Princeton, NJ: Princeton University Press, 1991).

15 P. Grilli di Cortona, *From Communism to Democracy*; also idem, *Le Crisi politische nei regimi communisti* (Milan: Franco Angeli, 1980).

16 On the concept of center, see E. Shils, "Center and Periphery" in idem, *Center and Periphery, Essays in Macrosociology* (Chicago, IL: University of Chicago Press, 1975), 3–34. On center-periphery relations on modernity, see S. N. Eisenstadt, *Tradition, Change and Modernity* (New York: John Wiley, 1973), chaps. 9–11, 203–58, and idem, "Post-Traditional Societies and the Continuity and Reconstruction of Tradition," in S. N. Eisenstadt, ed., *Post-Traditional Societies* (New York: W. W. Norton, 1972), 1–29. On the general prospect of modernity, see J. Habermas, *The Philosophical Discourse of Modernity* (Cambridge, MA: MIT Press, 1987).

17 N. Bobbio, *Il Futuro della Democrazzia* (Torino: Giulio Einaudi Editore, 1984); idem, "Postfazione," in N. Bobbio, *Profilo Ideologico del Novecento Italiano* (Torino: Giulio Einaudi, 1986), 177–85. N. Matteucci, "Democrazia e autocrazia nel pensiero di Norberto Bobbio," in *Per una Teoria Generale della Politica – Scritti Dedicatti Norberto Bobbio* (Firenze: Passigli Editori, 1983), 149–79. See also E. Frankel, "Strukturdefekte der Demokratie und deren Überwindung" and "Ratennythos und Soziale Selbstbestimmung," in E. Frankel, *Deutschland und die Westlichen Demokratien* (Frankfurt am Main: Suhrkamp, 1990), 68–95 and 95–137, respectively. A very strong statement against the emphasis on "common will" in the name of "emancipation" can be found in H. Lubbe, *Freiheit statt Emanzipationszwang: Die Liberalen Traditionen und das Ende der Marxistischen Illusionen* (Zurich: Edition Interfrom, 1991).

18 On some aspect of "postmodern" developments, see: J. Habermas, "Die Neue Unübersichtlichkeit, Die Krise des Wohlahrtsstaates und die Erschöpfung Utopische-energien," in J. Habermas, *Die Neue Unübersichtlichkeit* (Frankfurt am Main: Suhrkamp, 1985), 141–67; A. Melucci, *L'invenzione del Presente, Movimenti Sociali nelle Societa Complesse* (Bologna: Societa Editori Il Mulino, 1982); idem; "The Symbolic Challenge of Contemporary Movements," *Social Research* (Winter 1985), 789–816; S. N. Eisenstadt, "Some Observations on 'Post-Modern' Society," in Volker Bornschier *et al.*, eds, *Diskontinuität des Sozialen*

Wandels (Frankfurt: Campus Verlag, 1990), 287–96; C. Offe, "New Social Movements: Challenging the Boundaries of Institutional Politics," in idem, 817–09; Saage, *Das Ende der Politische Utopie?*

19 A. Przeworski, "Democracy as a Contingent Outcome of Conflicts," in J. Elster and R. Slagstad, eds., *Constitutionalism and Democracy* (Cambridge: Cambridge University Press and Norwegian University Press, 1988), 59–81. Ackerman, "Neo Federalism?" 153–95. J. Nedelsky, "American Constitutionalism and the Paradox of Private Property," 241–75. J. Lambert, *Tocqueville et les deux démocraties* (Paris: Presses Universitaires, 1983).

20 A. Pizzorno, *I. Soggetti del Pluralismo Classi Partiti Sindicati* (Bologna: Il Mulino, 1980).

21 See Charles S. Maier, ed., *Changing Boundaries of the Political* (Cambridge: Cambridge University Press, 1987).

22 See S. N. Eisenstadt, "Introduction" in idem, ed., *Democracy and Modernity*, International Colloquium on the Centenary of David Ben Gurion (Leiden: E. J. Brill, 1991), vii–xiv.

5

THE YEAR OF TRUTH

Timothy Garton Ash

British political historian and journalist Timothy Garton Ash's writings on the fate of Central Europe, the rise of independent movements challenging the Leninist regimes, the nature of the 1989 upheaval as well as its aftermath, have been remarkably prescient and influential. In this penetrating analysis of the annus mirabilis *of 1989, Garton Ash proposes a comparison between the European revolutions of 1848 and the great transformations which started with the events of 1989. He insists on the role of the intellectuals in formulating the language and the strategy of liberation. Without denying the importance of mass action, Garton Ash highlights the crucial importance of the intellectual rebellion against communist ideology. In his view, the demise of communism in East Central Europe in 1989 can be told as the result of a struggle between of a set of ideas whose time had passed and another one whose time had come.*

Like Jeffrey Isaac (but unlike G. M. Tamás and Tony Judt), Garton Ash sees the legacy of dissent as utterly significant for the shaping of the new political communities. He also offers an illuminating interpretation of the causes of the breakdown, insisting on the role of Gorbachev, the international environment (the Helsinki process), and the ruling elite's loss of belief in its own right to rule. Another important point in this contribution is the author's insistence on the role of civil society initiatives in the resurrection of the notion and practice of citizenry. Garton Ash's essay identifies some of the major risks confronting these societies, including national prejudice, inequality, poverty, and mass discontent. But, he states, even if the gloomy prospects were to be realized in some countries, the significance of 1989 as a passionate affirmation of Europe's democratic destiny will not be diminished.

Garton Ash uses the term "refolution," employing it as a way of capturing the dual nature of the ongoing transformation: a combination of gradual reforms and revolutionary changes, a mixture of continuity and discontinuity with the communist past. The changes of 1989 are thus seen as resulting from attempts to reform the system from above and efforts from below to change it fundamentally, i.e. to dismantle it.

* * *

This was the year communism in Eastern Europe died; 1949–1989 R.I.P. And the epitaph might be:

Nothing in his life
Became him like the leaving it

The thing that was comprehensively installed in the newly defined territories of Poland, Czechoslovakia, Hungary, Romania and Bulgaria, and in the newly created German Democratic Republic after 1949, the thing called, according to viewpoint, 'socialism', 'totalitarianism', 'Stalinism', 'politbureaucratic dictatorship', 'real existing socialism', 'state capitalism', 'dictatorship over needs', or, most neutrally, 'the Soviet-type system' – that thing will never walk again. And arguably, if we can no longer talk of communism we should no longer talk of Eastern Europe, at least with a capital 'E' for Eastern. Instead, we shall have central Europe again, east central Europe, south-eastern Europe, eastern Europe with a small 'e' and, above all, individual peoples, nations and states.

To be sure, even without a political-military reversal inside the Soviet Union there will be many further conflicts, injustices and miseries in these lands. But they will be different conflicts, injustices and miseries: new and old, post-communist but also pre-communist. In the worst case, there might yet be new dictators; but they would be different dictators. We shall not see again that particular system, characterized by the concentration of political and economic power and the instruments of coercion in the hands of one Leninist party, manifested sociologically as a privileged new class, in states with arbitrarily limited sovereignty.

Of course if we walk the street of Prague, Warsaw or Leipzig we can still find the grey, familiar traces: the flattened neo-classical Stalinist façades on all the Victory Squares, the Lenin boulevards, steelworks, shipyards, the balding middle-aged officials with their prefabricated lies, the cheap paper forms for completion in quadruplicate, the queues, the attitude of 'We pretend to work and you pretend to pay us'. Yet even the physical evidences are being removed at a speed that must cause some anxiety to conservationists. (In Poland there is a scheme for preserving all the old props in an entertainment park. The proposed name is Stalinland.)

If 1989 was the end, what was the beginning of the end? To read the press, or hear Mrs Thatcher talk, you would think history began with Gorbachev. At the other extreme, some would say communism in Eastern Europe was doomed at birth. This thesis may, in turn, be advanced in several forms. One can say that communism was incompatible with the political culture of East Central Europe, although why that political culture should suddenly stop at the quite arbitrary western frontier of the Soviet Union is not clear. Alternatively, one can say that communism was a wonderful idea that was doomed only because the people of Eastern

Europe did not find their way to it themselves, but had it imposed on them by a foreign power, which itself did not understand it. Or one can say that communism is incompatible with human nature, period. Whether by congenital deformity or merely as the result of a ghastly forceps delivery, the death was preordained at birth. In between these two extreme positions, some people in the countries concerned would point to various supposed 'missed opportunities' or turning-points at which East European history failed to turn. The years 1956 and 1968 are the leading candidates in this class.

As usual, there is an element of truth in all these claims, though in some more than others. Churchill declared, 'I have not become the King's First Minister in order to preside over the liquidation of the British empire', and proceeded to do almost exactly that. Gorbachev came to power proposing to save the Soviet empire and presided over its disintegration. That Moscow permitted the former 'satellite' countries to determine how they want to govern themselves was clearly a *sine qua non*. But the nature and direction of the processes of domestic political self-determination cannot be understood by studying Soviet policy. The causes lie elsewhere, in the history of individual countries, in their interactions with their East European neighbours and with the more free and prosperous Europe that lies to the west, north and south of them.

If I was forced to name a single date for the 'beginning of the end' in this *inner* history of Eastern Europe, it would be June 1979. The judgement may be thought excessively Polonocentric, but I do believe that the Pope's first great pilgrimage to Poland was that turning-point. Here, for the first time, we saw that massive, sustained, yet supremely peaceful and self-disciplined manifestation of social unity, the gentle crowd against the Party-state, which was both the hallmark and the essential domestic catalyst of change in 1989, in every country except Romania (and, even in Romania, the violence did not initially go out from the crowds). The Pope's visit was followed, just over a year later, by the birth of Solidarity, and without the Pope's visit it is doubtful if there would have been a Solidarity.

The example of Solidarity was seminal. It pioneered a new kind of politics in Eastern Europe (and new not only there): a politics of social self-organization and negotiating the transition from communism. The players, forms and issues of 1980–81 in Poland were fundamentally different from anything seen in Eastern Europe between 1949 and 1979: in many respects, they presaged those seen throughout Eastern Europe in 1989. If there is any truth in this judgement, then there was something especially fitting in the fact that it was in 1989 that the Russian leader and the Polish Pope finally met. In their very different ways, they both started it.

To find a year in European history comparable with 1989, however, we obviously have to reach back much farther than 1979, or 1949. 1789 in France? 1917 in Russia? Or, closer to home, 1918/19 in Central Europe?

But 1918/19 was the aftermath of World War. The closer parallel is surely 1848, the springtime of nations. In the space of a few paragraphs such comparisons are little better than parlour games. Yet, like parlour games, they can be amusing, and may sometimes help to concentrate the mind.

1848 erupted, according to A. J. P. Taylor, 'after forty years of peace and stability' while Lewis Namier describes it, with somewhat less cavalier arithmetic, as 'the outcome of thirty-three creative years of European peace carefully preserved on a consciously counter-revolutionary basis.' The revolution, Namier writes, 'was born at least as much of hopes as of discontents.' There was undoubtedly an economic and social background: lean harvests and the potato disease. But 'the common denominator was ideological.' He quotes the exiled Louis-Philippe declaring that he had given way to *une insurrection morale*, and King Wilhelm of Württemberg excusing himself to the Russian minister at Stuttgart, one Gorchakov, with the words: *'Je ne puis pas monter à cheval contre les idées.'* And Namier calls his magnificent essay, 'The Revolution of the Intellectuals'.

1989 also erupted out of celebrations of 'forty years of peace and stability in Europe'. Remember NATO's fortieth anniversary in May? With the 'Yalta Europe', as with the 'Vienna Europe' in the previous century, the question was always: peace and stability *for whom*? Ordinary men and women in Central and Eastern Europe felt the rough edge of both. Here, too, a stricter arithmetic might reduce the forty years to thirty-three, for perhaps it was only after crushing the Hungarian revolution of 1956 that Soviet leaders could be quite sure the West would not intervene militarily to disturb this peace – carefully preserved on a counter-revolutionary basis.

A revolution born as much of hopes as of discontents? Yes, again. To be sure, the economic 'discontents' were there, overwhelmingly in Poland and Romania, and persistently, though less dramatically, elsewhere. In this connection, the historian Fritz Stern has aptly recalled Mirabeau's declaration on the eve of the French Revolution: 'The nation's deficit is the nation's treasure.' Substitute 'hard currency debt' for 'deficit' and you have one of the main reasons why it was Poland and Hungary that led the field in the first half of 1989. But, unlike in Poland in August 1980, it was not a turn of the economic screw that precipitated mass popular protest in any East European country in 1989. It was political hopes – and outrage at the repression with which the local regimes attempted to curb those hopes.

Like 1848, this, too, might be called a 'revolution of the intellectuals'. To be sure, the renewed flexing of workers' muscle in two strike-waves in 1988 was what finally brought Poland's communists to the first Round Table of 1989. To be sure, it was the masses on the streets in demonstrations in all the other East European countries that brought the old rulers down. But the politics of the revolution were not made by workers or peasants. They were made by intellectuals: the playwright Václav Havel, the medievalist Bronisł aw Geremek, the Catholic editor Tadeusz Mazowiecki, the painter Bärbel

111

Bohley in Berlin, the conductor Kurt Masur in Leipzig, the philosophers János Kis and Gaspár Miklós Támás in Budapest, the engineering professor Petre Roman and the poet Mircea Dinescu in Bucharest. History has outdone Shelley, for poets were the acknowledged legislators of this world. The crowds on Wenceslas Square chanted, 'Long live the students! Long live the actors!' And the sociology of the opposition forums (New, Democratic, Civic), parties and parliamentary candidates was distinctly comparable with that of the Frankfurt Parliament or the Slav Congress at Prague. *Hundert zwanzig Professoren*. . . .

As in 1848, the common denominator was ideological. The inner history of these revolutions is that of a set of ideas whose time had come, and a set of ideas whose time had gone. At first glance this may seem a surprising statement. For had not the ideology ceased to be an active force many years before? Surely the rulers no longer believed a word of the guff they spouted, nor expected their subjects to believe it, nor even expected their subjects to believe that they, the rulers, believed it? This is probably true in most cases, although who knows what an old man like Erich Honecker, a communist from his earliest youth, still genuinely believed? (One must never underestimate the human capacity for self-deception.)

Yet one of the things these revolutions showed, *ex post facto*, is just how important the residual veil of ideology still was. Few rulers are content to say simply: 'We have the Gatling gun and you do not!' 'We hold power because we hold power.' Ideology provided a residual legitimation, perhaps also enabling the rulers, and their politbureaucratic servants, at least partly to deceive themselves about the nature of their own rule. At the same time, it was vital for the semantic occupation of the public sphere. The combination of censorship and a nearly complete Party-state monopoly of the mass media provided the army of semantic occupation; ideology, in the debased, routinized form of newspeak, was its ammunition. However despised and un-credible these structures of organized lying were, they continued to perform a vital blocking function. They no longer mobilized anyone, but they did still prevent the public articulation of shared aspirations and common truths.

What is more, by demanding from the ordinary citizen seemingly innocuous semantic signs of outward conformity, the system managed somehow to implicate them in it. It is easy now to forget that until almost the day before yesterday, almost everyone in East Germany and Czechoslovakia was living a double life: systematically saying one thing in public and another in private. This was a central theme of the essayistic work of Václav Havel over the last decade and one he movingly returned to in his 1990 New Year's address as president. The worst thing was, he said, the 'devastated moral environment. We are all morally sick, because we all got used to saying one thing and thinking another.' And: 'All of us have become accustomed to the totalitarian system, accepted it as an unalterable fact and therefore kept it running. . . . None of us is merely a victim of it, because all of us helped to create it together.' The crucial 'line of conflict', he wrote earlier, did not run between people and state, but rather through the middle of each individual 'for everyone in his or her own way is both a victim and a supporter of the system.' A banner I saw above the altar in an East Berlin church vividly expressed the same basic thought. It said: 'I am Cain *and* Abel.'

In order to understand what it meant for ordinary people to stand in those vast crowds in the city squares of Central Europe, chanting their own, spontaneous slogans, you have first to make the imaginative effort to understand what it feels like to pay this daily toll of public hypocrisy. As they stood and shouted together, these men and women were not merely healing divisions in their society; they were healing divisions in themselves. Everything that had to do with the word, with the press, with television, was of the first importance to these crowds. The semantic occupation was as offensive to them as military occupation; cleaning up the linguistic environment as vital as cleaning up the physical environment. The long queue every morning in Wenceslas Square, lining up patiently in the freezing fog for a newspaper called *The Free Word*, was, for me, one of the great symbolic pictures of 1989.

The motto of the year – and not just in Czechoslovakia – was 'Pravda Vitězí',the old Hussite slogan, adopted by Masaryk, 'Truth shall prevail', or, in the still more ancient Latin, *Magna est veritas et praevalebit*. As one talks in English of a 'moment of truth' for some undertaking, so this was a year of truth for communism. There is a real sense in which these regimes lived by the word and perished by the word.

For what, after all, happened? A few thousands, then tens of thousands, then hundreds of thousands went on to the streets. They spoke a few words. 'Resign!' they said. 'No more shall we be slaves!' 'Free elections!' 'Freedom!' and the walls of Jericho fell. And with the walls, the communist parties simply crumbled. At astonishing speed. By the end of 1989, the Hungarian Socialist Workers' Party had split in two, with the majority of its members leaving for good. In January 1990, the Polish United Workers' Party followed suit. Within three months, East Germany's Socialist Unity Party lost its leading role, its name and at least half its members. The inner decay of these parties recalled the remark of a German poet in 1848: 'Monarchy is dead, though monarchs still live.'

With the single, signal exception of Romania, these revolutions were also remarkable for the almost complete lack of violence. Like Solidarity in 1980–81 they were that historical contradiction-in-terms, 'peaceful revolution'. No bastilles were stormed, no guillotines erected. Lamp-posts were used only for street-lighting. Romania alone saw tanks and firing squads. Elsewhere the only violence was that used at the outset by police. The young demonstrators in East Berlin and Prague laid candles in front of the police, who responded with truncheons. The Marseillaise of 1989 said not 'aux armers, citoyens' but 'aux bougies, citoyens'. The rationale and tradition of non-violence can be found in the history of all the democratic oppositions of East Central Europe throughout the 1980s. Partly it was pragmatic: the other side had all the weapons. But it was also ethical. It was a statement about how things should be. They wanted to start as they intended to go on. History, said Adam Michnik, had taught them that those who start by storming bastilles will end up building their own.

Yet almost as remarkable, historically speaking, was the lack (so far, and Romania plainly excepted) of major *counter*-revolutionary violence. The police behaved brutally in East Germany up to and notably on the state's fortieth anniversary, 7 October, and in Czechoslovakia up to and notably on 17 November. In Poland the systematic deployment of counterrevolutionary force lasted over seven years, from the declaration of a 'state of war' on 13 December 1981 to the spring of 1989. But once the revolutions (or, in Poland and Hungary, 'refolutions') were under way, there was an amazing lack of coercive counter-measures. The communist rulers said, like King Wilhelm of Württemberg, 'I cannot mount on horseback against ideas.' But one is bound to ask: why not? Much of the modern history of Central Europe consisted precisely in rulers mounting on horseback against ideas. Much of the contemporary history of Central Europe, since 1945, consists in rulers mounting tanks against ideas. Until 1989 the most fitting motto for any history of this region was not 'Pravda Vítězí' but some lines from the nineteenth-century Polish poet, Cyprian Norwid:

> Colossal armies, valiant generals,
> Police-secret, open, and of sexes two –
> Against whom have they joined together?
> Against a few ideas . . . nothing new!

So why was it different in 1989? Three reasons may be suggested. They might be labelled 'Gorbachev', 'Helsinki' and 'Tocqueville'. The new line in Soviet policy, christened by Gennady Gerasimov on 25 October the Sinatra doctrine – 'I had it my way" as he actually misquoted the famous line – rather than the Brezhnev doctrine, was self-evidently essential. In East Germany, Moscow not only made it plain to the leadership that Soviet troops were not available for purposes of domestic repression, but also, it seems, went out of its way to let it be known – to the West, but also to the population concerned – that this was its position. In Czechoslovakia, the Soviet Union helped the revolution along by a nicely timed retrospective condemnation of the 1968 Warsaw Pact invasion. Throughout East Central Europe, the people at last derived some benefit from their ruling elites' chronic dependency on the Soviet Union, for, deprived of the Soviet Kalashnikov-crutch, those elites did not have another leg to stand on. Romania was the exception that proves the rule. It is no accident that it was precisely in the state for so long most *in*dependent of Moscow that the resistance of the security arm of the power-that-were was most fierce, bloody and prolonged.

None the less, the factor 'Gorbachev' alone does not suffice to explain why these ruling elites did not more vigorously deploy their own, still formidable police and security forces in a last-ditch defence of their own power and privilege. Is it too fanciful to suggest that the constant, persistent harping of the West on certain international norms of domestic conduct, the East European leaders' yearning for international respectability, and the sensed linkage between this and the hard-currency credits they so badly needed, in short, the factor 'Helsinki', played at least some part in staying the hands of those who might otherwise have given the order to shoot?

Yet none of this would have stopped them if they had still been convinced of their right to rule. The third, and perhaps the ultimately decisive factor, is that characteristic of revolutionary situations described by Alexis de Tocqueville more than a century ago: the ruling elite's loss of belief in its own right to rule. A few kids went on the streets and threw a few words. The police beat them. The kids said: 'You have no right to beat us!' And the rulers, the high and mighty, replied, in effect: 'Yes, we have no right to beat you. We have no right to preserve our rule by force. The end no longer justifies the means!'

In fact the ruling elites, and their armed servants, distinguished themselves by their comprehensive unreadiness to stand up in any way for the things in which they had so long claimed to believe, and their almost indecent haste to embrace the things they had so long denounced as 'capitalism' and 'bourgeois democracy'. All over Eastern Europe there was the quiet flap of turning coats: one day they denounced Wałęsa, the next they applauded him; one day they embraced Honecker, the next they imprisoned him; one day they vituperated Havel, the next they elected him president.

1848 was called the Springtime of Nations or the Springtime of Peoples: the *Völkerfrühling, wiosna ludów*. The revolutionaries, in all the lands, spoke in the name of 'the people'. But the international solidarity of 'the people' was broken by conflict between nations, old and new, while the domestic solidarity of 'the people' was broken by conflict between social groups – what came to be known as 'classes'. 'Socialism and nationalism, as mass forces, were both the product of 1848,' writes A. J. P. Taylor. And for a century after 1848, until the communist deep freeze, central Europe was a battlefield of nations and classes.

115

Of what, or of whom, was 1989 the springtime? Of 'the people'? But in what sense? *'Wir sind das Volk'*, said the first great crowds in East Germany: 'We are the people'. But within a few weeks they were saying *'Wir sind EIN Volk'*: 'We are one nation.' In Poland, Hungary, Czechoslovakia, Romania, the crowds were a sea of national flags, while the people raised their voice to sing old national hymns. In Hungary and Romania they cut the communist symbols out of the centre of their flags. In East Germany there were, at first, no flags, no hymns. But gradually the flags came out, plain stripes of red, black and gold without the GDR hammer and dividers in the middle: the flag of Western – and before that of united – Germany.

In every Western newspaper commentary on Eastern Europe one now invariably reads that there is a grave danger of something called 'nationalism' reviving in this region. But what on earth does this mean? Does it mean that people are again proud to be Czech, Polish, Hungarian or, for that matter, German? That hearts lift at sight of the flag and throats tighten when they sing the national anthem?

Patriotism is not nationalism. Rediscovered pride in your own nation does not necessarily imply hostility to other nations. These movements were all, without exception, patriotic. They were not all nationalist. Indeed, in their first steps most of the successor regimes were markedly less nationalist than their communist predecessors. The Mazowiecki government in Poland adopted a decisively more liberal and enlightened approach to both the Jewish and the German questions than any previous government, indeed drawing criticism, on the German issue, from the communist–nationalists. In his first public statement as President, Václav Havel made a special point of thanking 'all Czechs, Slovaks and members of other nationalities'. His earlier remark on television that Czechoslovakia owes the Germans an apology for the post-war expulsion of the Sudeten Germans was fiercely criticized by – the communists. In Romania, the revolution began with the ethnic Romanian inhabitants of Timişoara making common cause with their ethnic Hungarian fellow-citizens. It would require very notable exertions for the treatment of the German and Hungarian minorities in post-revolutionary Romania to be worse than it was under Nicolae Ceauşescu.

Of course there are counter-examples. One of the nastier aspects of the German revolution was the excesses of popular support for a Party-government campaign against Polish 'smugglers and profiteers', and abuse of visiting black students and Vietnamese *Gastarbeiter*. In Hungarian opposition politics, the fierce infighting between the Hungarian Democratic Forum and the Free Democrats was not without an ethnic undertone, with some members of the former questioning the 'Hungarian-ness' of some members of the latter, who replied with charges of anti-Semitism. Thousands of Bulgarians publicly protested against the new government giving the Turkish-Muslim minority its rights.

If one looks slightly further ahead, there are obviously potential conflicts over other remaining minorities: notably the Hungarians in Romania, the Romanians in the Soviet Union (Moldavia), the Germans in Poland, Romania and the Soviet Union, and gypsies in several countries. There are the potential political uses of anti-Semitism. There is the difficulty of finding a combination of Czecho- and -Slovakia fully satisfactory to both Slovaks and Czechs. And there are the outstanding frontier questions, above all that of the post-1945 German–Polish frontier on the Oder–Neisse line.

Yet compared with Central Europe in 1848 or 1918/19 this is a relatively short list. Most nations have states, and have got used to their new frontiers. Ethnically the map is far more homogenous than it was in 1848 or 1918: as Ernest Gellner has observed, it is now a picture by Modigliani rather than Kokoschka. (The main artists were, of course, Hitler and Stalin: their brushes, war, deportation and mass murder.) National and ethnic conflicts may grow again both between and within these states, as they did in Eastern Europe before the last war, especially if their economic situation deteriorates. Or those national and ethnic conflicts may progressively be alleviated, as were those of Western Europe after the last war, especially if these countries' economic situation improves in a process of integration into a larger European common market and community. We shall see. But the historical record must show that 1989 was not a year of acute national and ethnic conflict in Eastern Europe west of the Soviet frontier. Quite the reverse: it was a year of solidarity both within and between nations. At the end of the year, symbolic and humanitarian support for the people(s) of Romania came from all the self-liberated states of East Central Europe. A springtime of nations is not *necessarily* a springtime of 'nationalism'.

In any case, what was most striking was not the language of nationhood. That was wholly predictable. What was striking was the other ideas and words that, so to speak, shared the top billing. One of these was 'society'. In Poland, a country often stigmatized as 'nationalist', the word most often used to describe the people as opposed to the authorities was not 'nation'; it was *społeczeństwo*, 'society'. In Czechoslovakia the word 'society' was used in a similar way, though less frequently, and here it could not simply be a synonym or euphemism for 'nation' because it covered two nations. In both cases, it was as meaningful to talk of social self-determination as it was to talk of national self-determination. Everywhere stress was laid on the self-conscious unity of intelligentsia, workers and peasants. Of course, in part, this unity was created by the common enemy. When communist power had been broken, and real parliamentary politics began, then conflicting social interests were robustly articulated. Thus, probably the most distinctive and determined group in the new Polish parliament was not communists or Solidarity, left or right, but peasant-farmers from all parties, combining and conspiring to advance their sectional interests.

None the less, the social divisions were nothing like as deep as in the nineteenth- or early twentieth-century, and they did not undercut the revolutions. There is an historical irony here. For in large measure communism created the social unity which contributed decisively to the end of communism. The combination of deliberate levelling and unintended absurdities, resulted in a distribution of wealth throughout most of society that was not so much egalitarian as higgledy-piggledy. A professor would earn less than a miner, an engineer less than a peasant-farmer. A plumber with a few dollars or Deutschmarks would be better off than a prince without hard currency. A worker lived in the same house as a doctor, an engineer or a writer; and the ground plan of their apartments was almost certainly identical, even if the décor differed. At the same time, they were all united by consciousness of the one great divide between the communist upper/ruling class, the *nomenklatura,* and all the rest. In all these countries the latter were 'them': *oni* (a word made famous by Teresa Torańska's book of interviews with Polish Stalinists), the *Bonzen.* 'They' were identified by their clothes, their black curtained cars, their special hospitals and shops, their language and their behaviour. When the dense crowds in Prague were asked to clear a path for an ambulance, they did so chanting, 'We are not like them! We are not like them!'

At the same time, there was a remarkably high level of popular political awareness. Again, this was partly a result of the system. Everyone had at least a basic education, and from the earliest years that education was highly politicized. Many people reacted against this politicization with a determined retreat into private life, and an almost programmatic apoliticism. But because of the politicization of education, and the ubiquity of ideology, no one could be in any doubt that words and ideas mattered, having real consequences for everyday life.

A concept that played a central role in opposition thinking in the 1980s was that of 'civil society'. 1989 was the springtime of societies aspiring to be civil. Ordinary men and women's rudimentary notion of what it meant to build a civil society might not satisfy the political theorist. But some such notion was there, and it contained several basic demands. There should be forms of association, national, regional, local, professional, which would be voluntary, authentic, democratic and, first and last, not controlled or manipulated by the Party or Party-state. People should be 'civil'; that is, polite, tolerant, and, above all, non-violent. Civil and civilian. The idea of citizenship had to be taken seriously.

Communism managed to poison many words from the mainstream of European history – not least the word 'socialism'. But somehow it did not manage to poison the words 'citizen' and 'civic', even though it used them, too, in perverted ways; for example, in appeals to 'civic responsibility', meaning 'Keep quiet and let us deal with these troublesome students.' Why it did not manage to poison those words is an interesting question – to which I have no ready answer – but the fact is that when Solidarity's parliamentarians came to give their group a name, they called it the *Citizens'* Parliamentary Club; the Czech movement called itself the *Civic* Forum; and the opposition groups in the GDR started by describing themselves as *Bürgerinitiativen*, that is, citizens' or civic initiatives. (In the East German case, the actual word was probably imported from West Germany, but the fact remains that they chose this rather than another term.) And the language of citizenship was important in all these revolutions. People had had enough of being mere components in a deliberately atomized society: they wanted to be citizens, individual men and women with dignity and responsibility, with rights but also with duties, freely associating in civil society.

There is one last point about the self-description of the revolution which is perhaps worth a brief mention. As Ralf Dahrendorf has observed, Karl Marx played on the ambiguity of the German term *bürgerliche Gesellschaft*, which could be translated either as 'civil society' or as *'bourgeois society'*. Marx, says Dahrendorf, deliberately conflated the two 'cities' of modernity the fruits of the Industrial and the French Revolutions, the bourgeois and the *citoyen*. I thought of this observation when a speaker in one of the mass rallies in Leipzig called for solidarity with the *bürgerliche Bewegung* in Czechoslovakia. 'The bourgeois movement!' But on reflection there seems to me a deeper truth in that apparent malapropism. For what most of the opposition movements throughout East Central Europe and a large part of 'the people' supporting them were in effect saying was: 'Yes, Marx is right, the two things are intimately connected – and we want both!' Civil rights and property rights, economic freedom and political freedom, financial independence and intellectual independence: each supports the other. So, yes, we want to be citizens, but we also want to be middle-class, in the senses that the majority of citizens in the more fortunate half of Europe are middle-class. We want to be *Bürger* AND *bürgerlich*! Tom Paine, but also Thomas Mann.

So it was a springtime of nations, but not necessarily of nationalism; of societies, aspiring to be civil; and above all, of citizens.

The springtime of citizens has already changed the face of Europe. What seemed only possible at the beginning of 1989 seemed certain at the beginning of 1990. There would be a new Europe, for which the term 'Yalta' would no longer be an appropriate shorthand. This Europe would have a different place for the countries formerly described as East European, and, at the very least, a less divided Germany.

1848 ended badly because of the combination of internal and external forces of reaction; but the external ones were decisive. No comparable external forces of reaction were visible at the beginning of 1990. The Prussians were making their own revolution, not crushing those of their neighbours. Austrians were not repressing the Hungarian reform-revolution, but helping it along. And the Russians? Here the transformation was miraculous, to the point where senior American and British officials indicated that they might actually welcome a Soviet military intervention to smash the Securitate death squads in Romania. But no, for Romania, as for Czechoslovakia, Hungary, Poland and Bulgaria, Soviet leaders and commentators from Gorbachev down assumed a saintly expression and said they would never dream of interfering in the internal affairs of another sovereign state.

Yet the popular movement for national and social self-determination did not stop neatly at the western frontier of the Soviet Union. What happened in Eastern Europe directly encouraged the Baltic States, not to mention the Romanians of Soviet Moldavia. And what if the political earth began to move in the Ukraine? At the beginning of 1990 it was therefore all too possible to imagine some backlash or reversal inside the Soviet Union. But it seemed reasonable to doubt whether even a conservative-military leadership in Moscow would attempt to use armed force to restore Russian domination west of the Soviet frontiers of 1945. Would they not have more than enough on their hands trying to preserve the empire inside the post-war Soviet frontiers? Logically, if they invaded one East European country they should now invade them all. And then, what would they 'restore'? The shattered humpty-dumpties that were yesterday's East European communist parties? Obviously a reversal inside the Soviet Union would make life much less comfortable in the new Europe, and directly affect developments in a Germany still partly occupied by Soviet troops. But it would not in itself suffice to turn the map back to what it was before 1989.

About this new Europe there are countless questions to be asked, of which the most obviously pressing is 'How can the West help the transition of formerly communist states into liberal democracies?' I ask myself a less obvious question: not 'How can we help them?' but 'How might they help us?' What, if anything, can these nearly hundred million Europeans, with their forty years of hard experience, bring to the new Europe, and to us in the West? The Czechs were delighted to point out that '89 is '68 turned upside down. But one of the notable differences between '68 and '89 was the comparative lack of Western intellectuals discovering, in these exotic regions, new utopias, 'socialism with a human face' and the fabled Third Way.

Of course there is a whole kaleidoscope of new parties, programmes and trends, and it is little short of impudence to subsume them in one 'message'. Yet if you look at what these diverse parties are really saying about the basic questions of politics, economics, law and international relations, there is a remarkable underlying consensus. In politics they are all saying: there is no 'socialist democracy', there is only democracy. And by democracy they mean multi-party, parliamentary democracy as practised in contemporary Western, Northern and Southern Europe. They are all saying: there is no 'socialist legality', there is only legality. And by that they mean the rule of law, guaranteed by the constitutionally anchored independence of the judiciary. They are all saying, and for the left this is perhaps the most important statement: there is no 'socialist economics', there is only economics. And economics means not a socialist market economy but a social market economy. Not Ota Šik but Ludwig Erhard. Of course there are grave differences in these countries between, for example, Friedmanites and Hayekites. A good word might even be heard for Keynes. But the general direction is absolutely plain: towards an economy whose basic engine of growth is the market, with extensive private ownership of the means of production, distribution and exchange. The transition to such a system poses unique problems, for which original solutions will have to be found. In most of these countries there is still widespread support for relatively egalitarian distribution of the wealth thus created, and for a strong welfare state. But the basic model, in the three essentials of politics, law and economics, is something between the real existing Switzerland and the real existing Sweden.

Sweden – or, as one leading Soviet economist carefully stressed, *southern* Sweden – now seems to be the accepted ideal for virtually everyone who styles themself a socialist from Berlin to Vladivostok. But if Marx came back to earth, would he not describe the dominant mode of production in Sweden as capitalist? In other words, the fundamental argument from the left seems no longer to be about the best way to produce wealth, only about the best way to distribute it. (The more fundamental critique of the successful forms of production comes from Greens rather than socialists.)

For purely practical and historical reasons, the state will clearly play a larger part in most formerly East European countries than in most West European countries, for some years to come. But this does not necessarily mean that people will want it to. On the contrary, having had so much state interference for so long, they might decide they want as little of it as possible. Public opinion polls and sociological surveys are not much use here, since most people have only just begun to think about these issues, let alone to confront them in the harsh reality of economic transition. The proof of the pudding will be in the eating. Among the intellectuals who have begun to confront these issues there is, it seems to me, rather an opposite danger: that of regarding the free market as a cure for all ills, social and political as well as economic. Hence the popularity of Hayek. One might almost say that the free market is the latest Central European utopia.

It is easy now to forget that communism claimed to have found not only new and better forms of politics, law and economics, but also a new and better way of organizing relations between states. This new way was called 'socialist internationalism', and counterposed to 'bourgeois nationalism'. What we have seen in practice is the rise of socialist nationalism and bourgeois internationalism. There are many examples of bourgeois internationalism – G7, OECD, IMF, NATO, GATT – but in the perspective of European history the most dramatic is the European Community. Now there are proposals, too numerous even to list, for new forms of interstate relations in the former Eastern Europe. To give but one example, leading Polish politicians have revived the idea of a confederation of Poland and Czechoslovakia. But if you ask what is the underlying model for the new relations between these states, and for the resolution of their outstanding national, ethnic and economic conflicts, then the answer is clear. The model is the European Community.

This means not only that they would like to join the present EC, as fully as possible and as soon as possible. It also means that they hope their outstanding historic conflicts and enmities can be overcome in the same way that, say, those between France and Germany have been overcome. This is true, it seems to me, even of those groups that would not explicitly acknowledge the EC as a model. Certainly, you have to go far in Western Europe to find such enthusiastic 'Europeans' – that is, supporters of a supranational community called Europe – as you will find at every turn in Eastern Europe. Travelling to and fro between the two halves of the divided continent, I have sometimes thought that the real divide is between those (in the West) who have Europe and those (in the East) who believe in it. And everywhere, in all the lands, the phrase people use to sum up what is happening is 'the return to Europe'.

Yet what, to repeat the question, can these enthusiasts bring to the new Europe? If I am right in my basic analysis, they can offer no fundamentally new ideas on the big questions of politics, economics, law or international relations. The ideas whose time has come are old, familiar, well-tested ones. (It is the new ideas whose time has passed.) So is all they have to offer us their unique, theoretically intriguing but practically burdensome problems? Do they come like mendicants to the door bearing only chronicles of wasted time? Or might they have, under their threadbare cloaks, some hidden treasures?

Travelling through this region over the last decade, I have found treasures: examples of great moral courage and intellectual integrity; comradeship, deep friendship, family life; time and space for serious conversation, music, literature, not disturbed by the perpetual noise of our media-driven and obsessively telecommunicative world; Christian witness in its original and purest form; more broadly, qualities of relations between men and women of very different backgrounds, and once bitterly opposed faiths – an ethos of solidarity. Here the danger of sentimental idealization is acute, for the privileged visitor enjoys these benefits without paying the costs. There is no doubt that, on any quantitative or utilitarian reckoning, the costs have been far higher than the benefits. Yet it would be even more wrong to pretend that these treasures were not real. They were. And for me the question of questions after 1989 is: What if any of these good things will survive liberation? Was the community *only* a community of fate, a *Schicksalsgemeinschaft*? Were these *just* the uses of adversity?

Even if there is no reversal in the Soviet Union, no violent backlash or illiberal turn in this or that East European country, won't these treasures simply be swept away in the rush – the all too understandable rush – for affluence? As a Hungarian friend wryly remarked: 'I have survived forty years of communism, but I'm not sure that I'll survive one year of capitalism.' And this will not just be the atomizing impact of developed consumerism, one of the most potent weapons known to man. It will be the still rougher and more traumatic impact of the attempted transition from a planned to a market economy, with all the associated blows of unemployment, dislocation and injustice.

Wishful thinking helps no one. You can, alas, paint with a rather high degree of analytical plausibility a quite dark picture of the prospect for the former Eastern Europe in the 1990s: a prospect in which the post-communist future looks remarkably like the pre-communist past, less Central Europe than *Zwischeneuropa*, a dependent intermediate zone of weak states, national prejudice, inequality, poverty and *Schlamassel*. 1989 might then appear, to participants and historians, as just one brief shining moment between the sufferings of yesterday and those of tomorrow.

This fate is not inevitable. Whether it can be avoided depends to a very significant degree on the commitment and ingenuity of the West in general, Western Europe in particular, and above all on West Germany – or rather, to put it in terms more appropriate to the new Europe, on a Germany remaining Western.

Yet even if the darker prospect were to be realized, something would remain, at least in memory, in culture, in spirit. At the very least the Europeans from over there would have offered us, with a clarity and firmness born of bitter experience, a restatement of the value of what we already have, of old truths and tested models, of the three essentials of liberal democracy and the European Community as the one and only, real existing common European home. Intellectually, dare I say spiritually, '1989' in Eastern Europe is a vital complement to '1992' in Western Europe.

'*Litwo! Ojczyzno moja! ty jesteś jak zdrowie,*' begins the most famous of all Polish poems, Adam Mickiewicz's 'Pan Tadeusz':

> *Lithuania, my fatherland, thou art like health;*
> *How much we should value thee, he alone learns,*
> *Who has lost thee.*

If we put in place of 'Lithuania' the word 'Europe', we may have the deepest lesson of that year of wonders, '89.

Note

Source Reprinted by permission of the author from Timothy Garton Ash, *The Magic Lantern* (London: Vintage, 1990), pp. 131–56. Copyright © 1990, 1993 Timothy Garton Ash.

6

THE MEANINGS OF 1989

Jeffrey C. Isaac

*American political theorist Jeffrey C. Isaac in this thoughtful article offers a cri-
tical interpretation of the prevailing, often contradictory, viewpoints regarding
the revolutions of 1989 and the role of dissident notions of freedom and rights
in the dismantling of the Leninist regimes. Inspired by Karl R. Popper's critique
of historicism, Isaac rejects monistic interpretations that assign one single meaning to these events and proposes a multifaceted approach that would recognize the
plurality of significations associated with them. The most important element in his
analysis is the effort to recuperate and deepen the vision of political life and action
developed in the thinking and practice of East Central European dissent. In this
respect, his approach is radically different from G. M. Tamás's and Tony
Judt's visions of dissidents as naive dreamers, deprived of profound connections
with the societies they claimed to speak for.*

*Readers should notice Isaac's plea for an open-minded, nondogmatic vision of
democratic politics. Acknowledging the merits of liberalism, he argues that the
legacy of what East European critical intellectuals used to call "antipolitics"
should not be lightly dismissed. In other words, unlike those who herald the
advent of liberal democracy as a nonproblematic accomplishment, Isaac thinks
that the new ideas and styles of politics generated in the experience of dissent,
including nonparliamentary forms of participation and the ethos of civil society,
represent democratic possibilities relevant for the future of democracy in the
"East" and the "West."*

*　*　*

History, as an entirety, could exist only in the eyes of an observer outside it
and outside the world. History only exists, in the final analysis, for God.
(Camus, 1956, p. 189)

The historicist does not recognize that it is we who select and order the
facts of history . . . Instead of recognizing that historical interpretation
should answer a need arising out of the practical problems and decisions
which face us, the historicist believes that . . . by contemplating history we

125

may discover the secret, the essence of human destiny. Historicism is out to find The Path on which mankind is destined to walk; it is out to discover The Clue to History or The Meaning of History . . . [Yet] *history has no meaning.*

(Popper, 1971, p. 269)

In 1789 the Ancien Regime fell, accompanied by the crash of falling ramparts (Camus, 1956, p. 26). Punctuating an age of democratic revolution, the upheaval caught the attention of the world.[1] Immanuel Kant spoke for many "enlightened" thinkers when he observed that: "The revolution of a gifted people which we have seen unfolding in our day may succeed or miscarry . . . this revolution, I say, nonetheless finds in the hearts of all spectators . . . a wishful participation that borders closely on enthusiasm . . ." (1963, p. 148). Almost exactly two hundred years later ramparts again came crashing down, this time in the East of Europe. Symbolized so dramatically by the demolition of the Berlin Wall, the entire edifice of Communist rule – a truly immense superstructure weighting down upon its people – and with it the "Iron Curtain" dividing Europe from itself, came tumbling down, and democratic oppositions long subjected to persecution and marginality were swept into power.[2]

What do these events mean? What is their significance for the citizens of what used to be called Eastern Europe? What is their significance for democrats at the dawn of a new century? Intellectual history since 1789 proves that it is impossible to arrive at a single interpretation of events of such magnitude. For over two hundred years writers have argued about the meaning of the French Revolution. As we continually reassess ourselves, our political communities, and the problems facing them, we quite naturally reconsider those foundational episodes and events that have shaped our past and help to define our political identities. In this sense, history has no absolute or final meaning; it is continually, *historically*, interpreted and reinterpreted. On this most philosophers and historians would probably agree.

There is surely a range of possible interpretations of 1989. And yet at present a powerful consensus has taken shape on behalf of an avowedly liberal interpretation. The most famous, indeed notorious, exponent of this view is a writer who, intoxicated with Hegel, has clearly not yet properly learned the lessons of historicism. Francis Fukuyama, in his influential essay "The End of History" and later in his book by the same name, proclaimed that we have reached "the end point of mankind's ideological evolution and the universalization of Western liberal democracy as the final form of human government" (1989, p. 4).[3] Fukuyama was not alone in his enthusiasm. Marc Plattner, co-editor of the *Journal of Democracy* (founded in 1996), seconded this view, declaring that we now find ourselves in "a world with one dominant principle of legitimacy, democracy" (1992).

Such Hegelian optimism has been challenged by many liberal democrats. Jean Francois Revel has cautioned against "an overhasty assumption that the movement toward democracy represented a sort of reverse millennium, the arrival of the eternal kingdom of history" (1991, pp. 14–15). Perhaps the most serious statement of such skepticism has been articulated by Samuel P. Huntington. "To hope for a benign end to history," he writes, "is human. To expect it to happen is unrealistic. To plan on it happening is disastrous" (Huntington, 1989, pp. 3–11). Yet one need not be Hegelian in order to hold that the revolutions of 1989 represent the triumph of liberalism. Indeed, Huntington's own sophisticated account of the current "third wave" of liberal democratic transformation is one of many efforts to develop more realistic, constructive policies to assure the triumph of liberal democracy that Fukuyama only prematurely heralds.[4] In spite of significant disagreements, many liberal analysts concur that the transition to liberal democracy is the principal issue on the agenda today.

While I believe that there is much merit to this liberal interpretation, I consider it both politically and morally flawed. It is politically flawed because it marginalizes and/or ignores important forms of politics that were practiced by the Central European democratic oppositions, forms not adequately covered by liberalism. It is morally flawed because, in doing so, it prematurely forecloses some very complex questions about the meanings and legacies of 1989, thereby precluding certain important avenues of political action. More specifically, it minimizes the importance of nonelectoral, nonparliamentary forms of political activity – in particular the kinds of civic initiatives that played an important role in resisting communism – in opposing authoritarianism and constituting genuine spaces of democratic politics. While the "high politics" of normal liberal democratic institutions are important, these need to be supplemented by – and sometimes challenged by – more vigorous, grass-roots forms of citizenship. This is particularly true at a time when masses of people experience economic difficulty and frustration, and the institutions of mass democratic politics cannot compensate for these sufferings and indeed are often viewed as part of the problem. The liberal interpretation of 1989 that I criticize fails to see this.

It bears emphasis that in criticizing this liberal interpretation I do not wish to indict liberalism as a whole. A number of liberal democrats have developed criticisms of really existing liberal democracy that overlap substantially with the democratic arguments defended in this paper.[5] It would be a serious mistake to lump all liberals together and declare them celebrants of existing liberal institutional arrangements. Yet there is currently prevailing a liberal viewpoint that *does* celebrate such arrangements and that seeks to incorporate the democratic revolutions of 1989 neatly within them. This version of liberalism – a monist liberalism if there ever was one – merits criticism.

In the spirit of Popper's critique of historicism, I will reject the idea that 1989 has a single meaning. It has many meanings. While in some ways it suggests a triumph of liberalism, in other ways it presents more democratic and participatory possibilities. While it would be mistaken to overestimate these possibilities or their significance, it would equally be mistaken to ignore them. For at a time in which liberal democracy is suffering from its own forms of legitimacy crisis, these more democratic possibilities have relevance for the future of democracy in the "East" *and* the "West."[6]

The triumph of liberalism?

While Fukuyama's 1989 essay articulated a sense of liberal enthusiasm that was fairly widespread among politicians and media commentators,[7] liberal scholars who saw the weaknesses of his historicism did not fully dissent from his prognosis regarding the end of ideology. Stephen Holmes, for example, in his scathing review of Fukuyama's book, noted that, "Throughout the post-Communist world . . . we are observing waves of radical change that look so far like a liberal revolution." "Is liberal revolution," he asked rhetorically, "not the most significant fact of contemporary political life?" (Holmes, 1992a, pp. 27, 33). Contra Fukuyama, liberalism is not eschatological; but it is stable, fair, open, and free. What is taking place, Holmes suggests, is surely a liberal transformation, one more complex, and problematic, than the triumph proclaimed by Fukuyama but a vindication of liberalism nonetheless.

As Gale Stokes writes in his recent history of the Central European revolutions: "Theirs was not a revolution of total innovation, but rather the shucking off of a failed experiment in favor of an already existing model, pluralist democracy" (Stokes, 1993, p. 260). This is surely the dominant interpretation of 1989. Thus, Bruce Ackerman identifies 1989 with "the return of revolutionary democratic liberalism," the revival of a political project inaugurated by the framers of the United States Constitution (Ackerman, 1992, p. 1). Ralph Dahrendorf, in his subtle *Reflections on the Revolution in Europe*, writes that: "At its core, the European revolution of 1989 is the rejection of an unbearable and, as we have seen, untenable reality, and by the same token it is a reaffirmation of old ideas. Democracy . . . pluralism . . . citizenship . . . are not exactly new ideas." What has triumphed, Dahrendorf insists, is nothing but the idea of an "open society," a liberal idea whose progenitors include Locke, Hume, Madison, Kant, and, more recently, Raymond Aron and Karl Popper (Dahrendorf, 1990, pp. 27, 75–6). This thesis has been stated most forcefully by Timothy Garton Ash, who maintains that the European revolutions "can offer no fundamentally new ideas on the big questions of politics, economics, law or international relations. The ideas whose time has come are old, familiar, well-tested ones" – liberal ideas about the rule of law, parliamentary government, and an independent judiciary (Garton Ash, 1990a, p. 154).[8]

Those who subscribe to this view do not necessarily believe that the triumph of liberalism has yet been assured. Indeed, most emphatically do not believe this. Valerie Bunce (1990) articulates a common concern when she notes that "the question foremost on the minds of people in the East and the West alike . . . is whether the new regimes in Eastern Europe will succeed in their desire to become genuine liberal democracies."[9] Because this *is* a question, liberal political scientists and constitutional theorists have turned their attention to matters of constitutional and political engineering. As Stephen Holmes notes in the inaugural issue of the *East European Constitutional Review*, the journal of the newly established Center for the Study of Constitutionalism in Eastern Europe at the University of Chicago Law School: "From Albania to the Baltics and, more recently, in Russia itself, attempts are being made to design liberal-democratic political institutions . . . Chances for a successful transition to liberal democracy vary from country to country . . . [but] institutional design will have important long-term consequences for the stability and effectiveness of democratic government" (Holmes, 1992b). Bruce Ackerman echoes this sentiment. At a time of enormous turbulence and uncertainty, he insists, "the challenge for statecraft is to use these fleeting moments to build new and stronger foundations for liberal democracy" (Ackerman, 1992, p. 27). Western analysts have turned their attention to this challenge of statecraft with a vengeance. A proliferation of books and scholarly articles debate the virtues and vices of alternative electoral schemes, the perils of presidentialism or parliamentarism, the character of judicial review, and the logic of constitutionalism. New journals, like the *Journal of Democracy* and *East European Constitutional Review*, focus their attention on how better to effect a transition to functioning and stable liberal democracy in Central Europe.

Yet the view that 1989 set Central Europe on the path of liberal democratic transition is not simply the view of many important Western theorists; it is given credence by the reflections of Central Europeans themselves, including many who are quite famous for their roles in the democratic oppositions to Communism. János Kis, for example, has maintained that:

> The alternative Hungary is facing now is to create a constitutional, multiparty democracy and a mixed, market economy, or to regress into economic decay and political Balkanization. The chance for the former to happen seems to be slim. Still, this is our only chance for the next generations. We cannot choose another terrain, more

favorable to the realization of the values of liberty, equality and fraternity. We have to try to use this tiny bit of chance, here and now.

(Kis, 1989, p. 241)[10]

Adam Michnik has frequently sounded a similar theme – there are but two futures for Eastern Europe, the Western future of liberal democracy and political compromise or a descent into xenophobia and fractious tribalism (Michnik, 1990a, 1990b). In defense of the former, he writes that:

liberal values in the era of post-communism, values codified in the writings of John Stuart Mill and Alexis de Tocqueville, and also those of Hayek, are meeting with their true renaissance. Through their resistance to communism, they rediscovered their vision of civil liberty, their dreams of parliamentarism, of cultural and political pluralism, of tolerance, and their desire for a country free of any kind of ideological dictatorship.

(Michnik, 1991a, pp. 70–2)[11]

George Konrád, whose book *Antipolitics* was a veritable bible of democratic opposition to Communism, has perhaps best summed up this self-understanding: "Why am I a liberal? Because I am skeptical about everything human, about our collective self; because for me there are no institutions, persons, or concepts that are sacrosanct or above criticism . . . For me, liberalism, is, first of all, a style: worldly, civilized, personal, ironic . . ." (Konrád, 1990, p. 189).

What are we to make of this apparent convergence between Western scholars and Eastern former dissidents on a liberal interpretation of 1989? There is reason, I believe, at least to discount the liberal enthusiasm among Central European intellectuals. As one commentator has noted, it is not liberalism as a philosophical or political doctrine so much as liberalism as an *attitude* that has experienced the renaissance to which Michnik refers. "Liberalism," Szacki writes, "appears to Eastern Europe as a utopia, as a vision of the good society most glaringly opposed to the realities of the communist system" (1990, p. 472). The senses in which former oppositionists declare themselves to be liberals need to be unpacked; their own self-understandings, in other words, cannot be taken at face value if we wish to understand their current allegiances. Beyond this, there is no reason to privilege their views of the revolutions they helped to happen. Tocqueville long ago pointed out that revolutionaries can misperceive the events in which they participate. Unintended consequences, and possibilities too quickly foreclosed, seem almost inevitable features of revolutionary transformations. While the words of Michnik and Konrád tell us something important, then, there is no reason to treat them as the last words on our subject.

One way to get a better handle on the supposed triumph of liberal democracy would be to disaggregate this idea into a number of distinct claims, each of which needs to be judged on its own merit. The question, then, is not whether or not liberalism has triumphed, but *in which sense or senses* has it triumphed. Let me suggest that there are at least three distinct senses in which liberalism might be believed to have triumphed. In each sense liberalism has triumphed but not unambiguously.

First, we might speak of the practical triumph of liberal democratic institutions. It seems pretty clear that with the downfall of Communism monopolistic political regimes have given way to more "polyarchal" arrangements. The various "civic forum" type oppositional coalitions quickly gave way to Round Table negotiations between communist leaderships and democratic political elites about the transition to a liberal democracy. Constitutions, in some cases final, in some cases provisional, have been established, formally organizing public offices and containing bills of rights. Liberal democratic institutions – separation of powers, regular competitive elections, party systems – have been put into place. Political parties have supplanted and co-opted democratic opposition movements, channeling and "aggregating" political demands in manageable, politically "normalized" ways. More or less free and fair elections have been held, and successful alterations of government have been accomplished. In this sense we might speak descriptively of the institutionalization of liberal democracy, a process that could be explained partly by the structural imperatives of organizing political disagreement in a large-scale modern society, and partly by the financial requirements of a modern market economy operating in a global capitalist economy. It would be impossible to deny the political triumph of liberalism in this sense.[12]

And yet, of course, political processes in Central Europe are still very much in flux. Many crucial constitutional issues – the restitution of property nationalized under Communism, the so-called "lustration" of former Communists, and the status of the *nomenklatura* more generally – remain outstanding. The drastic and precipitous transformation of economic life, and with it the marked decline in the standards of living of many Central Europeans, have fed a widespread sense of popular resentment that has fueled chauvinistic ideologies. The problem of national minorities that is endemic to the region has exacerbated such ideologies. Authoritarian populism, in other words, is a real competitor of liberal democracy.[13] Perhaps equally ominous is the geopolitical uncertainty in the former Soviet Union and the brutal dismemberment of Yugoslavia, both of which add to the sense of popular anxiety and symbolize the insecurity of liberal democratic institutionalization in Central Europe. The tribalistic alternative against which Kis and Michnik caution still remains.

131

The limits of the triumph of liberalism in this first sense bring us to a second sense in which we might speak of a liberal vindication – the triumph of liberalism as an ethical-political imperative. Few liberal theorists would deny the great difficulties currently besetting liberalism in Central Europe. The point, I think, is that these are viewed as obstacles to the project of constructing liberal democracy rather than as plausible alternatives in their own right. From this point of view, while the success of liberalism is not yet assured, the alternatives to it are demonstrably undesirable. Whatever its problems, liberal democracy is, we might say, following Churchill's famous quip, the least bad form of government. If we wish to live in and enjoy the advantages of a modern market economy, and if we wish to avoid civil war in societies characterized by all kinds of ineliminable differences, then liberal democracy is the order of the day. What Holmes calls "constitutional design" and Ackerman "statecraft" thus becomes a pressing need.

There is much truth to this claim as well. It is impossible to consider the Bosnian tragedy, or the rise of chauvinistic ideologies in Slovakia, Romania, and the Baltic states, or the disturbing ascendancy of politicians like Zhirinovsky in Russia, or the anti-Semitic rhetoric of Csurka in Hungary and to question the attractiveness of liberal constitutionalism. The wave of anti-communist witch-hunting that has plagued political debate, threatening to engulf Central Europe societies in bitter recrimination about the past and offering fertile ground for political demagoguery, makes evident the importance of typically liberal civil liberties like the presumption of innocence and legal due process.[14] The insensitive and at times hostile ways in which national and religious minorities have been treated underscores the importance of liberal toleration.[15]

As Ulrich Preuss has argued, two competing logics of citizenship continue to jockey for position in Central Europe: a civil conception that defines as citizens those who are subject to a common law, and an ethnic conception that defines citizenship in terms of membership in a distinct ethnic or national group (Preuss, 1993).[16] The latter conception is profoundly hostile to the proceduralism of liberal representative government, and, mirroring the writings of Carl Schmitt, it relies upon appeals to an ethnically homogenous popular will against those "special interests" – national minorities, foreign capital, politicians – held to stand in the way of authentic popular sovereignty.[17] Such a vision, not without its appeal in Central Europe today, is simply another right-wing version of the "totalitarian democracy" long ago identified by Jacob Talmon (1970). In light of all this, it is hard to disagree with the judgment of Stephen Holmes:

> The most difficult problem facing the countries of Eastern Europe today is the creation of a government that can pursue effective reforms while retaining public confidence and remaining demo-

cratically accountable . . . The main political danger, conversely, is . . . the spirit of antiparliamentarism . . . Hence, the challenge in Eastern Europe today is to prevent extraparliamentary leaders from building public support on the basis of nondemocratic and nonelectoral forms of legitimacy.

(Holmes, 1993b, pp. 23–4)[18]

In this sense, liberal democratization *is* an ethico-political imperative. For the only macro-political alternative seems to be some combination of authoritarianism, civil war, and economic decline.[19] And yet even here some caution is in order. For what is the relationship between the liberal project and the other possibilities liberals like Holmes and Garton Ash frighteningly project? Are these alternatives simply obstacles to be combated? Do they answer to pressing concerns that derive from inadequacies of the liberal democratic transition itself, especially the endemic problems of economic dislocation and political alienation?[20] Can these challenges be so readily dismissed? For the purposes of my argument I will put aside what we might call the authoritarian populist alternative, for it is clearly both anti-liberal and anti-democratic, an alternative to be opposed however politically viable it may seem. But are there no other alternatives to liberal democracy? And might not a more radically democratic alternative in fact play some role in combating authoritarian populism?

Here things become complicated, and we move on to the third sense in which liberal democracy can be said to have triumphed, not simply as the practical result of structural forces or as an ethical-political imperative, but as the *fulfillment* of the democratic opposition to Communism. Let us return to some of the historical claims cited above, that "theirs was not a revolution of total innovation, but rather the shucking off of a failed experiment in favor of an already existing model . . . ," that "the common goal was not just throwing the rascals out, but also building liberal democracy" (Stokes, 1993, p. 260; Bunce, 1990, p. 403). Many liberal commentators have not simply offered a political prognosis but a historical interpretation, to the effect that liberal democratic institutions are the *intended outcome* of the revolutions, or at least of the most advanced democratic leaderships of the revolutions. Such a view recapitulates a nice, neat nineteenth-century progressivist scheme, pitting the forces of liberation against the forces of reaction, liberal democratic reformers against Communist reactionaries in league with nationalist ideologues. Revolutionary success versus reactionary failure. The choices seem clear.

Like the other senses in which liberal democracy can be said to have been vindicated, there is much truth to the view that liberal democracy has long been the goal of the revolutionaries themselves. The remarks of Michnik, Kis, and Konrád cited earlier certainly lend plausibility to it. At an even deeper level, the major democratic oppositions in Central Europe – the

Movement for Civil Liberties and later the Civic Forum in Czechoslovakia, the Democratic Opposition in Hungary, and the Committee for Social Self-Defense and Solidarity in Poland – had by 1989 all demanded an end to Communist rule and the institution of multiparty liberal democracy, demands that accurately reflected the long-standing positions of leading activists, many of whom had begun their careers as human rights dissidents.[21] At an even deeper level still, if we examine the major writings of the principal dissident intellectuals – Havel, Konrád, Michnik, Kuroń, Kis – it is not hard to discern that a recurrent theme is the need for limits in politics, surely a theme with liberal resonance.

And yet here too things are more complicated. For if we examine the views of the democratic oppositionists more deeply, we will discover that while they are democratic, it is not clear that they are unambiguously *liberal* democratic. This is *not* to say that they are antiliberal.[22] Liberal ideas of individual liberty and liberal institutions of constitutional government are surely valued as necessary ingredients of human freedom and dignity. But they are not viewed as sufficient for many of the democratic oppositionists. There is, if you will, a democratic "surplus value" that the liberal interpretation of 1989 quietly expropriates.

Indeed, liberals admit as much in passing. Ackerman, for example, both praises and criticizes the "antipolitical" vision shared by people like Konrád and Havel. Its resistance to totalitarianism was meritorious. But its calls for existential integrity, he maintains, are insufficiently practical for the task of liberal construction. Havel's "Heideggerian contempt for the Enlightenment in general and Western consumerism in particular has an authoritarian ring." Indeed, the very idea of "living in truth" – a hallmark of the democratic opposition – is "positively dangerous if the truth is understood with grim philosophical passion" (Ackerman, 1992, pp. 32–3).

Just what Ackerman means by this last remark about grim philosophical passion is made clearer by a similar observation offered by Timothy Garton Ash:

> Now we expect many things of politicians in a well-functioning parliamentary democracy. But "living in truth" is not one of them. In fact the essence of democratic politics might rather be described as "working in half-truth." Parliamentary democracy is, at its heart, a system of limited adversarial mendacity, in which each party attempts to present part of the truth as if it were the whole.
>
> (Garton Ash, 1990b, p. 52)

Garton Ash makes explicit what Ackerman keeps implicit – that too much integrity, conscientiousness, "authenticity" is anathema to liberal democracy, which requires a certain cavalierness about truth and honesty if it is to function properly.[23] The most sophisticated argument to this effect has been presented by Elisabeth Kiss, who maintains that while the vision of "antipolitics" developed by the democratic oppositionists played a very important role in inspiring and organizing opposition to Communism, this vision is insufficient as a model for ongoing, normal politics in a complex society. "The new social order that will emerge in East-Central Europe, and the extent to which it fosters democratic aspirations," she avers, "will depend in large measure on governments, parliaments, and parties." Because the "antipolitics" of the oppositionists abjured such institutions in favor of more genuine agencies, it "translates badly into the postcommunist era" (Kiss, 1992, pp. 230, 226).

Kiss frankly puts her finger on the problem with the idea that 1989 represents a fulfillment of the opposition vision by identifying the striking *tensions* between the liberal democracy currently being instituted and the aspirations of many of those who struggled most vigorously against Communism. With this in mind, we can return to Holmes's observation that the principal task facing liberal democrats is "to prevent extraparliamentary leaders from building public support on the basis of nondemocratic and nonelectoral forms of legitimacy." The question is simple. Are all extraparliamentary efforts to build public support on the basis of nonelectoral forms of legitimacy anti-democratic? Or are there forms of democratic politics that are democratic precisely by virtue of going beyond parliamentary and electoral institutions? What I will argue is that there are such forms of politics, and that they were pioneered by the democratic oppositionists. Among the many meanings of 1989, one is the continuing importance of such forms of politics.

Antipolitical politics revisited

In many ways the Central European democratic oppositions can be seen as animated by liberal principles of state neutrality, the rule of law, the accountability of government, and the inviolability of private life. Confronting an arbitrary and repressive Communist state, these oppositions began as human rights initiatives, monitoring governmental abuses, petitioning for redress of specific grievances, and publicizing egregious violations of human rights recognized by international law and the Communist constitutions themselves.

And yet such initiatives implicated a more radically democratic kind of political praxis. The political aspect of their activity derived in part from the simple fact that in a totalitarian state all independent initiatives of any kind assumed a political importance, at least implicitly challenging the party's monopoly of political legitimacy. In this sense it can be viewed as no more than a tactic or at best a strategy of achieving a liberal democratic opening over time. But what came to be known as "antipolitical

politics," whatever its initial motivations – which surely differed from
person to person – was more than a strategy. It developed into an alternative form of politics. Its very means – which were ever so scrupulously self-
monitored – became its ends. Antipolitical politics was, in short, what
antipolitical politics did. What it did was to organize forms of solidarity
and assistance for the persecuted and marginalized under conditions of
extreme duress.[24] A strong ethos of solidarity and participation was necessary to support such initiatives in the face of state repression and mass
indifference when not outright hostility. As one of the first appeals of
KOR, the Polish Committee on Social Self-Defense, put it:

> the independent social activity reemerging in the course of the past
> several years is based above all on the organization of authentic
> public opinion, on the defense against reprisals, on the formulation
> of genuine social demands, and on the interruption of the state
> monopoly over the dissemination of information. Participation in
> these activities is open to everyone . . . It is necessary to organize
> to defend one's rights.
>
> ("Appeal to Society," 1985, pp. 481–2)

In what ways did this practice of organizing "civil society against the state"
in order to "to defend one's rights" implicate a non-liberal but democratic
form of politics? I will suggest an answer by analyzing a single initiative, the
Czechoslovakian human rights group Charter 77.

As is fairly well known, Charter 77 was formed in 1976 as an ad hoc community of individuals who sought to protest the arrest of an avant-garde
rock bank called Plastic People of the Universe. The Charter was formed
around the drafting of a declaration of protest that appealed to the principles of legality affirmed by the Helsinki Accords, to which the Czech
regime had been a signatory. But it soon became the nucleus of a number
of independent initiatives aimed at the democratization of Czech society.[25]

In some ways Charter 77 *was* the declaration of protest, for from the very
beginning it forswore any formal organization or explicit membership.
Whoever signed the Charter simply was by the very act of having done
so a "Chartist."[26] The Chartists considered themselves a "civic initiative"
rather than a "classic opposition" or a "movement."[27] As one Charter
document (Document No. 9/1984) put it, a civic initiative is "an ongoing
common initiative by individual citizens of all ages, callings, political
opinions and religious beliefs. They are linked by a sense of public responsibility for the way things are and a determination to take action to correct
the present depressing state of affairs" ("Open Letter . . . ," 1984, p. 16). A
civic initiative is an open-ended form of voluntary association, an exercise
of civic responsibility for the "state of affairs." But it is not an interest
group or a mass movement, for it avoids formal organization and abjures

political power. It operates in the sphere of civil society, independent of official and formal political institutions, and it seeks to influence "public opinion" rather than directly to exercise political power.

In many ways this conception of civic initiative was adopted as a strategic necessity out of a desire to avoid a frontal challenge to totalitarian state power.[28] But it also reflected a specific theoretical understanding of modern politics consistently elaborated in Charter documents. The 1984 "Open Letter to the British Peace Movements," for example, states that:

> Charter 77 does not constitute a movement in the accepted sense. (These are not, however, "sour grapes" on the part of some crypto-oppositional group vegetating in a totalitarian society, but a policy we have pursued consistently on the basis of our conviction that it represents a new factor in overcoming the global political and moral crisis.) Charter 77 is far more concerned to promote and extend the aforementioned sense of responsibility than to become a mass movement and win the maximum possible number of supporters; it is hardly in any position, anyway, to set itself specific political goals, leastways not in the sense that the word "politics" has been understood heretofore [sic].
> ("Open Letter . . . ," 1984, p 16)

This point is made even more emphatically in one of the most serious and revealing Charter documents, the "Statement on the Occasion of the Eighth Anniversary of Charter 77." The Charter rejects formal political organization or objectives, it argues, not out of opportunism or strategic necessity. It does so because:

> its goal is really fundamentally different. It is deeper and more far-reaching: its goal is to rehabilitate people as the true subjects of history . . . [which] by its very nature radically transcends the framework of mere changes of the system of power, i.e., the framework of eventual exchange of one official ideology for another, one group of rulers for another. This effort represents potential criticism of every system because every system, even the best, conceals within itself a tendency to elevate itself above people. Therefore, Charter 77 has a valid purpose under any circumstances.
> (Document No. 2/1985, "Commission . . . ," 1988, p. 150)

Three key ideas are expressed in these documents: that there is a "global crisis" of political and moral responsibility, that the participation of ordinary citizens is necessary to address this crisis, and that this makes the Charter as a set of ideas and initiatives relevant "under any circumstances" as a response not simply to totalitarianism, but to a crisis of modern politics more generally.

These ideas have long been associated with the writings of Václav Havel. But the extraordinary diversity of Chartist documents makes clear that however influential Havel undoubtedly was, these ideas had fairly wide currency among the Czech democratic oppositionists. Indeed, while the Charter included individuals from many different political tendencies – radical democrats, democratic socialists, reform Communists, independent Trotskyists, liberals, religious conservatives – the very form of Charter initiatives led them to a remarkable convergence on a common understanding of the politics of their activities. They spoke of an "antipolitical politics" of a kind of ethical responsibility and initiative that went beyond politics "in the ordinary sense" or "as commonly understood."[29] This was a republican politics with deep Arendtian resonances.[30] It was anti-teleological in the sense that what was central to the Chartists was less the motives or the goals of action than the modes of action themselves. And it was an effort "to reach for a new type of politics, or rather, a revival of what was once understood by the term 'politics,' the way it was practiced, and which has, today, been almost forgotten" – an effort to revive active citizenship (Document No. 2/1985, "Commission . . . ," 1988, p. 161; Document No. 1/1987, "Commission . . . ," 1988, pp. 276–85). These themes were elaborated in a remarkable essay by Václav Benda entitled "The Parallel Polis," which was originally published in samizdat in 1978 and spawned a vigorous debate among the Czech democratic opposition.[31] A number of important themes emerged from this discussion.

First, the Czech democrats viewed politics in non-strategic, though not anti-strategic, terms. While they always sought particular objectives – indeed, in their revulsion against grandiose ideologies they turned particularity into a virtue – they had little aspiration directly to influence public policy. For them politics was primarily a way of being and acting so as palpably to experience one's power and affirm one's dignity. As Ivan Jirous, musical director of the Plastic People and an important cultural radical, wrote of the "parallel polis:"

> It does not compete for power. Its aim is not to replace the powers that be with power of another kind, but rather under this power – or beside it – to create a structure that respects other laws and in which the voice of the ruling power is heard only as an insignificant echo from a world that is organized in an entirely different way.
>
> (Benda et al., 1988, p. 277)

It is, of course, important to remember that the "entirely different way" to which he refers is the deadening and repressive mode of decaying totalitarianism. But his point has perhaps a broader relevance. In the face of a

political system whose power seems secure and beyond radical transformation, he insists on the necessity of creating independent poleis beneath and
beside it. Such communities do not principally direct themselves toward the
state or the formal political system; the activities they sustain "are their own
goals. In them, the intrinsic tendency of people to create things of value is
realized. By giving meaning to their lives and the lives of those close to
them, people are able to resist the futility that threatens to swallow them
up" (Benda et al., 1988, pp. 228–9).

Ladislav Hejdanek sounded a similar theme:

> Such a [democratic] regeneration is possible only in the form of free
> initiatives undertaken by individuals and small groups who are
> willing to sacrifice something in the interest of higher aims and
> values . . . The beginning of all independence is taking our lives
> seriously, deciding for something that is worth taking responsibility
> for, being prepared to devote our energy, our work, and our lives to
> something of value, or, more appropriately, to someone rather than
> something.
>
> (Benda et al., 1988, pp. 242–3)

The Arendtian resonances – creating value, resisting futility, regenerating
democracy – are striking. The Chartists saw themselves as resisting the
"worldlessness" and deracination characteristic of totalitarianism, and of
modern life more generally.

The Chartists described their community as a "small island in a sea of
apathy," the "visible tips of the iceberg" of discontent (Benda et al.,
1988, p. 232). For the Chartists, the insularity of the parallel poleis was
one of their prime virtues. Such insularity afforded protection from a
repressive state, but also established protective walls around activities
otherwise threatened with being "swallowed up" by the conformity and
consumerism of modern industrial society.[32] As Havel wrote: "It seems
to me that all of us, East and West, face one fundamental task from
which all else should follow. That task is one of resisting vigilantly, thought-
fully, and attentively, but at the same time with total dedication, at every
step and everywhere, the irrational momentum of anonymous, impersonal
and inhuman power – the power of ideologies, systems, apparat, bureaucracy, artificial languages, and political slogans" (Havel, 1987a, p. 153).

The islands of civic engagement and solidarity improvised by the Czech
democrats represented for them the most effective way to practice such a
resistance. The courage and conviction exhibited by the citizens of such
islands distinguished them from the mass surrounding them, threatening
to engulf them. The proximity of membership, and of objective, bound
them together in ways that mass organizations could never hope to accom-
plish. These citizens could see and hear their fellows. They could directly

experience the results of their action. They could personally be affirmed by their citizenship. Who were these citizens? Artists, writers, historians – persecuted, underemployed, insecure to be sure – but also shopkeepers, housewives, students, even factory laborers. They came from all walks of life, and what distinguished them was their commitment to principle, not their origins or their social status.[33]

Charter 77 and its adjuncts were not elites in the conventional sense. They were elites only in the sense of people bound together by a common refusal to be swallowed up by the conformity that surrounded them. Their members "lived in truth" where most lived a lie. Where most lived as subjects, accepting the disempowering structure of society, performing rituals of obedience in spite of their misgivings, the Chartists lived as *citizens* who had the courage of their convictions. Yet the Chartists refused to consider themselves a higher type of person, just as they refused to consider more ordinary, conformist individuals to be inherently corrupt. As Václav Havel noted in his famous essay, "The Power of the Powerless," it is impossible categorically to distinguish between the conforming member of society and the true, independent citizen, for the line separating the two "runs de facto through each person." Everyone is in some respects complicit in the ongoing structures of mass society; and no one is so utterly entrapped within them that he or she is incapable of some kind of independence on some occasion. The boundaries separating the islands and the seas are thus ever-shifting. At the same time, the connections between islands and seas vary. As Havel maintains: "It is probably not true to say that there is a small enclave of 'completely independent' people here in an ocean of 'completely dependent people' with no interaction between them. There is an enclave of 'relatively independent' ones who persistently, gradually, and inconspicuously enrich their 'relatively dependent' surrounding through the spiritually liberating and morally challenging meaning of their own independence" (Benda et al., 1988, p. 237). In this way the parallel poleis are not wholly self-absorbed in spite of their insularity.[34] They point beyond themselves, having a "radiating effect" on their environment, an effect caused by the force of their example, by the embarrassment of those who failed to act, by the indirect moral pressure exerted on the regime. At the same time they discover the appropriate locus of political responsibility – the civic initiative of concrete human beings acting on their own behalf, thinking and speaking for themselves (Havel, 1987b, pp. 103–4).

As should be clear, the independent initiatives of Charter 77, especially the vigorous quasi-public debate about opposition that itself constituted perhaps its most significant kind of initiative, implied *a theory of democratic power*, the most articulate statements of which were Havel's famous essays, "The Power of the Powerless" and "The Politics of Conscience." On this view, totalitarianism was a most extreme, malignant, and grotesque version of the more general tendency of modern society to subject individuals to "the irrational momentum of anonymous, impersonal, and inhuman power – the power of ideologies, systems, apparat, bureaucracy, artificial languages, and political slogans." Modern politics, in other words, including liberal democratic politics, is a politics of civic disempowerment justified by the advantages – sometimes palpable, often illusory – of a mass society. As Havel put it, man is treated as "an obedient member of a consumer herd"; "instead of a free share in economic decision-making, free participation in political life, and free intellectual advancement, all people are actually offered is a chance freely to choose which washing machine or refrigerator they want to buy" (Havel, 1992a, p. 60). The Chartists, agreeing with radical democrats like John Dewey and Hannah Arendt, considered this a Faustian bargain that doomed modern individuals to a life of passivity, conformity, and political irresponsibility. The acquiescence to totalitarianism was only the extreme form of such irresponsibility, but it was hardly the only form. For problems of human rights, ecological disaster, economic insecurity, and the threat of war all point toward the need for the kind of civic initiative that cuts against the grain of a modern industrial society.

It was this broader sense of civic responsibility that animated the Czechoslovakian democratic opposition, and, it would not be hard to demonstrate, it also played an important role in animating the other Central European democratic oppositions. This sense of responsibility led these oppositions to resist totalitarian power and to advocate liberal democratic institutions. But it also led them to consider such institutions insufficient insofar as "every system, even the best, conceals within itself a tendency to elevate itself above the people" (Document No. 2/1985, "Commission . . . ," 1988, p. 150). Because liberal democracy is itself a system, it is itself liable to this corruption. Yet in spite of their critique of liberal democratic party politics and its own "technologies of power," the Chartists recognized the value of liberal constitutionalism at the same time that they recognized its limits in an age of consumerism and bureaucratic power. Both of these points were brought home in Charter 77's open letter to the British peace movement:

> Your "sideways" stand, as it were, in relation to the classical democratic structures and political mechanisms is very close to the sense and forms of our own efforts. (Here, again, we must stress, however, our deep conviction that these structures constitute a vital basis which has been denied or falsified always at the cost of greater evil; but at the same time we are aware that the decline of those structures has done much to create the present global

crisis, and that without radical new impulses and regenerating transformations no way out of the crisis can be found).

(Document No. 9/1984, "Open Letter . . . ," 1984, p. 17)

Liberal democratic institutions, in other words, are "a vital basis" of human freedom. But they need to be supplemented, and reinvigorated, by "radical new impulses," civic initiatives that challenge the way these institutions typically function and the corruption to which they are perpetually liable.

Civic initiative and liberal democracy

As I have already alluded, in many ways this vision of civic initiative that resists intolerable power seems liberal. It affirms the importance of setting limits to this exercise of collective authority. It values liberal democratic political institutions. Its emphasis on the importance of protest and dissent is surely consistent with liberal political theory and the practices of liberal constitutionalism.[35] In all of these respects, the politics of Central European democratic opposition falls squarely within liberal parameters. On an even deeper level, the injunction to "live in truth" seems perfectly consistent with the Rawlsian view that there are a multitude of ways to live "the good life," and that the great evil in politics is to make one of them mandatory (Rawls, 1993). For the Central European antipolitics of civil society was explicitly voluntary and self-consciously insular. While open to all who might be interested, it never intended to incorporate masses of people into a hegemonic political project, much less coerce people to live "authentically." In this sense, it saw itself as one way of being among many others and was remarkably respectful of other ways of being, a political orientation wholly consistent with liberal theory and practice.[36]

And yet it would be a mistake to infer from this that it therefore fits neatly into a liberal perspective. Antipolitical politics is clearly not antiliberal. But this does not make it liberal. While there is much common ground with liberalism, there are also important points of tension.

At the political level, there is a profound empirical disagreement not about the importance of liberal democratic institutions, but about the way that they typically function in a modern industrial society. In the liberal democratic view, the principal task of politics is to provide limited, accountable institutions that are responsive to claims of justice. The great virtue of really existing liberal institutions – representative parliaments, competitive parties, independent judiciaries, impartial legal systems, civil service bureaucracies – is that they fulfill this task not, to be sure, perfectly, but better than all possible alternatives. For this reason, the imperative of liberal democratic politics is to strengthen these institutions and, through "institutional design," to make them work better, more fairly and responsively.

Antipolitical politics questions whether existing liberal institutions do fulfill this task. What emerges clearly from the Chartist literature, and from the literature of Central European dissent more generally, is the belief that the impersonality and consumerism of modern society, the bureaucratization of political agencies, and the debasement of political communication through the cynical manipulation of language and images produce a shallow politics, a disengaged citizenry, and the domination of well-organized, entrenched corporate interests.

In this sense, there is a striking parallel to the writings of pragmatist critics of American democracy like John Dewey and C. Wright Mills. Like these writers, the Chartists seem to believe that in an age of mass consumerism and bureaucratic administration the utopian energies of liberalism have been depleted. In 1956 C. Wright Mills wrote that:

> Perhaps nothing is of more importance . . . than the rhetorical victory and the intellectual and political collapse of American liberalism . . . liberalism has been organizationally impoverished . . . liberalism-in-power devitalized independent liberal groups, drying up the grass roots, making older leaders dependent upon the federal center and not training new leaders. . . . It is much safer to celebrate civil liberties than to defend them; it is much safer to defend them as a formal right than to use them in a politically effective way . . . as a rhetoric, liberalism's key terms have become the common denominators of the political vocabulary; in this rhetorical victory . . . liberalism has been stretched beyond any usefulness as a way of defining issues and stating policies.
>
> (Mills, 1956, pp. 333–35)[37]

Mills's point was not that there is anything wrong with liberal values of individual autonomy or liberal practices of constitutional government. It is that the actual institutions of liberal societies pay lip service to but do not effectively support such values and practices.

A very similar sentiment is developed by the Chartists when they note that while liberal democratic structures are vitally important and cannot be dismissed, "we are aware that the decline of those structures has done much to create the present global crisis, and that without radical new impulses and regenerating transformations no way out of the crisis can be found" (Document No. 9/1984, "Open Letter . . . ," 1984, p. 17). Because the liberal democratic structures have "declined," it is necessary to foster new impulses and undertake civic initiatives simply in order to realize liberal values. Because the Central European democrats operated with a highly critical understanding of the actual functioning of liberal democratic politics, they saw such civic initiatives as being significant not only as a way of opposing communism, but as a way of sustaining individual freedom and empowerment in a modern mass society.

The kind of civic initiatives that they practiced – petitions, protests, vigorous critical debate, civil disobedience – are not illiberal. But they are in deep tension with the "normal" institutions of liberal politics.[38] They are, as Holmes says, extraparliamentary. They impose ethical demands upon politicians contrary to the organized "adversarial mendacity" of which Garton Ash speaks. They involve a different style of politics, one more rebellious and more participatory than the normal forms of liberal democratic politics. They do not present themselves as wholesale alternatives to liberal democracy. For the Chartists, it is both inconceivable and undesirable that everybody could "live in truth" together in a modern, industrial society. Most people are preoccupied with other things, and the institutions of liberal democracy, imperfect as they are, typically suit them just fine. But these institutions are chronically liable to corruption, and the advantages they confer – security, economic opportunity – are, therefore, precarious. A more rebellious politics is, therefore, necessary to reinvigorate them and keep them honest.

Just as these political practices are in tension with normal liberal politics, so too are their guiding ideals in tension with certain liberal values. Liberal political philosophy is often distinguished by what Rawls has aptly called a "thin theory of the good" (Rawls, 1971). In this view, liberal justice is the codification of certain basic rights and liberties which allow individuals to pursue their own versions of the good life. Liberal politics is the legitimate avenue for protecting basic rights and liberties, for making sure that the exercise of political power is responsive to public opinion yet does not infringe upon individual liberties. This view of "the priority of right" over public goods has concisely been stated by Benjamin Constant: "Our freedom must consist of peaceful enjoyment and private independence. The share which in antiquity everyone held in national sovereignty was by no means an abstract presumption as it is in our own day . . . Lost in the multitude, the individual can almost never perceive the influence he exercises. Never does his will impress itself upon the whole; nothing confirms in his eyes his own cooperation" (Constant, 1988, p. 316). Constant does not deny that politics is important. Liberal representative government is a device intended to regulate common affairs so that individuals can pursue their private goods. It is thus essential for individuals to monitor their government and hold it accountable through the political process. But for Constant politics is in the service of a civil society that is itself properly beyond politics. Like Rawls, he sees the creation of any public goods beyond a certain "thin" minimum as threatening to the civil liberty that modern liberal individuals prize.[39]

Writers like Havel and Konrád share the liberal belief that the effort to constitute a single, homogeneous "general will" is tyrannical. They support the idea that any free society must provide spaces for autonomous individual initiative. But they question the faith that liberals place in representative institutions, and implicitly they challenge the view of civil society as properly beyond politics.[40] Recall Ivan Jirous's remark that civic initiatives allow people "to resist the futility that threatens to swallow them up." For antipolitical politics, the impersonality, bureaucratization, and domination characteristic of modern society threaten to swallow people up in manifold ways. On this view, Constant's description of liberal man – that "nothing confirms in his eyes his own cooperation" – is an all too accurate description of the political disempowerment and alienation characteristic of modern industrial society. If such experiences are not to produce frustration and resentment, they need to be channeled in healthy ways and resisted by civic initiative. Wherever injustice is experienced, then, it needs to be challenged. And while the state is a principal source of much injustice in our world, it is not the only source.[41]

Freedom, then, requires a conscientious engagement in public affairs. While such engagement is not contrary to liberal individualism, it relies upon a stronger sense of solidarity than that typically supported by liberal political theory or liberal political institutions. While liberal ideals tend to emphasize the importance of protecting individuals from extra-individual – typically political – forces, antipolitical politics involves a more Arendtian view of individuals as inhabiting a common world that in complex ways imposes on them certain ethical responsibilities. To ignore these responsibilities is to lack care for the world; it is also to be untrue to yourself, to exchange your dignity for certain advantages, to submit yourself to some kind of *diktat* in the name of convenience or sociability. Such submission is dangerous, short-sighted, wrong – it is hard to find exactly the right moral term here – though it does not follow from this that it could or should be proscribed. Civic responsibility is, thus, not a strictly political imperative; it would be both impossible and undesirable to mandate it. Indeed, the effort to mandate it is inconsistent with it, for civic initiative is essentially voluntary. But it is more than a moral imperative in a Rawlsian sense, a matter of simple and wholly capricious individual choice. It is an ethical imperative, a strong obligation to act in the name of a dignity that is jeopardized by the tendencies of modern social life.[42] It occupies a middle ground between individual liberty and state power, and its proper sphere of expression and assertion is civil society.[43]

It is understandable why people like Kis, Konrád, and Michnik would gravitate toward liberalism, both because its rights-based philosophy offers a powerful antidote to the kind of collectivism long enforced by Communism, and because it is the only feasible macropolitical alternative to right-wing populism. The practice of antipolitical politics under the conditions of postcommunism has great risks, for it is an unsettling politics, and the conditions of postcommunism seem to demand settlement and order;

145

and it is an ethically exacting politics at a time when most people seem to want normality. If Holmes is correct, and the building of stable parliamentary institutions is the order of the day, it would seem a strategic imperative to abjure antipolitical politics, and to take the liberal side. But two important caveats are in order.

First, it is important to see that such a move would involve a taking of sides, a marked *shift* from a politics of civic initiative and suspicion of institutionalized power to a politics of political "normalization." In this sense, we must reject the Whiggish reading of liberal democratization as a fulfillment of the democratic opposition. Second, having learned, with Popper, of the dangers of acting according to a confidence that our tasks are prescribed by History, we should proceed with caution before the suggestion that a single choice is "the order of the day." Indeed, many of the democratic oppositionists sympathetic toward liberalism, like Havel and Konrád, *have* proceeded with such caution. They have managed to navigate a difficult path in which support for liberal democracy is combined with more radical civic initiatives. This path deserves more attention. In the spirit of Popperian skepticism, then, we must see that the antipolitics of the Central European democratic oppositions is not *passé*, that it is of continuing relevance, both to the "emerging democracies" of Central Europe and to democratic politics in advanced industrial societies more generally.

The legacies of antipolitical politics

Stephen Holmes is right; the institutionalization of parliamentary democracy is a pressing task. But we need to see that he is only partly right. For it does not follow from this that all energies must be channeled in this direction, nor that those energies that are channeled elsewhere constitute extraparliamentary threats to a democratic transition. While in the postcommunist era antipolitical politics cannot claim to be the sole vehicle of democratic politics, this does not mean that it must now be liquidated in the name of democracy.[44] Indeed, I would suggest, in many ways antipolitical politics can be seen to occupy the same space that it occupied under communism – that of a marginalized minority of democrats undertaking civic initiatives in the hope, perhaps faith that "a purely moral act that has no hope of any immediate and visible effect can gradually and indirectly, over time, gain in political significance" (Havel, 1990, p. 115). There are at least three ways in which such a politics remains of continuing relevance to Central European politics. A brief consideration of these ways will also lead us to a broader assessment of the relevance of antipolitics to democratic politics in general.

The first is organizational. Put simply, antipolitical civic initiatives continue to operate in the postcommunist era. Charter 77, for example, has not dissolved, in spite of the fact that many of its founders and leaders have now become active in partisan politics. While in many ways it has been deprived of its principal *raison d'être* – opposition to the Communist party-state – it continues to act on behalf of human rights and in support of democratic civil liberties.[45] It also continues to have a "radiating effect" on democratic efforts in other parts of Central Europe.

In late 1991, for example, many members of the Hungarian democratic opposition constituted Charter '91, a "civic initiative" in many ways like the Czech Charter 77. Reacting to the perception that the Hungarian government – led by the conservative party called Hungarian Democratic Forum – was endangering constitutional liberties, the Charter presented seventeen points on behalf of liberal democracy. Within two months over 5,000 people had signed. George Konrád, one of the co-founders, described Charter '91 as

> a made in Hungary civic initiative . . . Civil society continually searches for and experiments with appropriate forms for expressing itself. It does not want to replace representative democracy, only to place the political class, and, more narrowly, the governing administration, in the environment of a democratic society. . . . It is important that politics, or the polis, namely the discussion of all of our affairs, should not become some far-off chattering on high.

Konrád emphasizes that the Charter is not a new discovery but "a further development of the tool-box of the democratic movement, in the genre of self-organization of civil opinion, the genre, above all, for individuals" (Konrád, 1992, pp. 36–7).[46]

The Charter is an explicitly pro-liberal democratic initiative. But it is also explicitly extraparliamentary and "antipolitical," seeking to raise the level of public debate about the political system and to nourish a more participatory political culture. It sees a liberal democratic political class as being necessary *and* dangerous, in need of support *and* intense, skeptical civic monitoring and criticism. As one commentator points out, the Charter emerges out of the disaffection of many former members of the democratic opposition with "the new power-oriented and bureaucratized politics." The Charter

> shows that this intelligentsia is partly returning to its pre-1989 role: as the "mediacracy" in the forming of cultured public opinion . . . Because its voice will no longer be as influential as it was; it will be lost in the din of battle between different social interests. The former Democratic Opposition's task will be to articulate the opinions of different politicizing groups, and once again to expand and explore the space between state and society. In this

respect, the Democratic Charter has given the old opposition a chance to find a new role for itself.

(Bozoki, 1992, pp. 13–17)

Another initiative drawing on the experience of antipolitical politics is the Helsinki Citizens' Assembly, an outgrowth of the international links formed between Central European dissidents and West European peace activists. Inspired by Charter 77's famous 1985 "Prague Appeal," the Assembly was established in 1990 in order to nurture an "international civil society," a network of citizens' organizations and initiatives that transcends the borders of the nation-state. As Mary Kaldor, one of the Assembly's founders, has described its politics: "It is not addressed to governments except in so far as they are asked to guarantee freedom of travel and freedom of assembly so that citizens' groups can meet and communicate. It is a strategy of dialogue, an attempt to change society through the actions of citizens rather than governments . . . in short, to create a new political culture. In such a situation, the behaviour of governments either changes or becomes less and less relevant" (Kaldor, 1989, p. 15). As the Assembly's 1990 Prague Appeal states: "overcoming the division of Europe is the job above all of civil society, of citizens acting together in self-organized associations, movements, institutions, initiatives and clubs across national boundaries" ("Helsinki Citizens' . . . ," 1991, p. 72).

The Assembly is organized into six ongoing working commissions on problems of democratization. It monitors human rights and discrimination against minorities and women, publishes a regular newsletter and special reports, and provides networking and support for civic initiatives throughout Central Europe. It sees itself not as an antagonist or rival of, but as a *democratic adjunct to* the formal process of liberal democratization, offering outlets for a more vigorous and direct participation in grass-roots politics and the formation of public opinion. As Kaldor notes:

> So what kind of organization are we? . . . We are not a representative of civil society; we are a part of civil society. If we were representative of civil society we would be no different from a parliament. . . . In fact, we don't represent anyone except the movements and institutions in which we are involved. In many cases, we represent no one but ourselves. And our power rests not on whom we represent but in what we do – in what we say, in our ideas, in our quest for truth, in the projects we undertake. It rests on our energy and commitment.
>
> (Kaldor, 1991, p. 215)

As Bozoki points out, such initiatives will necessarily be marginalized in the postcommunist period, by the structural logics of liberalization and marketization, and by the general banality brought on by the ascendancy of consumerism.[47] But they were marginalized under the Old Regime as well. A cynic could claim that when Kaldor states that the Assembly's power rests on civic initiative, she is really saying that it has no power at all, for the power of civic initiative surely pales in comparison with the power of more organized, well-connected political forces. Indeed, whether the issue is European integration, the rights of minorities, or peace in Yugoslavia, it is clear that the Assembly's efforts have borne little fruit. And yet their failure to make a clear and immediate impact on policy does not make them without moral and even political significance.[48] If the experience of democratic opposition under Communism has taught anything, it is that such efforts can have a surprising, and incalculable, impact below the surface of appearances, helping to incubate certain values so that they might surface with effect under the right circumstances.

This leads us to the second sense in which antipolitical politics remains relevant, the more directly *political* sense. While any such assessments are necessarily impressionistic and incomplete, it is possible to make some judgments on this score, and the Czech case is instructive. There is first the example of Havel himself, who in a matter of months went from being an imprisoned dissident writer to President of a newly liberated republic. What is most remarkable about Havel is that he seems to represent a new type of politician, someone capable of personal reflection and public articulation of the difficulties of practicing democratic politics and the need for more responsible forms of citizenship. Havel has issued a steady stream of public addresses on the challenges of the new situation. In his Address to the Opening Session of the Helsinki Citizens' Assembly he reflected on the readjustments made necessary by the transition from dissidence to leadership. He observed:

> It turns out that no matter how difficult it is to bring down a totalitarian system, it is even more difficult to build a newer and better system from its ruins. Since we entered the world of high politics, we have realized that in this world one has to take account of various interests, of various ambitions, of the balance of power represented by different groupings. . . . Thus a person in the world of high politics is forced to behave diplomatically, to maneuver. Simply, we now find ourselves in a different area . . . and have a totally different kind of responsibility from when we were in opposition.

This sounds like a concession to Garton Ash; "living in truth," it would seem, is now *passé*. And yet Havel continues that the requirements of "high politics" cannot alter "the essence of our efforts and ideals, even

though the forms and the ways in which these ideals are being implemented have been modified" (Havel, 1991, p. 74).

The refusal to allow the new circumstances to change his essential ideals
and efforts explains, of course, why this head of state, alone among European heads of state, considered it worthwhile to address the Assembly.
Havel's book, *Summer Meditations* (Havel, 1992b), presents a telling and
personal account of his efforts to advance and incarnate the ideals of
"living in truth" in a way that remains consistent with the requirements
of public office. What is the significance of this? Is Havel simply a unique
individual whose leadership style has no general importance? What good
has this leadership style gotten him anyway? It certainly failed to prevent
the breakup of Czechoslovakia; nor has it been able to stem the tide of
political recrimination. These are legitimate questions. But, in the case of
Czechoslovakia, it is worth considering how much more difficult things
might well have turned out had Havel not been the kind of President
that he is.

Yet the political relevance of antipolitics extends beyond the question of
Havel's rhetoric or leadership style. For Havel recently has engaged in a
highly charged and politically significant public debate with Czech Prime
Minister Václav Klaus over the meaning of civil society. Klaus, following
Hayek, has maintained that civil society is the sphere of individual trans-
actions. Havel, conversely has insisted that civil society "gives people
social space to assume their share of responsibility for social developments,
cultivates the feeling of solidarity between people and love of one's community, and makes it possible to live a full, varied life." At stake in this
philosophical debate are a number of very important political issues.

One is the pace and character of economic reform. Klaus sees the rapid
expansion of the market as the essence of freedom; Havel sees the
market as a necessary institution but one that also threatens many important forms of association and thus needs to be regulated, and embedded, in
certain ways.[49] The second is regional administrative reform. While Klaus
sees decentralization as a way of weakening the political agencies of economic shock therapy, Havel sees it as a way of providing important avenues
of democratic citizenship. Perhaps the most interesting debate concerns the
adoption of a law on nonprofit organizations. Havel has made clear that he
sees such organizations as crucial elements of civil society and has strongly
supported a law clearly laying out the rules for nonprofit organizations and
exempting them from the payment of taxes. As Radio Free Europe reported,
in his 1994 New Year's Day speech, "Havel made it clear that he considered
the decentralization of state administration and the adoption of a law on
nonprofit organizations to be the two most important steps the Czech
Republic should take in creating the social and legal conditions for civil
society."[50] Havel's position in these debates suggests that antipolitical
politics can inform important public-policy questions, placing an emphasis

on the ways in which legal and political arrangements can provide support for the development of voluntary associations and civic initiatives. While civic initiatives are always voluntary and never the creation of the state, a democratic state may be able to nourish such initiatives. Between the "democratic tool-box" of grass-roots activity and the "institutional design" of political elites, then, there may be room for some creative political learning.[51]

Antipolitical politics, then, continues to exist organizationally and to have some impact on Central European political culture and public policy. But perhaps its greatest relevance is hermeneutic or interpretative. Even if antipolitical politics currently had no palpable existence and no evident influence whatsoever, it would still remain relevant as a crucial historical moment of the recent past. In his *The Book of Laughter and Forgetting*, Milan Kundera presents a striking scene:

> In February 1948, Communist leader Klement Gottwald stepped out on the balcony of a Baroque palace in Prague to address the hundreds of thousands of his fellow citizens. . . . Gottwald was flanked by his comrades, with Clementis standing next to him. There were snow flurries, it was cold, and Gottwald was bare-headed. The solicitous Clementis took off his own fur cap and set it on Gottwald's head. The party propaganda section put out hundreds of thousands of copies of a photograph of that balcony with Gottwald, a fur cap on his head and comrades at his side, speaking to the nation. . . . Four years later Clementis was charged with treason and hanged. The propaganda section immediately airbrushed him out of history, and, obviously, out of all the photographs as well. Ever since, Gottwald has stood on that balcony alone. Where Clementis once stood, there is only bare palace wall. All that remains of Clementis is the cap on Gottwald's head.
> (Kundera, 1981, p. 3)

Kundera's target was the Communist obliteration of history, a common target of dissident writers. He points out the absurdity of the attempt to air-brush history, and indicates that the effort can never wholly be successful, for traces of the past remain. Kundera's point has a broader relevance. "The struggle of man against power," he insists, "is the struggle of memory against forgetting" (Kundera, 1981, p. 3).[52] Hannah Arendt offers a similar point: "What saves the affairs of mortal men from their inherent futility is nothing but this incessant talk about them, which in turn remains futile unless certain concepts, certain guideposts for future remembrance, and even for sheer reference, arise out of it" (Arendt, 1977, p. 220). The political initiatives of the Central European democratic opposition present a testimony to what conscientious and responsible citizens can do in order to defend their dignity and empower themselves under difficult circumstances. Such efforts may not be part of the normal repertoire of liberal democratic politics. They may represent fleeting moments of democratic action, destined to fade away or be incorporated by more bureaucratic organizations and institutions.[53] But this is all the more reason to remember them. For the traces of such initiatives remain in the freedoms now recognized by the law, in the current initiatives that continue to be inspired by them, and in the fertile embryos of initiatives yet to be undertaken.

Timothy Garton Ash is onto this when he asks whether or not the onset of consumerism will sweep the "treasures" of the opposition period away in the rush of affluence. He answers that in such an eventuality, "something would remain, at least in memory, in culture, in spirit. At the very least the Europeans from over there would have offered us, with a clarity and firmness born of bitter experience, a restatement of the value of what we already have, of old truths and tested models . . . of liberal democracy" (Garton Ash, 1990a, p. 156). Garton Ash is right that the democratic initiatives leading to 1989 furnish a valuable symbolic legacy. But I find his view of them too reassuring. Surely they may remind us that liberal democracy itself is worth struggling for, and that liberal democracy is indeed the outcome of hard fought struggle. As Frederick Douglass long ago noted with reference to the American Revolution:

> To say now that America was right, and England wrong, is exceedingly easy. Everybody can say it, the dastard, not less than the noble brave, can flippantly discant on the tyranny of England. . .
>
> It is fashionable to do so; but there was a time when . . . [it] tried men's souls. They who did so were accounted in their day plotters of mischief, agitators and rebels, dangerous men. To side with the right against the wrong, with the weak against the strong, and with the oppressed against the oppressor! Here lies the merit, and the one which, of all others, seems unfashionable in our day.
>
> (Douglass, 1950)

But for Douglass, the point of remembering the Revolution was not to assure Americans about the value of what they already had; it was to *disturb* their pervasive sense of assurance, to unsettle them, and to defend new, abolitionist initiatives that went beyond the constitutional politics of the day. Historical recollection of the antipolitics of democratic opposition, and the glorious revolutions of 1989 that it helped to bring about, can serve a similar function. It can also remind us of a kind of courage and conviction, and a kind of creative political agency, that cuts against the grain of liberal democratic normality.

Here we return to the question with which we began. Does 1989 simply represent the triumph of old, liberal values or of something new. It should now be clear that neither alternative as baldly stated is plausible. Liberal democracy has triumphed but haltingly and with uncertain results. Anti-political politics does resonate with liberalism, and yet it is not unambiguously liberal. It is new, but it is not wholly new. The kinds of civic initiatives pioneered by the democratic oppositions did not spring up *de novo*. They had antecedents and exemplars and surely were inspired by previous revolts against Communism and by nonviolent political struggles in the twentieth century more generally. Garton Ash refers to them as a "treasure." Perhaps unwittingly, this language recalls Hannah Arendt's discussion of "the revolutionary tradition and its lost treasure" (Arendt, 1977). There were surely novelties in the "democratic tool-box" of the Central European dissidents – the concept of a "self-limiting revolution," the successful practice of nonviolence against a post-totalitarian dictatorship, perhaps even the very idea of a "civic initiative." But on a deeper level antipolitical politics can be seen as simply one of a number of instances in modern history where ordinary citizens have improvised new forms of democratic agency and new forms of opposition to oppressive power.[54] It was not "new"; but neither was it assimilable to the repertoire of normal liberal democratic politics.

Such a treasure is now in danger of being buried. But it has not yet receded from politics, nor has it receded from memory. It will continue to play some role in Central Europe, a marginal one to be sure, but perhaps a significant role in sustaining a democratic political culture and in offering outlets for healthy political participation. Yet its significance is not limited to the postcommunist world. Indeed, it has a profound relevance for the "Western" world, the world of advanced capitalism and liberal democracy. For if I am correct, while antipolitical politics can remind us of the value of what we have, it can also remind us of the *limits* of what we have.[55]

In the East, the tasks of liberal construction impose constraints on antipolitics. Political resources and energies are scarce, and while the "contest" between liberal democratic transition and civic initiative does not constitute a zero-sum game, there are surely many times when it must seem as though it does.[56] And however much political theorists may endorse a healthy sense of the tragic ambiguities in politics, there are times in politics when important stakes are on the line and one must act. If liberal democrats in parliament are under attack from authoritarian populists, there are times when it may be necessary for a democrat to hold one's tongue and allow liberal parliamentary mendacities to pass. At a time when anarchy threatens, it may be necessary to avoid civil disobedience even though it seems wholly justifiable in principle. In Central Europe, antipolitical politics still has a role to play, but there are times when it will take a back seat to more conventional liberal democratic politics. It is wrong to overestimate

153

the "threat" that civic initiatives might pose to constitutional order. Indeed, as Charter '91 exemplifies, there are times when civic initiative provides indispensable support for such order. But there are other times when the claims of "normalization" will win out.

But if postcommunist societies experience a deficit of liberalism, liberal democratic societies might well experience a *surfeit* of liberalism. It is becoming increasingly obvious that liberal democracy in the West is suffering from a kind of legitimacy crisis, a growing and widespread concern that its institutions are no longer adequate, that they fail to live up to their own professed ideals, to support coherent public policy, a meaningful way of life, or a sense of popular empowerment. There are many symptoms of this crisis – a pervasive feeling of frustration with politicians, political parties, "special interests," and the mass media; the rise of "new social movements" that operate outside of established channels and politicize new realms of social life, whether they be gender, sexuality, race, or ecology; the conservative and often xenophobic backlash against these movements that has acquired a powerful rhetorical force.[57] If democracy involves some kind of identification between citizens and the laws that govern them, what is most striking about the current moment is the pervasive sense of alterity and alienation experienced by ordinary citizens of liberal democracies. Just as Constant described, most citizens feel "lost in the multitude"; nothing confirms in their own eyes their "own cooperation." As Constant saw, the "danger" of liberal democracy is that people will become so absorbed in private life that sources of power will evolve beyond their control. Lacking a sense of empowerment, and lacking a vision of healthy civic initiative, such a citizenry is fertile ground for anxiety, resentment, and authoritarianism.[58] It is this virtually total eclipse of democratic public life in Western liberal democracy that makes the experience of antipolitical politics supremely relevant, both as a source of inspiration and as a source of concrete examples.[59] While the Central Europeans have much to learn from "us" about the workings of liberal democracy, we have much to learn from them about the practice of democratic citizenship.

What, then, are the meanings of 1989? One is that liberal democracy is the most attractive way to organize politics at the level of the nation-state, and that the transition to liberal democracy in Central Europe, and in other parts of the world, is an ethico-political imperative. Another is that civic initiatives continue to possess a remarkable power to resist "the irrational momentum of anonymous, impersonal, inhuman power" (Havel), and that it is imperative for civic initiatives to resist the corruption endemic to liberal democracy. How to reconcile these conclusions? Need they be reconciled? Perhaps the strategic requirements of political maneuvering or constitutional design require that a choice sometimes be made. But perhaps we should heed the words of Albert Camus: "In the difficult times we face, what more can I hope for than the power to exclude nothing and to learn to weave from strands of black and white one rope taughtened to the breaking point?" (1968, p. 169). If 1989 has a single meaning, it is that any kind of monism, even liberal monism, is hostile to freedom, and the effort to exclude certain perspectives in the name of expediency of History is doomed to failure.

Notes

Source Reprinted by permission of the publisher from *Social Research* (an international quarterly of the social sciences) 63:2 (Summer 1996): 291–344.

Acknowledgment This paper was originally presented at the Political Theory Colloquium at the Department of Politics, Princeton University, and the Colloquium on Democratization, the Department of Political Science, Indiana University. I would like to thank Dana Chabot, Jacek Dalecki, Judy Failer, Matt Filner, Norm Furniss, Amy Guttman, Daryl Hammer, Ilya Harik, Jeff Hart, Greg Kasza, George Kateb, Elisabeth Kiss, David Korfhage, Stephen Macedo, Lawrence Mead, Dina Spechler, Ian Shapiro, Yael Tamir, Nadia Urbanati, Michael Walzer, and John Williams for their helpful questions and comments.

1 See Palmer, 1959, and Miller, 1989.

2 See Stokes, 1993.

3 See also Fukuyama, 1992, especially pp. 39–51.

4 See Huntington, 1991. See also di Palma, 1990, and the essays collected in Diamond and Plattner, eds., *The Global Resurgence of Democracy*.

5 See Note 6.

6 See Maier, 1994a.

7 "A new breeze is blowing and a world refreshed by freedom seems reborn," declared President George Bush in his Inaugural Address, "for in man's heart, if not in fact, the day of the dictator is over" (*Vital Speeches* . . . , 1989, p. 258). "The quest for democracy is the most vibrant fact of these times," proclaimed Secretary of State James Baker. See "The Battle for Democracy," *U.S. News and World Report* (May 22, 1989), p. 38.

8 See also Garton Ash, 1990b.

9 Similar expressions of concern can be found in the special issue of *East European Politics and Society*, 5:1 (Winter 1991), on 'Rediscovery of Liberalism in Eastern Europe," especially George Schopflin, "Obstacles to Liberalism in Post-Communist Politics;" Bunce and Csanadi, 1993; Ost, 1993; Bermeo, 1994. See also Roberts, 1990.

10 A very similar prognosis is offered by Mihaly Vajda (1990, pp. 51–3).

11 Michnik also mirrors Dahrendorf's assertion that the crucial issue now is simply between those who prefer "what Popper calls 'the open society,' and those who prefer a closed society" (Paradowska, 1991, p. 101).

12 This claim is different from the view of Fukuyama, for it does not rely upon any historical metaphysic and can be causally explained in historically specific ways.

13 See Bozoki and Sukosd, 1993.

14 See Elster, 1992, and the special section, "Dilemmas of Justice" (1992).

15 See, for example, Ogrodzinski and Szlajifer, 1992, and Michnik, 1990b. See also Gebert, 1991. For deeper explorations of the social psychological roots of exclusivism, see Michnik, 1991b, Siklova, 1991, and Kohak, 1992.

16 Jürgen Habermas has developed a similar distinction in Habermas, 1989, and more recently in Habermas, 1992.
17 See Schmitt, 1988, especially pp. 11–17, 68–76. For criticisms, see Holmes, 1993a, pp. 37–60, and Keane, 1988, pp. 153–90.
18 Timothy Garton Ash has issued a remarkably similar assessment:

> The immediate question, therefore, is: What variant of democratic politics can, on the one hand, provide sufficiently strong, stable, consistent government to sustain the necessary rigors of fiscal, monetary, and economic policy over a period of several years, while, on the other hand, being sufficiently flexible and responsive to absorb the larger part of the inevitable popular discontents through parliamentary or, at least, legal channels, thus preventing the resort to extraparliamentary, illegal, and ultimately anti-democratic means?
>
> (Garton Ash, 1990c, p. 54)

19 For a pessimistic assessment of the prospects for liberal democracy combined with an interesting defense of a third possibility – an *authoritarian* liberalism – see Jowitt, 1992, especially pp. 299–331.
20 The literature on the economic difficulties of liberal democratic transition is immense. See especially Przeworski, 1991; Offe, 1991; Comisso, 1991. On the problem of political demobilization and alienation, see Bozoki and Sukosd, 1993, and Arato, 1994.
21 See Tismaneanu, 1992; Stokes, 1993; and, for the clearest account of the final days of Communism, Garton Ash, 1990a.
22 The great weakness of Stephen Holmes' passionately argued and insightful *The Anatomy of Antiliberalism* is its refusal to take seriously the difference between the antiliberalism of writers like Schmitt and the nonliberalism of writers like Arendt or Lasch. In an ironic way, Holmes reiterates a classic Cold War rhetorical figure – one is either with liberalism or against it. He elaborates on the Hobbesian anxieties that underly such a "liberalism of fear" in Holmes, 1994.
23 The most penetrating philosophical account of this position offered by a contemporary liberal is Shklar, 1984.
24 For important general accounts of antipolitics, see Garton Ash, 1990d, and Goldfarb, 1989.
25 On the formation of Charter 77, see Skilling, 1981. On the many initiatives that sprung up in conjunction with it, see the very informative Skilling 1989, especially pp. 26–32 and 43–156.
26 The Charter originally had 241 signatories, of whom 40 percent were workers; by 1987, 1,300 people had signed. Its influence extended far wider. As Ladislav Hejdanek, one of its principal founders, noted:

> To act and live in the spirit of Charter 77 was quite possible, even without signing. The purpose of the Charter was not to gain as many signatures as possible but to persuade as many people as possible that they could and should act toward the state as free and courageous citizens and that – this was the main thing – they could and ought to act toward their fellow citizens as friends, companions and comrades.
>
> (quoted in Skilling, 1981, pp. 41–3)

27 See, for example, the interview with Marta Kubisova, Václav Havel, Peter Uhl, and other Charter leaders ("Polish KOR . . . ," 1979).

28 The classic exploration of this strategy was Michnik, 1985. Written in 1976 during the formation of KOR, the Polish Workers' Defense Committee (later reorganized as the Social Self-Defense Committee), this essay had a strong impact on democratic oppositionists in Czechoslovakia and Hungary as well.

29 See, for example, Havel, 1987a. See also the influential Konrád, 1984.

30 See Isaac, 1994.

31 Benda's essay and many responses to it were published as a book (Skilling and Wilson, 1991). For a more abbreviated version of the debate, see Benda *et al.*, 1988.

32 As the Hungarian dissident György Bence noted, "what the dissidents wanted to do was to erect their own ramparts and to live, behind them, a communal life worthy of free individuals" (quoted in Stokes, 1993, p. 22).

33 See Havel, 1987b, pp. 78–80, on how "dissident" is a label attached to "ordinary people with ordinary cares, differing from the rest only in that they say aloud what the rest cannot say or are afraid to say."

34 While the insularity of civic initiatives was one of their principal virtues, it also posed problems that were continual sources of debate among Chartists, relating to questions of strategic effectiveness and a dangerous sense of moral superiority. On the first question, see, for example, Anonymous, 1988. On the second, see "Discussion . . . ," 1979.

35 On civil disobedience, see Rawls, 1971, and Zwiebach, 1975. On political nonconformity and contestation more generally, see Kateb, 1992, pp. 1–107, 240–66.

36 Perhaps the most powerful articulations of this respectfulness are Adam Michnik's essays "Why You Are Not Signing . . ." and "Maggots and Angels" in his *Letters from Prison*. There was also a fascinating debate among the Chartists on this theme, provoked by Vaculik, 1979.

37 For Dewey's similar assessment, see Dewey, 1927.

38 See Carter, 1973. See also the discussion of "repertoires" of social movement and activity in Tarrow, 1994.

39 There are, of course, liberal democrats who would go much further than Rawls in allowing the importance of participation in politics and the public sphere more generally. See Dahl, 1989, Guttman, 1993, and Ryan, 1993. These liberal democrats still tend to place more emphasis upon "constitutional design" than upon civic initiative and insurgency. But there are important points of contact between such participatory liberal democrats and Chartist views. For the clearest point of contact, see Walzer, 1984. Just as I have argued that one can only speak of the triumph of liberal democracy in specific senses, so I would argue that one needs to distinguish between different senses of liberalism and different kinds of liberalism and cannot speak about liberalism in general. For a clever suggestion to this effect, see Kolakowski, 1990.

40 On this see Cohen and Arato, 1992, pp. 29–82, 345–420.

41 See Lefort, 1985.

42 The moral credo of antipolitics would go something like this: It is wrong to coerce, inconsistent with the demands of conscience and the requirements of civility; liberalism is the best system of politics insofar as it refuses to license legal coercion. but liberalism is insufficient in a world of injustice and evil. It is morally imperative to resist the sources of disempowerment, including those linked to liberal institutions themselves. But we cannot hope to achieve perfect justice. A self-limiting, modest search for justice is all that can be hoped for. We will practice civic initiatives, and hope that they will have some effect, without condemning those who do not or seeking to force them to do so. We

accept liberal democratic values and institutions. But it is necessary and good that civic initiatives challenge them and contest their injustices.

43 For an interesting discussion of some of the implications of such a view, see Walzer, 1991.

44 As Claude Lefort insists: "Those who exercise public responsibility are under no obligation to swear allegiance to the constitution. It is possible, for example, that a certain individual's disdain for elections, for the majority's decisions, for party demagoguery be combined with desire for independence, freedom of thought and speech, sensitivity for others, self-examination, curiosity for foreign or extinct cultures – all of which bear the mark of the democratic spirit" (1990, p. 1).

45 See Hromadkova, 1992, p. 69. See also Hejdanek, 1990, pp. 96–8, and Trojan, 1990, pp. 100–2.

46 The Charter itself is reproduced on pp. 35–7 of Konrád, 1991. See also pp. 27–8.

47 See Siklova, 1993, and Pithart, 1993.

48 This is not to deny that the new conditions have created problems for the former dissidents, who have had great difficulty adjusting to the complexities of the new environment and the noticeable decline in their stature now that communism has been supplanted. See, for example, Bauman, 1993, pp. 113–30, and Michael, 1991, pp. 141–54. Michnik has himself commented on this quite frankly: "Yes, today politics is becoming normal, and for those who did not treat politics as a game but as a way to defend basic values it is becoming difficult to find a space. It will become even harder in the future. This could have been anticipated, and there is no need for despair" (Paradowska, 1991, p. 96).

49 In this Havel is close to the views of many Western liberal democrats, who reject the dogmatism of Hayekian philosophy. See Dahl, 1990, pp. 224–8, and Dahrendorf, 1990, pp. 90–108.

50 See Pehe, 1994, pp. 12–18.

51 For some interesting reflections on this theme, see Cohen and Rogers, 1992, and the responses by Paul Hirst, Jane Mansbridge, Phillippe Schmitter, Andrew Szasz, and Iris Marion Young. See also Wainwright, 1989, 1994, especially pp. 115–236, and Walzer, 1994, pp. 189–91.

52 Jeffrey Goldfarb presents a penetrating discussion of these texts (1989, pp. 109–18).

53 The view of them as fleeting is most often associated with the writings of Hannah Arendt, especially her *On Revolution* (1977). For the most insightful discussion of this theme in her work, see Miller, 1979. See also Wolin, 1994. For the view of them as being part of a process of "dualistic politics," whereby the normal routines of liberal democracy are periodically reconfigured by radical movements, see Ackerman, 1991, and Cohen and Arato, 1992, especially pp. 492–563.

54 For a similar argument regarding the United States civil rights movement, see the wonderful King, 1992. On a more theoretical level, it could be argued that antipolitical politics represented a radical democratic reappropriation of the nineteenth-century bourgeois public sphere under the transformed conditions of a late-modern industrial society, a view associated with the work of Habermas and developed by Arato and Cohen. Habermas himself suggests such an interpretation in Habermas, 1991.

55 This point is also made in different ways by Lefort, 1990; Reidy, Jr., 1992; and Elshtain, 1993.

56 See Arato, 1993, especially pp. 631–46.
57 See Maier, 1994b; Kitschelt, 1993. With specific regard to the American case, see Greider, 1992; Dionne, 1992; and, most recently, Phillips, 1994.
58 For an interesting discussion, see Brown, 1993.
59 Harry Boyte, for example, writes about grass roots community organizing in a Chartist vein in Boyte, 1989. See also Flacks, 1993.

References

Ackerman, Bruce, *We The People* (Cambridge, MA: Harvard University Press, 1991).

Ackerman, Bruce, *The Future of Liberal Revolution* (New Haven, CT: Yale University Press, 1992).

Anonymous, "Beyond the Dissident Ghetto," *Uncaptive Minds* (June–August 1988): 35–9.

"Appeal to Society," reproduced in Jan Jozef Lipski, *KOR: A History of the Workers Defense Committee in Poland, 1976–1981* (Berkeley, CA: University of California Press, 1985).

Arato, Andrew, "Interpreting 1989," *Social Research*, 60:3 (Fall 1993).

Arato, Andrew, "Constitution and Continuity in the East European Transitions, Part I: Continuity and Its Crisis," *Constellations*, 1:1 (April 1994).

Arendt, Hannah, *On Revolution* (Harmondsworth: Penguin, 1977).

Bauman, Zygmunt, "The Polish Predicament: A Model in Search of Class Interests," *Telos* (1993).

Benda, Václav, et al., "Parallel Polis, or an Independent Society in Central and Eastern Europe: An Inquiry," *Social Research*, 55:1–2 (Spring/Summer 1988).

Bermeo, Nancy, "Democracy in Europe," *Daedalus*, 123:2 (Spring 1994).

Boyte, Harry, *Commonwealth: A Return to Citizen Politics* (New York: Free Press, 1989).

Bozoki, Andras, "The Democratic Charter One Year On," *East European Reporter* (November/December 1992).

Bozoki, Andras and Sukosd, Miklos, "Civil Society and Populism in the Eastern European Democratic Transitions," *Praxis International*, 13:3 (October 1993).

Brown, Wendy, "Wounded Attachments," *Political Theory*, 21:3 (August 1993).

Bunce, Valerie, "The Struggle for Liberal Democracy in Eastern Europe," *World Policy Journal* (1990).

Bunce, Valerie and Csanadi, Maria, "Uncertainty in the Transition: Post-Communism in Hungary," *East European Politics and Society*, 7:2 (Spring 1993).

Camus, Albert, *The Rebel* (New York: Knopf, 1956).

Camus, Albert, "Return to Tipasa," in *Lyrical and Critical Essays* (New York: Knopf, 1968).

Carter, April, *Direct Action and Liberal Democracy* (New York: Harper, 1973).

Cohen, Jean and Arato, Andrew, *Civil Society and Political Theory* (Cambridge, MA: MIT Press, 1992).

Cohen, Joshua and Rogers, Joel, "Secondary Associations and Democratic Governance," *Politics and Society*, 20:4 (December 1992).

Comisso, Ellen, "Property Rights, Liberalism, and the Transition from 'Actually Existing Socialism,'" *East European Politics and Society*, 5:1 (Winter 1991).

"Commission on Security and Cooperation in Europe: United States Congress," *Human Rights in Czechoslovakia: The Documents of Charter 77, 1982–1987* (Washington D.C.: U.S. Government Printing Office, 1988), pp. 139–62.

Constant, Benjamin, "The Liberty of the Ancients Compared with That of the Moderns," in Biancamaria Fontana, ed., *Political Writings* (Cambridge: Cambridge University Press, 1988).

Dahl, Robert A., *Democracy and its Critics* (New Haven, CT: Yale University Press, 1989).

Dahl, Robert A., "Social Reality and 'Free Markets,'" *Dissent* (Spring 1990).

Dahrendorf, Ralf, *Reflections on the Revolution in Europe* (New York: Random House, 1990).

Dewey, John, *The Public and its Problems* (Chicago, IL: Swallow Press, 1927).

Diamond, Larry and Plattner, Marc, eds., *The Global Resurgence of Democracy* (Baltimore, MD: Johns Hopkins University Press, 1992).

"Dilemmas of Justice," *East European Constitutional Review*, 1:2 (Summer 1992).

Dionne, E.J., *Why Americans Hate Politics* (New York: 1992).

"Discussion within the Charter: The Ethics of Opposition," *Labour Focus on Eastern Europe*, 3:2 (May/June 1979): 16–21.

Douglass, Frederick, "Fourth of July Oration," in Phillip S. Foner, ed., *The Life and Writings of Frederick Douglass* (New York: International Publishers, 1950).

Elshtain, Jean, "Politics Without Cliche," *Social Research*, 60:3 (Fall 1993).

Elster, Jon, "On Doing What One Can," *East European Constitutional Review*, 1:2 (Summer 1992).

Flacks, Richard, "The Party's Over," *Social Research*, 60:3 (Fall 1993).

Fukuyama, Francis, "The End of History?" *The National Interest* (Summer 1989).

Fukuyama, Francis, *The End of History and the Last Man* (New York: Free Press, 1992).

Garton Ash, Timothy, *The Magic Lantern* (New York: Random House, 1990a).

Garton Ash, Timothy, "Ten Thoughts on the New Europe," *New York Review of Books* (June 14, 1990b).

Garton Ash, Timothy, "Eastern Europe: *Après le Déluge, Nous,*" *New York Review of Books* (August 16, 1990c).

Garton Ash, Timothy, *The Uses of Adversity: Essays on the Fate of Central Europe* (New York: Vintage, 1990d).

Gebert, Konstanty, "Anti-Semitism in the 1990 Polish Presidential Election," *Social Research* 58:4 (Winter 1991).

Goldfarb, Jeffrey C., *Beyond Glasnost: The Post-Totalitarian Mind* (Chicago, IL: University of Chicago Press, 1989).

Greider, William, *Who Will Tell the People: The Betrayal of American Democracy* (New York: Touchstone, 1992).

Guttman, Amy, "The Disharmony of Democracy," in John W. Chapman and Ian Shapiro, eds., *Democratic Community: NOMOS XXXV* (New York: New York University Press, 1993).

Habermas, Jürgen, "Historical Consciousness and Post-Traditional Identity: The Federal Republic's Orientation Toward the West," *The New Conservatism* (Cambridge, MA: MIT Press, 1989).

Habermas, Jürgen, "What Does Socialism Mean Today? The Revolutions of Recuperation and the Need for New Thinking," in Robin Blackburn, ed., *After the Fall: The Failure of Communism and the Future of Socialism* (London: Verso, 1991).

Habermas, Jürgen, "Citizenship and National Identity: Some Reflections on the Future of Europe," *Praxis International*, 12:1 (April 1992).

Havel, Václav, "Politics and Conscience," in *Living in Truth* (London: Faber and Faber, 1987a).

Havel, Václav, "The Power of the Powerless," in *Living in Truth* (London: Faber and Faber, 1987b).

Havel, Václav, *Disturbing the Peace* (New York: Knopf, 1990).

Havel, Václav, "Address to the Helsinki Citizens' Assembly Opening Session," *East European Reporter*, 4:4 (Spring/Summer 1991).

Havel, Václav, "Dear Dr. Husak," in *Open Letters: Selected Writings, 1965–1990* (New York: Vintage, 1992a).

Havel, Václav, *Summer Meditations* (New York: Knopf, 1992b).

Hejdanek, Ladislav, "Democracy Without Opposition is Nonsense," *East European Reporter* (Autumn/Winter 1990).

"Helsinki Citizens' Assembly," *East European Reporter*, 4:4 (Spring/Summer 1991).

Holmes, Stephen, "The Scowl of Minerva," *The New Republic* (March 23, 1992a).

Holmes, Stephen, "Introducing the Center: A project to promote clear thinking about the design of liberal-democratic institutions," *East European Constitutional Review*, 1:1 (Spring 1992b).

Holmes, Stephen, *The Anatomy of Antiliberalism* (Cambridge, MA: Harvard University Press, 1993a).

Holmes, Stephen, "Back to the Drawing Board: An Argument for Constitutional Postponement in Eastern Europe," *East European Constitutional Review*, 2:1 (Winter 1993b).

Holmes, Stephen, "Liberalism for a World of Ethnic Passions and Decaying States," *Social Research*, 61:3 (Fall 1994).

Hromadkova, Alena, "Whatever Happened to Charter 77?" *East European Reporter* (January/February 1992).

Huntington, Samuel P., "No Exit: The Errors of Endism," *The National Interest* (Fall 1989).

Huntington, Samuel P., *The Third Wave: Democratization in the Late Twentieth Century* (Norman, OK: University of Oklahoma Press, 1991).

Jowitt, Ken, *New World Disorder: The Leninist Extinction* (Berkeley, CA: University of California Press, 1992).

Kaldor, Mary, "Introduction," in Mary Kaldor, Gerald Holden, and Richard Falk, eds., *The New Detente* (London and Tokyo: Verso and United Nations University, 1989).

Kaldor, Mary, "Speech to the Closing Session of the Helsinki Citizens' Assembly," in Mary Kaldor, ed., *Europe From Below: An East–West Dialogue* (London: Verso, 1991).

Kant, Immanuel, *On History*, Lewis White Beck, ed. (Indianapolis, IN: Bobbs-Merrill, 1963).

Kateb, George, *The Inner Ocean: Individualism and Democratic Culture* (Ithaca, NY: Cornell University Press, 1992).

Keane, John, *Democracy and Civil Society* (London: Verso, 1988).

King, Richard, *Civil Rights and the Idea of Freedom* (Oxford: Oxford University Press, 1992).

Kis, Janos, "Turning Point in Hungary: A Voice from the Democratic Opposition," *Dissent* (Spring 1989).

Kiss, Elisabeth, "Democracy Without Parties? 'Civil Society' in East-Central Europe," *Dissent* (Spring 1992).

Kitschelt, Herbert, "Social Movements, Political Parties, and Democratic Theory," *Annals of the American Academy of Political and Social Science*, 528 (July 1993).

Kohak, Erazim, "Ashes, Ashes . . . Central Europe After Forty Years," *Daedalus*, 121:2 (Spring 1992).

Kolakowski, Leszek, "How to be a Conservative–Liberal–Socialist: A Credo," in *Modernity on Endless Trial* (Chicago, IL: University of Chicago Press, 1990).

Konrád, George, *Antipolitics* (New York: Harcourt Brace, 1984).

Konrád, George, "Chance Wanderings: Reflections of a Hungarian Writer," *Dissent* (Spring 1990).

Konrád, George, "A Colorful Scene Ahead," *East European Reporter* (Spring/ Summer 1991).

Konrád, George, "What is the Charter?" *East European Reporter* (January/February 1992).

Kundera, Milan, *The Book of Laughter and Forgetting* (New York: Penguin, 1981).

Lefort, Claude, "Politics and Human Rights," in *The Political Forms of Modern Society* (Cambridge, MA: MIT Press, 1985).

Lefort, Claude, "Renaissance of Democracy?" *Praxis International* 10:1/2 (April and July 1990).

Maier, Charles S., "Democracy and its Discontents," *Foreign Affairs*, 73:4 (July/ August 1994a).

Maier, Charles S., "The Moral Crisis of Democracy," *Foreign Affairs*, 73:4 (July/ August 1994b).

Michael, John, "The Intellectual in Uncivil Society: Michnik, Poland, and Community," *Telos* (Summer 1991).

Michnik, Adam, "The New Evolutionism," in *Letters from Prison* (Berkely, CA: University of California Press, 1985).

Michnik, Adam, "After the Revolution," *The New Republic* (July 2, 1990a).

Michnik, Adam, "The Two Faces of Eastern Europe," *The New Republic* (November 12, 1990b).

Michnik, Adam, "The Presence of Liberal Values," *East European Reporter*, 4:4 (Spring/Summer 1991a).

Michnik, Adam, "Nationalism," *Social Research*, 58:4 (Winter 1991b).

Miller, James, "The Pathos of Novelty: Hannah Arendt's Image of Freedom in the Modern World," in Melvyn A. Hill, ed., *Hannah Arendt: The Recovery of the Public World* (New York: St. Martin's Press, 1979).

Miller, James, "Modern Democracy From France to America," *Salmagundi*, 84 (Fall 1989).

Mills, C. Wright, *The Power Elite* (Oxford: Oxford University Press, 1956).

Offe, Claus, "Capitalism By Democratic Design? Democratic Theory Facing the Triple Transition in East Central Europe," *Social Research*, 58:4 (Winter 1991).

Ogrodzinski, Piotr and Szlajifer, Henryk, "Is the Catholic Church a Threat to Democracy?" *East European Reporter* (May/June 1992): 17–20.

"Open Letter to the British Peace Movements CND and END," *Bulletin No. 25* (London: Palach Press, 1984).

Ost, David, "The Politics of Interest in Post-Communist East Europe," *Theory and Society*, 22 (1993).

di Palma, Giuseppe, *To Craft Democracies: An Essay on Democratic Transitions* (Berkeley, CA: University of California Press, 1990).

Palmer, R.R., *The Age of Democratic Revolution: The Challenge* (Princeton, NJ: Princeton University Press, 1959).

Paradowska, Janina, "The Three Card Game: An Interview with Adam Michnik," *Telos* (Summer 1991).

Pehe, Jiři, "Civil Society at Issue in the Czech Republic," *Radio Free Europe/Radio Liberty Research Report*, 3:32 (August 19, 1994).

Phillips, Kevin, *Arrogant Capital* (New York: Simon and Schuster, 1994).

Pithart, Pitr, "Intellectuals in Politics: Double Dissent in the Past, Double Disappointment Today," *Social Research*, 60:4 (Winter 1993).

Plattner, Marc, "The Democratic Moment," in Larry Diamond and Marc Plattner, eds., *The Global Resurgence of Democracy* (Baltimore, MD: Johns Hopkins University Press, 1992).

"Polish KOR interviews Charter 77 Representatives," in *Labour Focus Eastern Europe*, 2:6 (January/February 1979).

Popper, Karl, *The Open Society and its Enemies, Vol. II* (Princeton, NJ: Princeton University Press, 1971).

Preuss, Ulrich K., "Constitutional Powermaking for the New Polity: Some Deliberations on the Relations Between Constituent Power and the Constitution," *Cardozo Law Review*, 14 (January 1993): 646–51.

Przeworski, Adam, *Democracy and the Market: Political and Economic Reforms in Eastern Europe and Latin America* (Cambridge: Cambridge University Press, 1991).

Rawls, John, *A Theory of Justice* (Belknap: Harvard University Press, 1971).

Rawls, John, *Political Liberalism* (New York: Columbia University Press, 1993).

Reidy, Jr., David A., "Eastern Europe, Civil Society and the Real Revolution," *Praxis International*, 12:2 (July 1992).

Revel, Jean-Francois, *Democracy Against Itself: The Future of the Democratic Impulse* (New York: Free Press, 1991).

Roberts, Brad, *Securing Democratic Transitions* (Washington D.C.: Center for Strategic and International Studies, 1990).

Ryan, Alan, "The Liberal Community," in John W. Chapman and Ian Shapiro, eds., *Democratic Community: NOMOS XXXV* (New York: New York University Press, 1993).

Schmitt, Carl, *The Crisis of Parliamentary Democracy* (Cambridge, MA: MIT Press, 1988).

Shklar, Judith, *Ordinary Vices* (Cambridge, MA: Harvard University Press, 1984).

Siklova, Jirina, "Backlash," *Social Research*, 60:4 (Winter 1993).

Skilling, H. Gordon, *Charter 77 and Human Rights in Czechoslovakia* (London: Allen & Unwin, 1981).

Skilling, H. Gordon, *Samizdat and an Independent Society in Central and Eastern Europe* (Oxford: Macmillan Press, 1989).

Skilling, H. Gordon and Wilson, Paul, eds., *Civic Freedom in Central Europe: Voices from Czechoslovakia* (New York: St. Martin's Press, 1991).

Stokes, Gale, *The Walls Came Tumbling Down: The Collapse of Communism in Eastern Europe* (Oxford: Oxford University Press, 1993).

Szacki, Jerzy, "A Revival of Liberalism in Poland?" *Social Research*, 57:2 (Summer 1990).

Talmon, Jacob, *The Origins of Totalitarian Democracy* (New York: Norton, 1970).

Tarrow, Sidney, *Power in Movement: Social Movements, Collective Action, and Politics* (Cambridge: Cambridge University Press, 1994).

Tismaneanu, Vladimir, *Reinventing Politics: Eastern Europe from Stalin to Havel* (New York: Free Press, 1992).

Trojan, Jacub, "Democracy and its Spiritual Foundations," *East European Reporter* (Autumn/Winter 1990).

Vaculik, Ludvik, "Notes on Courage," reproduced in *Labour Focus on Eastern Europe*, 3:2 (May/June 1979): 16–21.

Vajda, Mihaly, "Past, Present, Future: The Collapse of Socialism," *East European Reporter*, 4:3 (Autumn/Winter 1990).

Vital Speeches of the Day, 55:9 (February 15, 1989).

Wainwright, Hilary, "The State and Society: Reflections from a Western Experience," in Mary Kaldor, Gerald Holden, and Richard Falk, eds., *The New Detente* (London and Tokyo: Verso and United Nations University, 1989).

Wainwright, Hilary, *Arguments for a New Left* (Oxford: Blackwell, 1994).

Walzer, Michael, "Liberalism and the Art of Separation," *Political Theory* (1984).

Walzer, Michael, "The Idea of Civil Society: A Path to Social Reconstruction," *Dissent* (Spring 1991): 193–304.

Walzer, Michael, "Multiculturalism and Individualism," *Dissent* (Spring 1994).

Wolin, Sheldon, "Fugitive Democracy," *Constellations*, 1:1 (April 1994).

Zwiebach, Burton, *Civility and Disobedience* (Cambridge: Cambridge University Press, 1975).

7

NINETEEN EIGHTY-NINE:
THE END OF *WHICH*
EUROPEAN ERA?

Tony Judt

In this essay, historian Tony Judt explores the role of political myth in the shaping of the postcommunist European identity. In many respects the aftermath of the revolutions of 1989 is similar to the situation following World War II: there is a strong need to identify the "guilty" people and exert retributive justice. There is also a rampant temptation to externalize blame and avoid a lucid coming to terms with the past. New myths about national resistance to communism have surfaced to avoid thorough-going analyses of widespread forms of complicity and collaboration with the Leninist regimes. This article highlights the disturbing resurgence of populism, nationalism, and anti-Semitism in the postcommunist societies and the rise of counter-Enlightenment movements. The long-accepted categories of "left" and "right" have lost their original meaning. Altogether, Europe has ushered in an era of ethnic anarchy and political discombobulation.

With this focus on disarray, frustrations, loss of morale, and widespread malaise, Judt belongs to those who are skeptical about the overall liberal implications of the 1989 revolutionary upheaval in East and Central Europe. His contribution offers a necessary counterpart to the more optimistic interpretations of the future of the region. Of particular note is Judt's insistence on the need to distinguish between different shades of anticommunism. Not all those who opposed the imposition of Stalinism were necessarily friends of democracy, and there is the risk that in the post-1989 euphoria such distinctions tend to be blurred. For Judt political, economic, and cultural uncertainties make East and Central Europe a propitious territory for self-congratulatory fantasies of heroic national traditions. These, however, are just the opposite of what liberal values tend to defend and could be conducive to fragmentation, divisiveness, and cynical demagoguery. Politically manipulated memories are thus presented as a daunting threat to the emergence of a democratic postcommunist Europe.

* * *

TONY JUDT

> Every epoch is a sphinx that plunges into the abyss as soon as its riddle has been solved.
>
> Heinrich Heine

Postwar Europe was erected upon a foundation of myths and forgetting. This is not as cynical or as dismissive as it may appear; the myths were often positive and helpful, there was much that needed to be forgotten, and the results, especially in the western half of the continent, were impressive. Nor are such exercises in collective self-construction necessarily foredoomed to futility. The treaties which ended the wars of the Reformation, the Thirty Years War, and the Napoleonic wars all depended upon comparably ambitious attempts to put the past away and all of them succeeded in some measure; their effects are with us still. But for reasons peculiar to the shape of twentieth-century history the post-1945 settlement has proven peculiarly illusory, something which was already clear in Eastern Europe by the early 1980s and which 1989 and subsequent developments have brought home to everyone. The purpose of this essay is to try to understand the era which has now closed in its historical context and to sketch an outline of the terms in which Europe might think of itself as it enters a new and distinctive stage in its history.

After 1945 there was much to forget. Most obviously, and this is a subject which I have addressed elsewhere, there was the experience of occupation and collaboration – or, in the case of those countries like Germany or Italy where fascism came to power by domestic means, the memory of more than a decade of dictatorship.[1] Beyond this lay the unhappy memory of World War I and its inadequate resolution; the resentments and injustices occasioned by the Treaty of Versailles; the economic debacle of the interwar decades, itself a heritage of World War I but exacerbated by autarkic and antagonistic commercial policies; unresolved nineteenth-century dilemmas of social inequity and imperial conquest; and, overshadowing it all, a deep, continent-wide sense of decline and decadence. This last sentiment, although the least tangible of Europe's inherited problems, was also in some sense the most important. It was shared by the generation that would come to power in 1945, and it accounts for their common disgust with the inadequate responses of the democracies to the interwar crisis and for their earlier susceptibility to the appeals of fascism and communism alike. It lay behind the sentiment of many intellectuals that "Auschwitz" stood for more than just a German atrocity: the Holocaust was the culmination and proof of the ultimate decline of European civilization. By May 1945 it was not only Europe's great cities which lay buried in rubble, it was the very spirit of the continent itself.

To put all that behind, to imagine a new, better Europe was a massive undertaking. It could not be done by policy and planning alone. Marshall, Beveridge, the welfare state, multiyear plans, and nationalization were the

166

necessary conditions of European reconstruction but alone they would have been insufficient. What gave them meaning were certain foundation myths, most of which concerned questions of guilt and forgiveness. The success of these myths is illustrated in the fact that the mistakes of 1919 were not repeated, even though in 1945 there was more real guilt around. For reasons at once prudential and strategic, Germany (both Germanys) was quickly incorporated into international communities on relatively non-discriminating terms. Potentially damaging civil wars in France and Italy were nipped in the bud by strong postwar governments at the price of burying old feuds and memories of fascist crimes or venal acts of collaboration.[2] The nationalist sentiments and national suspicions which had shaped European politics since the late nineteenth century were denied expression, consigned to a past whose ugly outcomes were now plain and by common consent unacceptable. The only acceptable collective objectives in Western Europe were now social (in the form of egalitarian redistributive legislation), economic (in the form of productivist goals), and internationalist (in the shape of a variety of possible institutions, both European and global).

In Eastern Europe something similar took place, its similarity masked by the ideological and geopolitical interests in which it was characteristically expressed. The bitter resentments of the small countries of the region – inadequately served at Versailles or Saint-Germain, truncated or abandoned in the course of diplomatic maneuverings thereafter, lacking in most cases a competent political class, economic resources, or the means to exploit them rationally, short on social justice or the means to express discontent, and most recently the chief victims of a war from which they would derive no benefits – were quickly buried beneath an obligatory myth of fraternal internationalism and the assertion (partially true) that a revolutionary transformation had taken place. Here too potential civil wars deriving from wartime or prewar divisions were snuffed out from above, and where retribution was applied it was mostly a cynical business, undertaken more to ensure the firm implantation of communist authority than to root out those responsible for collaboration with the Nazis or for domestic political crimes. In republican Italy, for analogous reasons, administrators, policemen, and others who had served the old regime and its foreign paymasters were often left in place, the reality of the continuity they represented overlain by a myth of renewal and revolution. In Eastern Europe, as in Western Europe, there was indeed real, radical change – geared to redistribution, production, and new international institutions – but here, too, the foundation myths came first and took precedence.

The need for such a radical break with the past – a discursive break no less than a political one – lay in the special circumstances of the moment.[3] In Western Europe the whole process was driven by a French search for security. After 1945 the French were doing what they had sought to achieve

167

after 1918, but this time with more success. After a series of false starts in the years from 1945 to 1947 French policymakers realized that their best hope lay not in pursuing the existing Franco-German antagonism to their own advantage, but in "Europeanizing" their problem: incorporating West Germany, with its resources and potential, into a European community where the Germans would be bound to the French and the French would cease to fear the Germans. The addition of Italy and the Benelux countries was, in this context, little more than a window dressing. Men such as Schumann and Monnet sought to ascribe a European dimension to France's interests. In this, on the whole, they succeeded, until 1990.[4]

The myth of a "united Europe" was not wholly illusory. At each stage – in 1950, in 1958, in the Single European Act, and in the project of Maastricht – European diplomats and their intellectual spokespeople were compelled to describe in normative, even ethical, terms a vision of the continent which had vastly outgrown the purposes or possibilities originally assigned to it. To do less would have seemed like failure, an acknowledgment that "Europe" was and could only be the sum of the separate interests of its members. Like a middleweight boxer blown up to heavyweight dimensions, the "European idea" put forth promises of pan-European unity and offered hope and prosperity to any and all states who qualified for inclusion. The reputation of the myth of "Europe" depended upon it never being put to the test. The inclusion of three poorer countries from Southern Europe (Greece in 1981, and Spain and Portugal five years later) stretched the resources of an entity which relied upon steady economic growth and great collective wealth. After 1989 the threats posed by the collapse of communism exceeded the absorbent capacities of Western Europe at a time when its economies were no longer expanding. The myth burst.

For some time Western Europeans have had their doubts about the "European idea." The first postwar generation was happy to believe in it, to put their faith in the thirty-year long miracle of sustained growth, and to share in the benefits of "Euro-travel," "Euro-fashion," and so forth. Their children, while dismissive of national identity and happy enough to be "Europeans," did not inherit faith in economic improvement and material security: in the 1960s they found it aesthetically unappealing and emotionally unsatisfying; after 1973 (and especially since 1987) they find it deeply unconvincing. Despite all the chatter about a common European currency, the impending removal of frontiers, 1992, and all that, a growing number of young (Western) Europeans well before 1989 had begun to take their distance from the postwar myth. This was less prominent in places like Greece or Spain, or even Italy, where "Europe" still offered the prospect of an unattained cosmopolitan modernity, than it was in Germany, Denmark, Britain, or even France, where its role as a screen behind which national interests could be pursued had worn thin.

The irony, of course, is that the place where "Europe" continued to function as a powerful myth and common project was in *Eastern* Europe, where dissidents, young people, and even reform-minded communist managers longed to share in the personal, political, and moral benefits of "Europeanness," to "return" to a Europe from which they had been cut off by their enforced attachment to a different and distinctly dysfunctional myth, "socialism." Here, too, "Europe" was a myth, a language, but it was part of a strategy for escaping from a hopeless past: by "returning to Europe" Poland, Czechoslovakia, Hungary, and their neighbors could not only overcome economic retardation with help from Brussels, but could find the strength to fight and defeat the forces of darkness in their own national traditions – much as de Gaulle and Adenauer had sought to do in their historic treaty of 1963.

What we have seen since 1989 is the steady erosion of these illusions in the liberated lands of Eastern Europe at the same time as the last remaining strands of the Western myth have fallen away. These are interrelated developments. Had it not been for German unification, itself the most immediate and important consequence of the events of 1989, neither Germany nor France would be facing their present dilemmas. The French would not be suffering the short-term effects of high German interest rates and the long-term realization that their Europe, in which France was the primary beneficiary of German economic strength, no longer exists; the Germans would not be facing, for the first time since 1950, the prospect of a seriously troubled economy and, with it, the need to rethink the degree of importance they should attach to being "Europeans" rather than Germans, given that the two may no longer be compatible. This Franco-German dilemma has not only damaged the European idea, it has revealed it as vulnerable and mythic. "Euro-talk" in Western Europe today rings cynical, when it does not sound merely naive.[5]

Meanwhile, the alacrity with which Western Europeans (notably the French) backed away from their earlier enthusiasm for a liberated Eastern Europe has seriously weakened the position of those in the former communist lands who are pro-Europe. Since the European Community is in no hurry to admit countries like Hungary or Poland (much less Lithuania, Romania, or Slovenia) into its midst, fearful of the added costs of subsidies and the competition from low-wage economies (not to speak of an increased flow of "immigrant" labor), the idea of Europe is looking more than a little tattered in Prague, Budapest, and Warsaw. As a result, those same intellectual dissidents who were most outspokenly "European" in their pronouncements and ideals are now multiply discredited with the local electorate: seemingly naive and out-of-touch with local sentiment, they are accused of being spokespeople for a foreign, cosmopolitan interest which is antagonistic to the needs of the nation. Adherence to the Western community is now the only foreign-policy option in most of Eastern Europe, but affection for "Europe" is at a discount.

With the decline of the European idea, reduced now to pragmatic economic practice and administrative uniformity, other postwar illusions have been shattered. The European economic miracle was built in part on the importation of cheap, non-European (or at any rate non-European Economic Community) labor. The "open door" policy of the 1950s had the further advantage of echoing postwar ideals concerning the right of asylum, the free movement of peoples, and an end to ethnic or national discrimination. No longer required, seen as an economic burden and a social threat, these "guest workers" and their children are now "immigrants" or "aliens." Since the late 1960s the British, the French, and the Scandinavians have been putting up barriers against outsiders, a process now at its zenith with the most recent legislation in France and Germany; the unification of Germany and related post-1989 developments have made uncomfortably obvious a process already under way.[6]

The Yugoslav civil war, which has contributed to the "immigrant problem" in no small measure,[7] has also shattered two other treasured postwar illusions. If World War I was mistakenly supposed to have been the war "to end all wars," World War II did indeed seem for many years to have been just that, at least as far as Europe was concerned. The threat of nuclear disaster, the creation of NATO, and the imposition of Soviet power seemed to forever exclude a military response to intra-European crises. Rare exceptions to this norm were attributed either to domestic instability occasioned by quasi-colonial crises (as in France or Greece), or to misapprehensions concerning the realities of global power (as in Hungary in 1956). That Europeans might come to blows over such traditional matters as borders, nationality, or ethnic territorial claims seemed unthinkable; that they might do so in ways uncannily redolent of earlier conflicts hitherto assigned to history books would have seemed horrific and absurd just five years ago.

Moreover, the events in Yugoslavia reveal not only the extent to which Europe has been unable to escape its past, but how hollow was another of the continent's myths: the newly acquired capacity for sustained collective action. We have not come to an end of intra-European wars, and it is now clear that there is little that a place called "Europe" can do about them. That there was ever any reason to believe otherwise was a myth sustained during a time, from 1949 to 1989, when Europe was, in fact, happily powerless, when action or inaction by the United States or the Soviet Union was the only significant variable in international politics.[8] The broader promises of the postwar world – the United Nations' reiterated desires to see the whole continent "reunited" and collective European action – depended upon them never being put to the test.

Perhaps the most telling sign that a profound change has taken place in recent years is the unsuitability, the irrelevance of many of the categories of description conventionally employed to make sense of European affairs. It no longer makes any sense to describe someone as a "socialist," for example; in Eastern Europe the term is heavily polluted (although nostalgia for the pre-1989 stability in countries undergoing traumatic economic upheaval may now be giving it a brief political afterlife). In Western Europe there are politicians and political parties who still operate under that label, but neither they nor their audience attach any historical significance to the word. The Labour Party in Britain is struggling to free itself from an association with labor, though to date it has lacked the courage of the Italian Communists who, like the Italian Christian Democrats, have changed their name in an effort to erase past associations.

But it is more than just a matter of names. In Eastern Europe the very terms "Left" and "Right" no longer mean what they once did, and those who operate under them are often seen by their opponents and even by their own electorate as belonging somewhere else on the spectrum. The older usage of "Populist" and "Westernizer" in places like Hungary or Slovakia to capture the historical cleavage between national conservatives and urban-liberal modernizers no longer makes sense – the lines are as blurred by conservative parties with rural roots pressing for Euromembership as they are by former communists trading on religious, provincial, and neo-Slavophile prejudices.

This problem of categories is especially acute in Eastern Europe, where for nearly fifty years collective national identity was in large measure determined by the nature of one's relations with the Soviet Union: how friendly they were, when and if they were punctuated by revolts and with what outcome, degrees of autonomy in matters of religion, economic policy, and foreign relations, etc. Since 1989 all that is gone (and consigned to a limbo between history and memory whence it will only be retrieved with difficulty). In a region whose recent past offers no clear social or political descriptors it is tempting to erase from the public record any reference to the communist era, as though it were but an unhappy and transient interlude – in its place we find an older past substituted as a source of identity and reference. This is deeply misleading. In Eastern Europe, as in Western Europe, something important happened in the years from 1939 to 1989; to explain the Czech–Slovak or Serb–Croat conflicts as "timeless historical antagonisms," as though the European past had just been waiting to get its revenge upon the illusory postwar interlude, is as meaningless as attributing the resurgence of neo-Nazi skinheads in Germany to some extrahistorical problem of "Germanness" reaching deep into the unresolved past.

This inclination to treat post-1989 Europe as a mere revival of the past could only make sense if one satisfactorily demonstrated that the era which has just ended was indeed the one which began with Yalta, or with Hitler's invasion of Poland, and that the passing of the postwar illusions leaves us more or less where we started. But the categories of 1939 are, as I have suggested, of little use; they are themselves part of the era which has now closed, and their current exploitation points to the present political vacuum. Where the promise of the future once helped to justify political and social programs and languages, the past, however distorted, is all that remains. Instead of mobilizing ideas and people in the name of things to come, national and ethnic leaders invoke times past. Reactionaries always did this, of course. What has changed is that now "reaction" occupies both its own terrain and that of the erstwhile radicals. This is as true for France as it is for Slovakia and Croatia.[9]

In the matter of defunct eras we are dealing today not only with 1945–1989 but also with 1917–1989. To say that Europe until recently operated under the sign of the Holocaust, or of Hitler, does not sufficiently or precisely explain what came apart in 1989. For both parts of Europe after 1945, just as for Europe (communist, fascist, and liberal) before 1939, the crucial reference was Lenin's Revolution. This was the event which not only shaped geopolitics in our century but also gave new life to the nineteenth-century tradition of revolution. Because of what happened in St. Petersburg in 1917 the prospect and the language of revolution made sense as an influential and seductive way of thinking about public life and collective action in our times. It is what gave the communist and even the noncommunist Left a common eschatology and provided them, at least until 1968, with a shared language, however distorted. Without that language and that reference there is no radical project in European political thought, and its absence has shaken European political sensibilities in ways that we have not yet fully understood.

Yet, 1917, too, was part of a distinctive and older tradition. Lenin provided the European Left with a means of sustaining the heritage of the French Revolution in social and international circumstances which by 1900 had threatened to render the language of 1789 hopelessly inadequate and imprecise. In other words, he saved the revolutionary political myth, albeit at the price of destroying much of its ethical credibility. This was a matter of some importance, since in the aftermath of the failed revolutions of 1848 most of the radical energies of Europe had gone into national movements of various kinds, or else had moderated their ambitions and entered the mainstream of liberal politics in fact if not in name. The confusion engendered by the shift of the revolutionary center from Paris to Frankfurt and then to Moscow was overcome by the characteristically nineteenth-century association of revolutionary progress with industrial production; if Russia could out-industrialize the West, then its revolutionary claims would be retrospectively legitimized.

If we have reached the end of the revolutionary era set in motion by Lenin, then we have in an important sense also closed the era opened by his French predecessors in 1789. This conclusion will come as no surprise to many in France who have been proclaiming the end of this epoch for some time now; but whereas their claims rested on domestic transformations in France, including the terminal decline of France's own Communist Party, they are now confirmed on a pan-European scale by the collapse of the Bolshevik regime, the institutional incarnation of the European revolutionary epoch. The implications are startling in that both the language and the projects of European political life rest squarely upon the terms of reference in which the heritage of the French Revolution has hitherto been grasped. Without it as a reference, the distinctive features of Left and Right blur, as they are already beginning to do in parts of Europe. Without the eschatology of revolution, "socialism" makes no sense. Perhaps more importantly, without the significance accorded to "1789," the building blocks of European political liberalism, the other great heritage of the revolutionary era, lose their form. It is for this reason that political theorists and philosophers in Hungary, Poland, Germany, France, Italy, and elsewhere have in recent years been turning to the somewhat different Anglo-American tradition of liberal political thought to see what might be grafted on to the faltering continental stem.

Revolutions, of course, are not the only mileposts of the past. Events since 1989 suggest that another era is coming to a close, that of the nineteenth-century nation-state. The demise of the nation-state was too hastily announced in recent decades, the presumptive outcome of a globalized economy and the successful Eurofication of at least the Western half of the continent. If anything, the reaction against Maastricht and the postcommunist backlash in the East would superficially suggest an altogether too healthy presence of the national idea. What, after all, are German unification, the rise of Jean-Marie Le Pen, the breakup of Czechoslovakia and the former Soviet Union, and the collapse of Yugoslavia if not the evidence of rampant national revivals?

The evidence is misleading because it confuses national identity with the nation-state.[10] The European nation-states of the last century came into being either through the successful expansion of an early-modern dynastic state into linguistically contiguous territory, or else through the breakup of an old empire – or both, as in the case of Germany and Italy. Whether formed early (i.e., Greece, Belgium, Serbia, and Italy) or in the last bout of state construction after World War I (i.e., Czechoslovakia, Austria, Poland, Yugoslavia, the Baltic states, etc.) these countries were never ethnically, culturally, or socially homogenous. Some of them became so in the course of World War II or as a result of enforced postwar population shifts. This merely underscored the point that such states were, in almost every case, the products of Great Power diplomacy (or its failure). *These* are the states which are now breaking up. The new fault lines vary, but the pattern is consistent. From Spain to Belgium, from Italy to Yugoslavia, from Czechoslovakia to the United Kingdom (a marginal case), European states are dividing into regions. The nineteenth-century settlement of Europe, itself the sediment of shifting imperial plates, is cracking.[11]

The era to which these events signal an end is the one that began in 1848, following the failure of the revolutions of that year. From then until 1945 nationalism and industrial progress substituted for revolution and social transformation across much of Europe. That nationalist sentiment and the ultimate configurations of European nation-states did not always match helps account for the domestic conflict of the new states and their angry quarrels with neighbors – Polish, Hungarian, German, and Italian nationalism took their cue from the perceived inadequacy of their geographical area and the presence of unwanted minorities within their territory. World War II and the enforced settlement that followed put an end to such disputes, but also contributed to a radical undermining of the fragile legitimacy of the newer states – between Soviet internationalism and the promise of Europe their raison d'être seemed elusive. Once free to pursue their own ends – or in the Western case to take advantage of the promise of a transnational Europe – Slovenians, Croats, Flemings, Lombards, and Catalans saw no good reason to accept the terms of earlier settlements which now seemed more restrictive than liberating.

Another way of thinking about the collapse of the nineteenth-century settlement (here taking the nineteenth century to have ended with the defeat of the Central Powers in 1919) is to note the alacrity with which the intelligentsia of much of the continent has thrown in its lot with the notion of extraterritorial identity. Until 1919, the idea of a "European intellectual" was almost unheard of and something of an oxymoron. An intellectual was, almost by definition, the representative, spokesperson, theorist of a nation (in the case of new or aspirant nations) or of a political or cultural stream within a nation (as in the French case). In the most extreme cases (i.e., the Czechs or the Croats) the intellectuals *were* the nation; nobility or urban bourgeoisie identified with the empire (Austrian, in this case), while peasants lacked any collective consciousness or representation. Intellectuals (forgiving the anachronism) invented, or reinvented, the nation, its myths, its language, its culture, and its demands. From Fichte to Masaryk, through Palacký and Kossuth, the mark of the intellectual was his place as nation-maker. Even Jaurès or Croce, not to mention Julien Benda or Giovanni Gentile, were primarily national intellectuals concerned with domestic debates, however great their international reputation.

After 1919, and with growing effect after 1945, intellectuals were internationalized – or else attached themselves disastrously (as in Germany, France, or Romania) to an aggressively fascist aesthetic. The European idea, as a substitute for the sort of nationalism which was thought to have produced 1914 and its heritage, acquired a certain appeal, reinforced after 1945 by the idea of the intellectual as spokesman for a morally troubled world. In a curious paradox this process was uniquely slowed down in France by the accident of French postwar intellectual ascendancy, which meant that a French intellectual could be both French and universalist without apparent contradiction. Elsewhere – in Italy or West Germany, for example – intellectuals consciously addressed themselves to a cosmopolitan audience and took up a new role as spokesmen *against* the national idea.[12] In Eastern Europe the nationalist intellectual was, of course, defunct after 1945, replaced by the progressive, socialist, or communist intellectual whose vision was necessarily nonnational, the more so because so many Eastern and Central European intellectuals were exiles in their own lands, often returning home after years spent abroad as refugees from domestic authoritarianism and foreign fascism alike. But with the declining legitimacy of communism, intellectuals in Eastern Europe took on a new and difficult role: they became critics of the Soviet-imposed regime not in the name of the oppressed nation but on behalf of the individual citizen and the ("European") idea of freedom and rights.

Intellectuals and the nation-state have a close and symbiotic relationship in modern European history. The fragmentation of this link signals a crisis for both parties. Deprived of intellectual justifications for their existence and lacking an empire or empires from which they seek liberation, the nation-states of Europe can only be grounded in economic and political necessity or local interest. In every case today this appears to point either to "Europe" (as fortress or protector) or else to multifurcation – or both, for regions like Lombardy, Slovenia, or Catalonia where the national entity of which they have hitherto been a part seems more of a drain than a benefit. For intellectuals in these places the local interest argument is unappealing. This is not to deny the very real presence of "nationalist" intellectuals in Hungary or Serbia, apologists for the retrenching and revanchist ambitions of their political leaders; but such intellectuals, men like Csurka, are thereby constrained to speak a language which is peculiarly repulsive to the sensibilities of an international intellectual community brought up on the lessons of World War II. Most European intellectuals, faced with the current crisis, may despair of "Europe" but it is all they have.

For this reason it may be that the era whose crisis we are now experiencing began not in 1945, nor in 1917, nor even in 1848, 1815, or 1789. We are living, in one special sense, the end of the European Enlightenment. On the surface this may seem an odd proposition. After all, Europe is still a continent whose political and cultural life is shaped by the dream of rationality, progress, and critical tolerance which we associate with the revolution in European sensibilities that unfolded in the century between the British and the French Revolutions – or, if you like, between the Scientific and the Industrial Revolutions. Indeed, to the extent that the characteristic political form of the European Enlightenment was enlightened despotism – of Maria Theresia and Joseph II, of Frederick the Great and Louis XVI – we live now more than ever in the glow of the Enlightenment idea. What is "Brussels," after all, if not a renewal of the goal of efficient universal administration, shorn of particularisms and driven by rational calculation and the rule of law, which the great eighteenth-century monarchs strove unsuccessfully to institute in their ramshackle lands? Indeed, it is the very rationality of the European Community ideal which has made it appealing to many European intellectuals – and especially to that educated professional intelligentsia which sees in Brussels an escape from hidebound practices and particularisms, much as eighteenth-century lawyers, traders, and writers appealed to enlightened monarchs over the heads of reactionary parliaments and diets. In this limited sense the European Enlightenment is alive and well and living in Jacques Delors.

And yet the Enlightenment *is* in crisis. By this I do not mean that we are about to forget the lessons of the early modern revolutions, abandon discursive rationality and experimental thought, reject the premises of social and political modernity – though we should not too hastily dismiss the notion that there are influential thinkers in Europe today who would do just that. But there is a new counter-Enlightenment in the air and its symptoms are important.

Among these the most obvious is the crisis of the European intellectuals. This may be read in two ways: In a functional sense, intellectuals are redundant and feel themselves to be so. In Eastern Europe their political influence is at a low ebb; they are perceived as culturally marginal and an embarrassment, a reminder of a time when most of their audience did not wish to associate with them and an annoying prolongation of the dissident conscience with which most Hungarians, Czechs, Slovaks, Poles, and others had, and still have, little in common. In their marginality they speak neither for the state nor to it. They have lost their role as self-appointed spokespeople for imprisoned peoples, the only role they ever truly had in Central and Eastern Europe, and in societies where there is no integrated cosmopolitan subcommunity they are adrift. The Jewish intelligentsia of fin-de-siècle Vienna or Budapest might have been marginal to the Empire as a whole, but they were a very real part of a very real micro-society, and from that base they could speak to the world. Today, Czech or Hungarian intellectuals have no such base and thus speak to the world from nowhere. This is not a comfortable or sustainable pose.

In a similar sense, the intellectuals of Western Europe are also adrift. In Paris, still the intellectual heartland of the continent, there is interminable, agonized debate over the lost role of the intellectuals. The classic role of the Western intellectual, as a surrogate authority for both the prince and the people, has been lost. The identity and importance of the state have been blurred by the apparent Europeanizing of power and the privatizing of resources, while the moral standing of the masses has dimmed along with the great theories of human progress which established the people – or privileged elements within it – as vehicles of rational change. In the words of Margaret Thatcher, "society" does not exist. Intellectuals may speak and write and make important ethical pronouncements, but *they themselves* no longer have a theory of why anyone should listen to them.

This is the second element in the decline of the intellectuals. The Enlightenment bequeathed an ideal of knowledge, the belief that understanding the natural, social, and spiritual realism was within the human grasp, and that those who grasped it – scientists, philosophers, social theorists – had a special claim on the attention of rulers and the ruled alike. This fundamental notion – the controlling vision of European modernity – has not come under attack from so many directions that we have forgotten how crucial it is. It has been condemned in its Marxist form as a hubristic and dangerous assertion of human power; in its scientific form as a naive and no less dangerous misunderstanding of the mysteries of nature; in its economic form as a monstrous and self-destructive confidence in the myth of productivity and transformation; and in its philosophical form as the quintessential fallacy of rational objectivism.

There is, of course, much about these attacks on the Enlightenment inheritance that is contradictory and confused. Neo-Heideggerians of the Right may see industrial society as the vicious stepchild of discursive rationality, but their own arguments are no less steeped in post-Enlightenment assumptions; neo-Heideggerians of the Left (Havel might be a case in point) express an almost mystical distaste for the political and economic damage wrought by thoughtless, overconfident modernity but set against it ideals of individual freedom and civic values which took their modern form in the Enlightenment era.

It is this confusion over what exactly its critics find unattractive about our world, and why, which makes it harder to see at first glance just how much the common theme is one corrosive of the assumptions under which we have practiced society since the eighteenth century. The direct attacks on rational discourse itself, although they are the most obviously dismissive of whatever it means to be "enlightened," are probably the least important because of their marginal and self-refuting quality.[13] Not many people are listening to the extreme Derridians, including Derrida himself. But the broader, shallower claim that there is nothing big left to believe in, that ideals are a sham, that progress is an illusion, and that short-term self-interest is the only sustainable private goal (there being no public ones) has now moved from the sphere of public cant into that of cultural discourse. The free-thinking man in the public sphere – Kant's vision of the Enlightenment – still exists; that is what an intellectual is. But for such a person to perform his crucial role – in the Habermasian sense of speaking rationally in and to a public sphere – he must share with his audience a common epistemology. There must be an agreed sense of what constitutes rational collective projects and for what ends it makes sense to pursue them. Today the European intellectual cannot credibly offer reasons beyond the prudential for the thoughts he is propounding, and that is truly a sea change in European thought. In Bertrand Russell's words, we are discovering that there is in fact *less* in heaven and earth than was dreamt of in our philosophy.

History, as Marx was not the first to note, has more imagination than men. Whatever is now happening in Europe will lead *somewhere*. The point I wish to make in this essay is that "somewhere" will look very different from the Europe we have known since 1945. It already does. The regional dislocation of Europe is a fact; Yugoslavia will never be the same again, nor will Italy. The recent Spanish elections came very close to giving the Catalan nationalists a veto over national legislation, a veto they would have exercised to give Catalonia a near monopoly of its resources. Such regionalization, identical to that sought by the Northern League in Italy and already achieved, at too high a price, by the relatively well-off northern states of Yugoslavia, will be disastrous for the southern extremities of Mediterranean Europe, the more so as it is they who sit closest to the ever increasing demographic pressures from Africa to the south and Asia to the east. In the same way, the likely compromise, whereby the western fringe of Central Europe (Poland, Hungary, and the Czech lands) will become a Euro-suburb while "Byzantine" Europe (from Latvia to Bulgaria) will be left to stew in its provincial juices, will further exacerbate the politics of nostalgic resentment in the latter region.

This does not signal a return to the past. Between the end of steady economic growth (itself now recognized, in historical perspective, as a moment of peculiar and contingent good fortune unlikely to be repeated) and the retreat of Great Powers and great ideas alike, we can reasonably expect to experience for the foreseeable future an era of uncertainty, and with it domestic and international resentments and instability. The crucial building blocks of international moral institutions in our era – human rights, social justice, national autonomy – were philosophical and sociological epistemes which contemporary thinkers have difficulty grounding in universally acknowledged propositions.[14] To convince ourselves and our neighbors that we should continue as though these were self-evident truths is going to be all the more difficult: second order assumptions guiding such ideals no longer obtain. Our present situation, with respect to the basic political ideas which shaped post-Enlightenment Europe, is thus comparable to that of the rudimentary organs of which Darwin wrote in the *Origin of Species*:

[They] may be compared with the letter in a word, still retained in the spelling but become useless in the pronunciation, but which serve as a clue in seeking for its derivation.

At best such guidelines for social behavior, at home and abroad, will have to be reconstructed as myths, as rule-utilitarian premises for human practice in a world where most people would dismiss anything more ambitious as "nonsense on stilts." This, however, fails to address the question of authority. Who in Europe today has the authority (moral, intellectual, political) to teach, much less enforce, codes of collective behavior? Who, in short, has power, and to what ends and with what limits? This is an unresolved inheritance from the Enlightenment – indeed it was the space opened up by the end of the Divine Right and the extinction of absolutism which first brought into the public place the very theories of representation and nation, progress and history in whose twilight we now sit. In the absence of any clear answer to this question, it seems only a little melodramatic to conclude that in a variety of ways Europe is about to enter an era of turmoil, a time of troubles. This is nothing new for the old continent, of course, but for most people alive today it will come as a novel and unpleasant experience.

Notes

Source Reprinted by permission of the publisher from *Daedalus* (Journal of the American Academy of Arts and Sciences), from the issue entitled "After Communism: What?," 123:3 (Summer 1994): 1–19.

1 See Tony Judt, "The Past is Another Country: Myth and Memory in Postwar Europe," *Daedalus* 121 (4) (Fall 1992): 83–119.
2 For the Italian case see the magisterial work of Claudio Pavone, *Una Guerra Civile. Saggio storico sulla moralitá nella Resistenza* (Turin: Bollati Boringhieri, 1992).
3 Which is not to deny that many in the previous decades had pressed for just such changes, but to no effect.
4 The relationship between France and the Federal Republic of Germany in the years 1949–1990 curiously echoes that between Austria and Prussia after the Congress of Vienna. In both cases one partner, ostensibly the senior one, sought to use the other as both a resource and a guarantee – in the Austrian case by encouraging Prussia to participate in and strengthen the German Confederation – only to discover, in the fullness of time, that the power relationship had reversed itself and the senior partner could no longer control or contain the ambitions of its economically superior associate.
5 For a full discussion of the European ramifications of German unification, and the uses of "Europe" in German political debate, see Timothy Garton Ash, *In Europe's Name: Germany and the Divided Continent* (New York: Random House, 1993).

6 Curiously, this reveals the enduring strength and relevance of at least one European idea, that of "Fortress Europe," a continent united in its Christian whiteness against cosmopolitan, exotic, and threatening forces, from within or without. *This* version of the European idea, with its roots in nineteenth-century racial theory was shared by Hitler and even by some of the intellectual critics of democracy of the 1930s. It has been revived by neo-fascists and "new Right" intellectuals in Germany, France, and Italy in recent years and appears to be thriving.

7 At least in those countries that have opened their doors to refugees – Austria and Germany in particular.

8 Except in small ex-colonies outside of Europe, where Britain or France might still intervene with relative autonomy – but precisely *as* Britain or France, which underscores the point.

9 A number of prominent French left-wingers, among them Max Gallo, Régis Debray, and Jean-Pierre Chevènement, have recently taken to nostalgic invocations of a sort of national republicanism, quite literally a "reaction" to the overselling of Europe and the demise of an *international* radical project.

10 For a fuller discussion of this theme, see Tony Judt, "The New Old Nationalism," *New York Review of Books*, 26 May 1994.

11 In the case of Belgium, the national settlement is coming apart as a result of pressure from two directions: domestically the Flemings and Walloons are splitting into a federated state, while internationally the image of "Benelux" in so many fields of economic and administrative action has eroded the specificity of "Belgium" as a distinctive entity.

12 Hans Magnus Enzensberger has argued cogently that the paradoxical consequences of this new role for German writers – filling a domestic political void but in a condition of existential discomfort over their national identity – were disastrous for modern German intellectual and political life.

13 "Some beliefs and truths are inescapable . . . there are constraints of fact and logic. A correct understanding of how, for instance, true factual beliefs are formed has no tendency to undermine them, while the opposite is typically true of ideological beliefs, for example. This is a truth, admittedly far from clear, at the heart of the Enlightenment enterprise." Bernard Williams, *Shame and Necessity* (Berkeley and Los Angeles, CA: University of California Press, 1993), p. 216, n. 52.

14 Witness the general reaction to the work of John Rawls, including his most recent attempt to devise a theoretical basis for liberalism – that it is only valid to the extent that it describes the sort of liberal societies where it is already practiced. Hence, too, the rather disembodied air of even the best-informed attempts to import such Anglo-American speculation into continental terrain.

8

THE LEGACY OF DISSENT

G. M. Tamás

Political philosopher G. M. Tamás was one of the main personalities of the Hungarian Democratic Opposition in the 1980s. After 1989 he remained politically active as a major figure of the Alliance of Free Democrats and author of numerous thought-provoking and deliberately controversial essays and commentaries. In this article he proposes an original explanation of the post-1989 mass disenchantment with the once presumably admired dissidents. His two-fold argument is that dissent had always been unpopular and that the dissidents' subcultures were fundamentally isolated from the population at large.

Tamás's approach tends to extrapolate the peculiar conditions of Hungary's dissident community and overlooks the exhilarating appeals of a mass social movement like Solidarity in Poland. Whatever one thinks of his bitter diagnosis of the dissidents' alienation from the societies they claimed to speak for, Tamás's essay captures accurately the ethical dimension of the critical intellectuals' calls for a new politics rooted in truth and respect for individual human rights. Particularly significant are his reflections on the ambivalence of the key strategic concept of "civil society" and the contrast he highlights between its East European and traditional Western liberal interpretations. Tamás concludes, in agreement with Poland's Adam Michnik, that the heroic times are over and that one of the legacies of dissent is a deep sense of ambiguity including a healthy suspicion regarding all political dogmas.

*   *   *

The dissidence of the 1970s and 1980s is rather unpopular in the Eastern Europe of today. With the exception of Poland (where there was an almost uninterrupted revolutionary tradition from 1976 on), former dissidents play but a token role in real politics, and their proudest symbols, like Walesa, Havel or Konrád, are decried as "communists," "traitors," "agents." In the Hungarian parliament, any mention of the erstwhile dissidence is greeted with hoots of laughter, catcalls, and jeers from the government benches. Its very existence is denied sometimes by official journalists and historians. Apart from the understandable fight for a respectable pedigree and the embarrassment felt by today's democratic leaders, who nearly without exception were collaborationists, former communist party officials, or at best pusillanimous "sleepers" who spent the last fifty years saying nothing, the antipathy felt for dissidents calls for some explanation.

Dissent was an anomaly. Dissidents, as we shall see, led a life where satisfactions, successes, defeats, and frustrations were very different from those felt by the population at large. While our academic or other intellectual colleagues looked for preferment, authorial fame, international travels, second homes, and the like, our pride lay in our work appearing in smudgy, primitively stencilled little pamphlets called by the Russian word "samizdat," and success was distributing a couple of hundred copies before the secret police arrived. "Why not fifty thousand copies?" a writer asked me in the early 1980s. "If you weren't such an idiot to have put yourself on the black list, you could now have a real impact, even if you couldn't perhaps flatter your adrenaline levels by cursing Andropov." A secret police officer – unforgettably dressed in a University of Texas T-shirt – asked me once, "You consider yourself an intelligent man, I suppose. Then how do you explain that you are acting against your own interests?" How indeed.

The minority of the body politic that was aware of "dissident activities" felt ambivalently about them. First, dissidents challenged the efficacy of reforms, seen by almost everyone as the only possible salvation. Second, with their emphasis on "rights" and "liberties," the dissidents challenged the dominant political discourse, which was based on interest and naked power. Third, they challenged the tacit assumption that all resistance was so dangerous that it was impossible. Fourth, therefore, dissidence challenged the moral stance of those who were silently opposed to the communist regime but did not dare to do anything about it.

This last challenge is the source of the most deep-seated prejudice against dissidence. "If it is obviously impossible for *me* to be a resister, how is it possible for *him*? He *must* have some sort of spiel with the authorities if he is not arrested or deported, since if *I* did the things he does *I would be*." These intellectuals in the so-called "reform dictatorships" believed that the essence of dissent was Silent Reproach. According to this view, the message of the dissidents was not so much "Go to Hell!" directed towards the leaders of the regime, but more "Shame on you!" directed towards the majority of bystanders. I have always hotly denied this, but I was so frequently accused of it that I started entertaining some doubts about the motives of my dissident acts.

There was a fifth reason for ambivalence. "Dissident activities" challenged another assumption of the populace, namely the common Eastern European view that all politics is filth, that *civisme* does not exist, that law

THE LEGACY OF DISSENT

is for the strong, etc. If people were visibly prepared to make sacrifices for their political beliefs, the world being what it is, they must be bonkers. My old arch-rival, the prime minister of Hungary, was certainly in tune with at least a part of popular opinion when he called my party, which emerged from the dissident tradition, "psychiatric opposition."[1] Do not think for a moment that the notion of "political psychiatry" in the Soviet Union and Romania was wholly cynical. The powers-that-be (and that now, thank God, have been) were puzzled, nay, appalled by the mere phenomenon of dissidence. Non-conformism and eccentricity are conflated with madness even in freer and more permissive societies than were those of Eastern Europe. Dissidence was regarded as an expression of anomie by many and, well, I could not deny that there were a few strange types among us, as fond as I may have been of them.

The dissidents said strange things. They began to talk about "parallel polis," "parallel public sphere," "dissident sub-culture," and the like, as though they were content with the quirky and murky underworld of political, artistic, and moral avant-garde. Their sit-ins, hunger strikes, civil disobedience were reminiscent of New Left tactics. Dissidents wore beards, did not save up to buy East German automobiles, spoke foreign languages, and were the first to carry their children in pouches. Many were Jewish. In 1968, when many good Hungarians and East Germans drunk themselves into oblivion with happiness at the sight of the humiliation of their ancient foe, Czechoslovakia, the dissidents took the side of the foreigner. In short, they were a pain in the neck.

Although dissent did not cause the collapse of the communist regime, beyond doubt it was an important historical phenomenon, and not only for Eastern Europe, Russia, and China. At a moment when the "thaw" and détente were making Soviet systems almost acceptable, when Admiral Gorshkov's fleet steamed gaily around Africa and Army General Yepishev's guerrillas installed "revolutionary dictatorships" all over the Third World, when Lieutenant General Markus Wolff's terrorists nearly forced West Germany to its knees, when peace (that is, unilateral disarmament) movements fostered an atmosphere of "moral equivalence" between the super-powers, and when, all in all, the intellectual initiative was on the socialist Left, it was then that the lonely voices of dissenters from behind the Iron Curtain made a difference.

They were feeble voices, of course, but they proved by the sheer fact of having spoken that the quest for liberty and justice remained universal, that state socialism was not a permanent fixture rooted in the ineffable traditions of the East, that the problems of mankind were at least inter-related. They showed that the curious, warped modernity imposed by Stalin and his followers was at last being resisted and criticized in the very place where it was dominant.

As in the West from the sixteenth to eighteenth centuries, it all began with a seemingly marginal battle for freedom of expression against censorship. Then, audacious French and English books were printed in the Netherlands, the freest nation of that age. Pseudonyms, false datings, smuggling ventures abounded. Similarly, in recent times, the authors of bold books that could not get past home censorship played to both a domestic and foreign audience. At the Sinyavsky–Daniel trial, the first important trial against dissident writers, the defendants were "unmasked" as the smugglers of their own pseudonymous novels to the West. The proceedings of this trial (and those of Joseph Brodsky's trial) were published in France. And while samizdat copies were distributed, without Western dissemination dissident authors could not have been effective; in some cases, Western fame even meant a little protection.

Dissidents came to understand that it was not enough to foil the communist secret police and to find an enthusiastic domestic audience ready for sacrifice. In order for them to get international clout, they had to please Western "civil libertarians," publishers, editors, journalists, academics, NGO (nongovernmental organization) functionaries, diplomats, spies, and other assorted busybodies who naturally wanted to make their own political points as well. And let us not forget that during most of this period – broadly speaking, the last thirty years – cold warriors and staunch anti-communists were not at all respectable in the West. CIA funding was necessary for launching the liberal anti-communist journals *Encounter*, *Survey*, *Preuves*, *Der Monat*, most of which are, alas, no more. Cold warriors were regarded as a nuisance by both Kissingerian *Realpolitikers* and the Left Establishment.

On the whole, dissident rhetoric shifted from the substantive, moralistic, and politically socialist oratory of 1956 and 1968 to a jargon of rights-centered liberalism. It became a self-conscious defense of the virtuous minority that lived on a bohemian reservation called "the parallel polis," and so the emphasis switched from workers' councils and self-management to exit visas and toleration of underground seminars on Heidegger.

At first glance, the interest of the Western Left in East European dissidence is a strange fact. But, the Left was always internationalist and had a quasi-religious interest in the great socialist experiment and its problems. The Left's local prestige depended on it. After the bloody crushing of the Hungarian revolt in 1956 and the Sino-Soviet split shortly thereafter, it was difficult to maintain the myth of world revolution led by a few, maybe bullyish, maybe harsh but nonetheless dedicated armed prophets who were the strict parents of their refreshingly naive and docile peoples. It was crucial to see whether there was still any hope of a Red Dawn from the East, even if it could not come directly from the Kremlin.

And indeed, the most profound analyses of 1956 came from the heretic ex-Trotskyite Cornelius Castoriadis and his magazine, *Socialisme ou Barbarie*, which presented the argument that the Hungarian revolutionary workers' councils of 1956 offered a non-capitalist solution to the woes of the Soviet system. The workers' councils were revolutionary, anarcho-syndicalist, democratic, anti-capitalist, and heroic – and they were really and truly all those things. The interpretation *Socialisme ou Barbarie* gave to the Hungarian uprising (accidentally coinciding with Hannah Arendt's views) was a vitally important, if subterranean influence on the rise of the New Left and the inception of a socialist critique of totalitarianism. The radical Left (still very strong in the 1970s) could keep some of its revolutionary faith, dissociate itself from the despicable communist parties, and unlike the decrepit social democrats who were ever dewy-eyed about Soviet "reforms" could attack *all* the established powers in the industrial world. The New Left began to take exception at Western governments' complacency about us brave fighters for democracy. One of the most influential Western periodicals reporting faithfully on the development of dissent was Sartre's *Les Temps modernes*, hardly known for its liberal-democratic leanings. (Similar periodicals in the U.S. were doing the same.) And, of course, the intellectual Left, which in those days had a dominant position in the media, the universities, research centers, think tanks, and increasingly in the civil service, foreign service, and other related bureaucracies, had an enormous stake in finding out whether those brave and glamorous freedom fighters and "human rights activists" in the East still subscribed to the general philosophy of the Left.

The traditional leaders of the Western nations were mainly interested in those conflicts within socialist societies that could have resulted in strategic realignments or even in *renversements des alliances*. Thus, the people to watch were the diverse factions within the ruling communist parties, the people who – in the memorable phrase of Prime Minister Thatcher (as she then was) – Western leaders "could do business with." At the same time, of course, the Western democratic powers mildly grumbled when really untoward things happened in the East.

This situation changed radically with the advent of neo-conservatism. Unlike home-grown American paleo-conservatives, the U.S. neo-cons had an internationalist tradition of their own from two sources. One was a continental social democratic, radical tradition opposed to both main forms of totalitarianism; these adherents had already fought communism ideologically from a left-liberal standpoint in the 1950s and 1960s and came to conservatism partly as a result of reflections on international politics. The other source was from the influence of Leo Strauss and his secret armies. Both sources were strongly German in heritage and greatly affected by the experiences of both Auschwitz and Kolyma.

Traditional conservatives are by inclination *Realpolitiker*, cautious and disillusioned schemers. But post-Auschwitz neo-conservatives were different. They were able to use the main weapon of the Left, namely a moral critique of politics, for unheard-of conservative purposes. You never saw crusading conservatives before. But the twin influences of Hayek and Solzhenitsyn changed this, perhaps forever.

There was, therefore, an audience for East European dissenters not only on the Left, as earlier, but also on the Right. Both New Left and New Right were influenced by the testimony of dissidence and, in terms of the history of ideas, they have a common origin: all three are reactions to modern socialism, just as the older kinds of conservatism and liberalism were reactions to the French Revolution. The history, and indeed the fate, of East European dissidence, the New Left, and the New Right are intertwined and mutually dependent in many respects. I shall try to show how this odd, distant symbiosis has fashioned the political thought of the dissidents themselves.

How are we to understand political thought expressed under duress, threats, and persecution? This thorny problem of cultural history was first examined by Leo Strauss in his classic book, *Persecution and the Art of Writing* (1952), where he contended that our acuity of analysis of the past was blunted by three centuries of free speech in the West. Most of cultural history has taken place in societies where the state was invested with an authority to fashion morality and to persecute vigorously all who were perceived as immoral or heretical or seditious. But even in free societies, a breach with received opinion can lead to social ostracism, marginalism, and isolation, or at least obloquy. Leo Strauss deduced from his studies of medieval Jewish and Muslim philosophy that practically all ancient thinkers had esoteric teachings that were sometimes hidden between the lines; Leo Strauss construed inconsistencies, wrong inferences, and strange lapses by authors of genius as discretely veiled allusions to heretical or perilous ideas that the authors did not dare express with point-blank candor. In the title essay, he says that

> [p]ersecution, then, gives rise to a peculiar technique of writing, and therewith to a peculiar type of literature, in which the truth about all crucial things is presented exclusively between the lines. That literature is addressed, not to all readers, but to trustworthy and intelligent readers only. It has all the advantages of private communication without having its greatest disadvantage – that it reaches only the writer's acquaintances. It has all the advantages of public communication without having its greatest disadvantage – capital punishment for the author.

The further twist in this story is that samizdat turned exactly against such debilitating self-censorship and double-entendre and practiced what the Hungarian dissident philosopher Janos Kis called "the conspicuous exercise of rights." Dissidents committed defiant acts when they thought they were within their rights guaranteed by international agreements, constitutional provisions, or even, some would argue, by natural law. This is what gave samizdat, and dissent in general, its moral force, pride, and dignity.

Still, if truth be told, there were limitations to the absolute truthfulness and sincerity of the underground literature and of other dissident pronouncements. First, openly seditious appeals would have been meaningless in a non-revolutionary situation. Second, if samizdat was to be effective, it had to be grafted on the body of existing social criticism, historical awareness, and conceptual vocabulary. (There was a sharp difference in perceptions between those of my contemporaries who read George Orwell, Arthur Koestler, Arthur London, Boris Souvarine, and Isaac Deutscher for the first time only in 1990 and those of us, like myself, for whom these books, together with Solzhenitsyn, were inspirations during our adolescence in the 1960s. The word "gulag" was unknown to most of my non-dissident academic acquaintances in the 1980s. You could not allude to these things – even *officially* published accounts of Stalinist terror, like the wonderful stories of Jozsef Lengyel, tended to be carefully ignored outside a very narrow circle of committed people.) Third, it was a conscious tactic of dissidence to intentionally blur the boundaries between dissident and "reformist" criticism in order to woo potential allies and encourage a more timid readership. Fourth, what we said had to be comprehensible and more or less acceptable to a Western audience of patrons, benefactors, and well wishers. They were the only people able to offer fame and protection and thereby indirectly influence policies here and more directly the human rights policies of Western democratic governments.

This last influence on dissidence was not wholly conscious, naturally. But writers and public speakers learn from reaction, and it was easy to see which dissident authors were celebrated and famous in the West. Dissidents knew that Mr. Solzhenitsyn was barred from the White House, while a small stretch of street was named Sakharov Plaza near to the Soviet embassy. So, when erstwhile ironies and ambiguities have been forgotten along with the context, and when dissident writings are considered "moralistic," "naïve," and even "rationalist-liberal" owing to a growingly literal-minded reading, we shall have to very carefully extricate out of all these hermeneutical difficulties what I believe to be the real meaning of dissident political thought, and only then assess what its consequences are today.

Both the darker strands and the innovation of dissident thought have been hidden. The reason for this lies in both the content of dissident teachings and their simplified contemporary post-communist reading; and it is devilishly difficult to tell the two apart. Leo Strauss, in another essay of the same book, "How to Study Spinoza's *Theologico-Political Treatise*," writes:

> To understand the words of another man, living or dead, may mean two different things which for the moment we shall call interpretation and explanation. By interpretation we mean the attempt to ascertain what the speaker said and how he actually understood what he said, regardless of whether he expressed that understanding explicitly or not. By explanation we mean the attempt to ascertain those implications of his statements of which he was unaware. Accordingly, the realization that a given statement is ironical or a lie, belongs to the interpretation of the statement, whereas the realization that a given statement is based on a mistake, or is the unconscious expression of a wish, an interest, a bias, or an historical situation, belongs to its explanation.

In what follows, I shall attempt both interpretation and explanation mainly of three concepts or notions that, in the wake of the velvet revolutions of 1988–1990, have received a new lease on life and are currently, quietly changing the character of liberal political thinking (the first time since Lenin and Trotsky that Eastern Europe has had such an influence). These key notions are, not surprisingly, civil society, human rights, and democracy.

Civil society

We inherited our concept of civil society from Locke, the Scottish Enlightenment, Burke, Hegel, and de Tocqueville. On the European continent, the latter three were the most important; it was their idea of a civil society that, in a simplified version, captured the imaginations of East European intellectuals. According to this idea, in a liberal society, where in comparison to the absolutist historical precedent the power of the state is inordinately weak, the conformity, loyalty, obedience, and initiative necessary for self-government is assured by voluntary associations. Civic order in a liberal society cannot be sustained without the activity of the citizens. Before the intercession of the state becomes necessary, competition between individuals for wealth, fame, status, imposition of moral preferences should be conducted in an orderly way among groups linking together people of similar inclinations, interests, or other common features of their lives. Civil society, in a way, was a price to be paid for liberty. The informal pressure of egalitarian public opinion threatened a new tyranny, and only the plurality and diversity of civil associations was presumed to be a defense against it – for that meant a public opinion *divided*. Stendhal's fear, expressed in *Lucien Leuwen*, that in America you had to flatter your shoe-maker if you wanted to get on was partly assuaged by the fact that there were many different cobblers of variegated religious and moral opinions. The problem for Burke, Hegel, and de Tocqueville was how to obtain cohesion, order, and civic virtue in a society both free and democratic – that is, egalitarian and lacking in chivalrous heroism, aristocratic panache, divine authority, or a religiously underpinned commitment for the common good that made civic and social altruism appear natural. The key question was how to keep society together in the absence of a pre-ordained hierarchy.

East European intellectuals critical of the communist regime had com-pletely different headaches. Their society seemed to be – at least this was the prevailing view – regimented, conformist, exacting, and possessing a more than desirable degree of cohesion, order, and discipline. Here, a coercive morality demanded sacrifice and altruism for a common good that was unequivocally identified by the rulers; here, quasi-religious doctrines forced themselves upon private citizens who were not free to follow their own sensibilities, inclinations, or beliefs. Burke, Hegel, and de Tocqueville had to ponder whether and how it was possible to make the autonomous individual in a free society be a citizen beyond mere passive law-abidingness; what, indeed, would hold together the body politic. My generation in Eastern Europe had to counter the crushing pre-ponderance, the all-pervasive omnipresence of the police state, central planning, capricious autocracy, and the rest.

These two situations make for rather different ideological strategies. The Eastern Europeans' worry was not that without voluntary associations, superogatory benevolence, and non-coercive co-operation, individuals would become "atomized," disoriented, amoral, and oblivious of duty. These are the permanent anxieties of free polities. On the contrary, our worry was that without diversified, pluralistic, voluntary associations, the dutiful citizens of the totalitarian state would become automatons, soulless executors of orders from on high. The problem was not the peril inherent in *too much* autonomy, but in *too little*. We do not need to debate whether this was or was not a realistic assessment of late socialist society; this was the dominant analysis.

Thus, the East European notion of civil society was pitched against the state, whereas the Whig idea was to complement the enfeebled state, to find new reasons for obedience and conformity after the wane of divinely anointed authority. The Whig idea was that voluntary, self-governing entities help to build a relatively non-coercive order, while the East European dissidents' idea was that they might help to destroy an overly coercive order. In a word, the Burkean–Hegelian–Tocquevillian, or Whig, idea was a *political* one; the East European dissident idea was *anti-political*.

What does "anti-political" mean in this context? The East European idea was, as seen in the works of Václav Havel and György Konrád, to escape politics altogether with the aid of a commonplace morality stressing the beauty of humdrum everyday life, small-scale integrity, a sense of humor, self-deprecatory modesty, and above all, authenticity. Everything grandiose was suspect. The nifty vivacity of the black market was favorably compared to the grandeur of the Siege of Leningrad; healthily promiscuous sensuality was shown to be superior to doctrinaire fanaticism.

The anti-institutional slant of the dissident idea of civil society made it "anti-political," although it was not a-political. Dissidents thought that the bigger chunk of human life was non-institutional anyway; this is where we should conquer and realize our independence. It was the old Stoic idea. Dissidents somehow imagined that the totalitarian state would whir in an abandoned back room like a washing machine, while the *real* things would be happening in the salon and in the bedroom. There were lyrical effusions about the civic virtue of lazing in the sun and surveying pretty girls from the pub door.

This utopia, of course, contradicted the dissident analysis of the totalitarian state. If the state was so all-pervasive, how could it be only a washing machine? No doubt, like all politics of authenticity, this was an expression of weakness. But, the consequences of this weakness were ruinous. According to the dissident view, morality had become an exclusively private affair, so private that all general normative or prescriptive judgments are unable to be brought to account for it. Institutional discourse, codes of behavior, lists of virtues and sins, ideas of justice, a sense of obligation, codes of propriety, and the abstract, universalistic language reminiscent of the dread Marxist-Leninist science were all rejected. Only disjointed, fragmentary talk would do. Morality at best can be expressed by paradox, by a wry joke, by an oblique allusion. So, we did it again: by adapting a Western, liberal (well, Whiggish) concept, we used it to reject the whole Western political tradition. The echoes of this in the deconstructionist-postmodernist mode of approach are no mere coincidence.

For the anti-institutional idea of East European dissidence was eagerly seized upon by disgruntled exponents of the Western Left. Its proponents could at least argue that their attack against the main Western political tradition was coming from sources above suspicion. Distrusts of ethics, ideology, and politics can mean different things. But the idea of a society where nothing good can be achieved by institutional means, where there is no authority, where every political act is voluntary, where education is impossible and obligation is always subject to individual analysis, where even contractual relations are subordinated to whim, this idea is irreconcilable even with anarchism. Civil society without a state would be a

Hobbesian state of nature. But dissidents presupposed a state, a totalitarian, dictatorial, autocratic state that would, as if by magic, be made irrelevant by the strengthening of voluntary associations and a non-political diversity of lifestyles. The ambiguously expressed idea of civil society was liked by adversary culture radicals and neo-conservatives alike. Neo-conservatives liked this idea of civil society because it seemed to them that it paralleled their own distaste for state intervention; radicals loved it because they could sniff the fragrance of their anti-institutionalism.

The dissident idea of civil society was the body politic, subtracting the politics.

Human rights

If civil society was the human entity that dissidents wanted to represent, human rights were the principle according to which they wished to represent it. Marxism proper was critical of such universalist Enlightenment notions, but communist revolutionaries, the true heirs of the Jacobins, could bring themselves occasionally to speak this language while signing documents such as the U.N. Charter or the CSCE's Helsinki Final Act, and similar covenants, pacts, and agreements. Between 1933 and 1945, the human rights discourse was directed against the Nazis, who had turned most overtly against natural law and other universal moral criteria. The communists committed the same crimes, but did not justify them by openly changing the basic rules of morality (see Trotsky's *Their Morals and Ours*), and instead excused them by rather conventional references to history and to the ends sanctifying the means. The communists, unlike the Nazis, never deviated consciously from the grand tradition of the primordial unity of mankind. Indeed, they did not think that the existence of the Gulag made their subscription to such lofty declarations look rather odd.

Still, "human rights," although not operative, have been a recognized principle, coming down from the venerable intellectual treasure of the American and French revolutions. It was an antidote to oppressive positive law (statutes) and was unencumbered by the metaphysical questions that beset natural right in its classical form. The first most important right for dissident intellectuals was the right to freedom of expression. But freedom of expression meant a license to tell the truth, especially the truth about the communist system, the truth about the martyrdom of East European peoples under the Gulag regime. The moral attitude that sprung from this simple idea of uncensored truth-telling was bearing witness: the chief genre of dissident writing is neither philosophical treatise, nor poetry, but testimony. Martyrs are – even etymologically – witnesses. The elocution of their martyrdom, where the whole community was martyred,

191

created a new symbolic community: the community of those who suffered and lived to tell and were ready again to suffer for the right to tell.

The irresistible force of this surge of testimony was lethal because, in spite of denial, in spite of a sometimes almost psychotic refusal to know, half-consciously everybody knew what happened. After all, this testimony was the basis of the Secret History of the communist avant-garde elite as well: the heroism à rebours of the show trials so well described by Arthur Koestler, Arthur London, and Bela Szasz. There was no apparatchik in the Soviet Union who did not know that Alexander Solzhenitsyn was right.

In the struggle for the right to historical truth, for the right to bear witness, where history and morals become one, dissidents were harassed, persecuted, and punished. They went on documenting these new abuses – one of the chief tasks of the dissident movement was to write its own chronicle, a testimony this time about the witnesses themselves – and more or less quietly protesting against them in a non-violent way. Dissenters did not at first demand the usual set of fundamental human rights: the stress was on the word. They did not set up political parties or organize conspiracies. They wanted to expose unspeakable, unimaginable crimes and to show the continuity of the Great Terror with the servility and mendacity of the present. They said to the rulers, "These communiqués and declarations signed by you guarantee the right to free speech, peaceful assembly and the like. Why cannot we say what we believe to be the truth?"

There was no good answer to this question for the very simple reason that communists in principle did not condone mass murder, or even the radical deprivation of people's liberty. Hitler never said he was a humanist, but Bolsheviks did. And this was their undoing. Liars are not heroic; exposed liars lose their authority. The incipient reformist criticism of the achievements of the socialist economy combined with the corrosion of moral self-confidence brought about by dissident testimony proved too much. Few people in the West are aware of the peculiarities of the communist aristocracy, the descendants of the Old Guard. Their radical forebears were motivated by what one could call critical passion, the passion that comes from a moral critique of politics. Radicals are always and invariably right when they say that life is disgusting. The rejection of this unsavory world is the reason why revolutionary radicalism is so alluring. Radicalism, however, cannot be sustained without the proof of sacrifice, without bearing witness. But the heroic testimony was offered against socialism. The communist elite could not help but realize that this time dissidents and "deviationists" experienced the same passion with which the heroes of the Narodnaya Volya went to the scaffold. The elite understood only too well, and it is but little wonder that their sons and daughters joined in the dissident movement in very significant numbers.

The West understood little of this passion for historical-moral truth, but its shaky faith in the universality of its own basic principles of human and civil rights was challenged by the East European dissidents: people were putting themselves at risk for the pious and dull commonplaces of the Helsinki Accords. "Will you live by your principles?" they asked. This unsolicited support for Western constitutional principles by people whose integrity was proven by their willingness to suffer for those very principles gave a new force to the idea of natural right and to the ideas of the American Revolution, which were put onto the political agenda once more. This was a universalist discourse common to both systems, and the debate conducted within that discourse was won by the West and its allies, the dissidents. *Realpolitik* could have never won that debate.

We should not forget, however, that this universalistic Enlightenment discourse is not really part of the East European tradition. Moreover, it was used for very peculiar purposes; the set of rights that counted most referred to the moral interests of committed people engaged in public speech and the pursuit of historical and moral truth. This pre-eminent set of human rights was selected so as to be anti-political, to interfere as little as possible with existing administrative, economic, military, and cultural structures of power. The demand for independent, non-Marxist-Leninist philosophical inquiry, for example, did not imply the replacement of the official dogma with apparently truer theses. But freedom of expression, of course, silently presupposed liberalism. No clamor for free speech is ever innocent of politics. But this was liberalism for people *outside the institutions*, with no expressed preference for institutions of any kind. The grand revolutionary narrative had been exposed as fraud and a space for free debate inaugurated. And while the human rights strategy did not condemn politics outright as immoral, it definitely turned its back to it, a result of communist might combined with a Western unwillingness to change the status quo.

But politics was not the only thing being rejected. Civic community, the state, and the law were suspect for most dissidents. These smacked of regimentation, indoctrination, and domination. Freedom seemed to reside in individual moral action. Human rights would leave the space of public action to a very small state manned by administrators, with all the "real men" being outside. The ever-increasing list of human rights, a universal phenomenon, will finally make nil any conceivable claim of the City on its citizens: the exodus of the citizen from the City is completed. Dissidents, leading this exodus, this desertion of the City, now find themselves in the wilderness, faced with a body of opinion that fails to recognize any institutional authority, any civic duty, any political obligation, any idea of the common good, and is ever impatient with disorder and squalor. The universalism of human rights (maintained by most dissidents with a true Gallo-American revolutionary fervor) concealed the fact that Western civilization's success did not rest only on liberal-democratic constitutional arrangements, nor merely on the market rules characteristic of liberal capitalism. The cohesive elements of Western civilization – the classical republican heritage, civic patriotism, Biblical religion, and an institutionalized political tradition – were necessarily ignored.

Government could not very well defend the civil rights of individuals and minority groups if it were not already held in high esteem by obedient citizens convinced of the natural authority of the polity they were ready to serve and were prepared to die for. One of my most frustrating and bitter experiences under communist dictatorship was the difficulty of identifying with my own political community and the lack of shared symbols. It was a state of affairs that made virtually every honest man and woman into a social recluse and an emigré in one's own country. "Internal exile," "inner emigration" – these were no empty phrases. They have cut across natural loyalties and make post-communist societies today into foci of disorder. Dissent could not possibly help it; the de-politicizing effect of modern tyranny has touched everybody, even those who resisted it. Tyrannical pseudo-politics, and the exercise of self-abasement before the mighty, has made real politics unpalatable.

And there is another, more subtle factor here. Liberal capitalism is the first and only political regime in history that is profoundly *controversial*, against which a permanent cultural revolution has been waged and traditionally by the best minds of their time. Liberal capitalism commands no authority, since both Christians and radicals regard it haughtily as materialistic and selfish to the point of being bestial. Since the ideal of the dissidents was the liberal-democratic West, they had no ideal, for the Western political order was far from being the West's own ideal. Unlike other revolutions in history, the East European revolutions did not and do not have a utopia of their own, owing to this Western–Eastern "dialectic" and the culturally controversial nature of liberal capitalism.

It is small wonder that Western influence was limited to that idea of Western civilization seemingly unaffected by the corrosive Marxian and Nietzshean critique of liberal societies, namely dissent, whereas the culturally undefended foundations of Western societies, those that allow them to function but which are derided and blushingly disavowed, could not play a role. The reluctance of conservatives in the West to defend the Western order – expressed most aptly by Michael Oakeshott's distaste for theory – is characteristic. Even conservatives can bear the reality of liberal capitalism only if it is cloaked in the garb of "What Is," tradition as such, with the unpleasant details grandly removed. Paradoxically, liberal capitalism is in better odor now with conservatives after the collapse of "real socialism" because an authentic revolution appears to have legitimized it. But that cannot hide that the Western inspiration for the East was that of the adversary culture, most of Western high culture being adversarial by nature and opposed to liberal society in substance, tone, manner, and taste.

Democracy

In 1988–1989, when it was certain that the communist system was finished and, unnoticed by the West, when there were great demonstrations demanding the ouster of the incumbent regime, free elections, a new constitution, and the departure of Soviet troops, we shouted on the streets of Budapest, "We Want Democracy!" Not "We Want the Rule of Law," mind you, not liberty, not justice, but democracy.

What people's idea of democracy was in those dizzy, exhilarating days, can be safely reconstructed from what people now consider non-democratic or anti-democratic and as such reject. Imposition of political will by an elite (law) is anti-democratic. Coercion used to elicit uniform behavior (public order) is anti-democratic. Political deliberation through public controversy conducted by a specialized group of people (representative government, a.k.a. parliamentarianism) is anti-democratic. Interference with private wealth (redistribution through levying of taxes and duties) is anti-democratic. Unequal concentration of wealth, fame, and influence (liberal capitalism) is anti-democratic. Indoctrination according to elite preferences (education) is anti-democratic.

Even what appeared at first sight to have been democratic nationalism was nothing but regionalism and autonomism based on crude a-political (racial or cultural) ethnicity, with the now obvious horrors resulting.

The East European democratic idea basically envisions a society without a state. The anti-institutional curse that seems to plague us leaves us the choice of a barbarous dictatorship or boundless chaos. In order to prevent either from happening we should understand why all the conventional expectations are being left unfulfilled. Nobody dared to confess that liberal democracy is *not* government by the people, that economic decisions are *not* to be taken by plebiscite. Nobody dared to point out that in liberal democracies there is a conspicuous, loud, assertive political elite (the butt of satirists since Aristophanes), that democratic conformism will be the rule rather than the exception, and that not only are these new elites dazzlingly and deafeningly *obvious*, but also *common*.

The aristocratic/anarchistic contempt for the bourgeois, for rich and vulgar plebeians, for perspiring and shouting demagogues is more or less blunted in the West by force of long habit; but this contempt flared up with unprecedented vehemence in the East. Without respect for impersonal institutions and without esteem for the rulers, political coherence and law-abidingness is nearly impossible to achieve. If Western analysts want to understand the roots of the East European debacle, they should open the latest issue of *Private Eye*, *The Village Voice*, or *Le Canard Enchaîné*. All the sentiments are there, only they are rendered ineffectual in the West by constant repetition and the feeling that attacks on liberal capitalism are somehow part of the political system, and nobody wonders anymore why the regime is not defended at all.

Westerners think that their political system is universally attractive, but they will not offer arguments on its behalf. The Western political order is fundamentally mute. This silence was the dissenters' inspiration. Thus, the work that is cut out for their heirs is not very different from what awaits those faithful to liberal democracy in the West: the apologia for liberty still has to be found.

After only a few years, Eastern Europe has reached the last consequence of both modern liberalism and modern socialism: an overwhelming desire for the obliteration of the public realm. It is best described by Hannah Arendt in her *Human Condition* (1958):

> A complete victory of society will always produce some sort of "communistic fiction," whose outstanding political characteristic is that it is indeed ruled by an "invisible hand," namely by nobody. What we traditionally call state and government gives place here to pure administration – a state of affairs which Marx rightly predicted as the "withering away of the state," though he was wrong in assuming that only a revolution could bring it about, and even more wrong when he believed that this complete victory of society would mean the eventual emergence of the "realm of freedom."

The French Revolution ended a situation so ancient that it seemed eternal: the condition of citizenship as a distinction or privilege reserved mostly for gentlemen of leisure. Citizenship has become the universal condition of mankind, made possible by the liberal, but anti-democratic artifice of representative government. Citizenship, though universal, was diluted, and politics became a profession, even if a strange one. The East European revolutions opposed a political order where citizenship was declared to be universal but was in fact non-existent. The activist grandeur of Bolshevism equated citizenship with "being mobilized," and the *populus* was replaced by the fanatical *plebs*, the reinvented crowd. The dissident withdrawal from politics, the exodus from the City, the idea of civil society as "private" society (a seductive oxymoron) this all led to a cult of the "private" conceived as the exclusively personal. It is unprecedented.

Hannah Arendt writes later in *The Human Condition*:

> This enlargement of the private, the enhancement, as it were, of a whole people, does not make it public, does not constitute a public realm, but, on the contrary, means only that the public realm has almost completely receded, so that greatness has given way to charm everywhere; for while the public realm may be great, it

cannot be charming precisely because it is unable to harbor the irrelevant.

Dissident literature seemed "charming" in this sense; it had given up grandeur, heroism, magnanimity, a passion for civic felicity, all of which seemed compromised. The very idea of duty, let alone sacrifice was reminiscent of tyranny. Growing up in an artificial childhood forced upon us by tyrannical rulers meant a loss of faith, not the acquisition of a new (or for that matter, an old) one. I find it quite ironic that the most resounding literary success of the last few years in Eastern Europe was an auto-biographical novella of that conspicuously non-dissident Czech writer, Bohumil Hrabal, who tells us the story of how he became a half-hearted informer for the communist secret police in exchange for an exit visa. He just wanted to see Greece, he says. After all, we are all humanists. The courage and altruism of that obnoxious little posse called dissidents could only offer the long-suffering East European societies absolution. We were all part of the great web, weren't we?

The heroic times, thank God, are over; a new world begins, a world of creative disorder. We cannot describe it, since the public words capable of speaking of things that are not personal were exiled together with all of us when we left the City, all together.

Note

Source Reprinted by permission of the publisher from *Uncaptive Minds* 7:2 (Summer 1994): 19–34.

1 Since this article was written, the prime minister referred to, Jozsef Antall, who was leader of the Hungarian Democratic Forum, died of cancer.

9

OVERCOMING TOTALITARIANISM

Jacek Kuroń

Jacek Kuroń is one of the most influential democratic thinkers and activists in East and Central Europe. For more than two decades, his ideas played an immense role in the development of the Polish anticommunist opposition. After 1989, he served in important political positions and continued to offer insightful analyses of both the past and the present. This essay examines the collapse of communism in Poland and explains the rationale behind the democratic opposition's readiness to engage in the roundtable negotiations that led to the end of communist dictatorship in that country.

Kuroń emphasizes the importance of gradualism and rejects the calls for a cataclysmic rebellion against the old regime. This "evolutionist" strategy helped Solidarity come to power without resorting to violence and allowed for the smooth transition from communism to democracy. As Adam Michnik points out in his contribution to this volume, some among the revolutionaries found this engagement in a negotiated transition frustrating. What Kuroń demonstrates in this article is that the roundtable negotiation between the communist rulers and an autonomous political force opposed to the existing system was in itself a revolutionary event and implicitly a denial of totalitarianism.

* * *

Poland's historic June 1989 elections were an outgrowth of "roundtable" discussions between the opposition, united around Solidarity, and the authorities. The very fact that the authorities in a totalitarian communist country met and negotiated with an autonomous political force opposed to the existing system was of primary importance. It was a very unusual event, and in a way a denial of totalitarianism.

Totalitarianism is an attempt to command all social life. It is based on the exclusive control of the power center over the organization of all activities. This monopoly is so total that if citizens gather and discuss freely a matter as simple as roof repairs on a block of apartments, it becomes a challenge to the central authority. Accompanying this monopoly of organization is a monopoly of information, meaning that every printed word – not to mention the electronic media – is controlled by the central authority. And these monopolies in turn lead to a monopoly of decision-making by the central authority. Obviously, this totalitarian ideal cannot be fully implemented, but even the attempt to implement it destroys a nation's economic and political life.

The holding of negotiations between an organized opposition and the authorities, negotiations which were transmitted uncensored by television and relayed to every household, signaled that totalitarianism had been broken, inasmuch as all three of these monopolies were infringed. But, of course, the roundtable talks were by no means the first step toward undoing the totalitarian monopoly of power. The real breakthrough took place in 1980, when a massive wave of strikes led to the founding of Solidarity, an independent trade union that the central government was forced to recognize. This was truly the moment when the totalitarian system in Poland was broken.

At that time I wrote an essay entitled "What Next?" in which I compared the political situation in Poland with the movement of trains. A railroad schedule in which every tenth train was allowed to operate independently, governed by an accord between the conductor and the passengers, would either compel a change in the principle on which the whole railroad was based or lead to a series of catastrophes.

That was the situation in Poland in 1980–1981, when an independent mass movement encompassing over half the population was created *within* a totalitarian system. Since the *nomenklatura*, the apparatus of power, did not want to make the necessary structural changes, catastrophe was inevitable. It came on 13 December 1981 with the imposition of martial law. The tanks rolled into the streets. All laws were suspended. The population was terrorized and forced to submit to a military and police dictatorship.

One might conclude that if totalitarianism had been broken in Poland in 1980 by the emergence of a mass opposition movement, then the suppression of that movement by martial law would have restored totalitarianism. But I believe this conclusion would be wrong, for certain social processes are indeed irreversible.

The explosion that gave birth to Solidarity was a denial of totalitarianism, but martial law was also a denial of totalitarianism. Because a totalitarian system is based on the three monopolies of organization, information, and decision-making, the more perfect the system, the better camouflaged it is. It becomes nearly invisible. In Poland before 1980, there existed a parliament and a nominal multiparty system, and a number of newspapers were available. One could have the illusion that this was a normal parliamentary democracy.

JACEK KUROŃ

In August 1980 this illusion was undermined by the peaceful popular uprising. But whatever remained of the illusion was shattered by the authorities themselves when they declared martial law and made it clear that they would use naked force to suppress Polish society. The fact that in a totalitarian system every person, every member of society, is in some measure involved creates a certain social compact. We in the opposition denounced this compact in August 1980. But the authorities destroyed this compact in December 1981.

A dictatorship based solely on force was created. The authorities then had two options. One was to maintain this dictatorship of naked force – a dictatorship that even more quickly than ordinary totalitarianism destroys everything, including the economy. The second option was to withdraw from that form of dictatorship. Finally, after a number of futile attempts at different solutions, the authorities decided that it would be possible to reach an accord with the society by making an agreement with the opposition. As a result, the conditions were created for the roundtable negotiations, negotiations aimed at allowing the society to organize itself and initiating a gradual movement toward democracy.

In other words, the roundtable talks marked a certain stage in the continuing struggle of the Polish people for democracy. But it became possible to reach this stage only after the enormous social activity in the legal days of Solidarity and the widespread clandestine resistance during the years of martial law.

Recent Polish history has disproven the assumption that totalitarianism can be broken only from the outside, that there are no internal forces capable of overcoming a totalitarian system. By building independent organizations, society can erode totalitarianism from within.

But how can society organize itself under a totalitarian system? To answer this question, I must point out that this movement toward the self-organizing of Polish society did not suddenly begin in August 1980. We started many, many years before. Recalling those early years, in light of what has now been accomplished, I look back in astonishment. It was so simple then. What we wanted was to read books, to talk to one another freely, to collect money for people needing help: the simplest human actions. Yet one can organize society around these simple actions and goals, and this very fact is like a time bomb ticking away under totalitarianism.

There is one more point to be made about our strategy. Many of our friends, members of the opposition in Poland, asked us: Why did you go to the roundtable negotiations? Wouldn't it have been better to continue organizing people and to increase the potential for social explosion – a social explosion that would wipe out the totalitarian system?

Our answer was "No." We don't want to destroy the system by force. Several reasons for this can be given. The simplest is that totalitarianism is a system artificially created and artificially designed, and such a system

200

destroys all life around it. If you destroy this political system, you cannot reclaim a system from the past or import a system from abroad. You have to create a new system. But that new system would also be artificially constructed and would only bring back all the faults of the old system.

Therefore, the road to democracy has to be a process of gradual evolution, of gradual building of democratic institutions. It is a revolution in the sense that we are radically changing the system. We are going from totalitarianism to democracy. But if we are to have a truly democratic revolution, it must be achieved through a gradual process.

Note

Source Reprinted by permission of the publisher from *Journal of Democracy* 1:1 (Winter 1990): 72–4. Copyright © 1990 Johns Hopkins University Press.

Part III

FUTURE

10

THE FUTURE OF LIBERAL REVOLUTION

Bruce Ackerman

Political theorist Bruce Ackerman is among those who see the revolutions of 1989 as part of the global revival of liberal values at the end of the twentieth century. His approach extends the range of analysis beyond the boundaries of Eastern Europe and explores the collapse of authoritarianism in South Africa and Latin America. Thus, the victory of liberal principles in the former communist countries is part of a process that defines this late stage of modernity and redeems some of the long-forgotten non-Jacobin, emancipatory promises of the French Revolution. Enduring democratic achievements in the East will have a major impact on the successful construction of a pluralist united Europe. His vision of the 1989 upheaval is related to the approaches of Jeffrey C. Isaac and S. N. Eisenstadt in their essays in this volume in that he emphasizes the non-totalistic and non-utopian nature of these changes. What makes this contribution original is the insistence on 1989 as part of the global resurgence of liberal revolution as a world-historical possibility.

Like Poland's Adam Michnik, Ackerman is concerned with the transition from the first to the second stage of these revolutions. He argues that the rise of new elites and the postcommunist cultural tensions, including the apparent marginalization of the former dissidents, does not mean the defeat of these revolutions. History has not come to an end, he states in opposition to such prophets of the inexorable triumph of liberal democracy like Francis Fukuyama. Together with Jeffrey C. Isaac and Ken Jowitt, Ackerman anticipates a strong resistance to liberal values coming from clericalism and ethnic fundamentalism and warns against Western self-congratulatory illusions.

* * *

It is one thing to sit on the sidelines and point emphatically to the window of opportunity closing upon the revolutions of Eastern Europe, quite another to act decisively and gain democratic consent to a constitution that defines the terms of political life for a new era. It would be wrong, moreover, to exaggerate the significance of my constitutional concerns.

Even if my fears are realized, it would hardly be the first time in world history that a rising political movement has failed to exploit its opportunities to the fullest. It will be more than satisfactory if most Eastern Europeans – through leadership, luck, and popular support – manage to muddle their way toward liberal democracy, avoiding the worst excesses of xenophobic nationalism that might serve as a cover for new authoritarianisms.

If this much can be accomplished, the revolutions of 1989 will have enduring importance for all of us, however removed we may be from the scene of the action. By exploiting a moment of Communist weakness, the Eastern Europeans have not only destroyed a great system of oppression but given us reason to rethink the promise of revolution itself. In spite of the tragic consequences of revolutionary mobilizations since 1917, the century closes with a great affirmation: men and women *can* make a new beginning and build a better world – one that won't look anything like utopia but that still promises more diversity and freedom than the grim bureaucratic tyranny it has replaced.

What are the rest of us to make of this triumph, if such it turns out to be? I have already emphasized the importance of this question for Western Europe. After briefly returning to this point, I shall consider people, like myself, who stand on the sidelines in Africa or the Americas or the rest of the world. Because liberals in these places confront very different problems, the Eastern European success carries very different meanings – but do these meanings suggest the continuing relevance of the revolutionary project?

As we have seen, the central challenge for liberals in Western Europe does not involve the construction of a rights-oriented market economy. It is posed by the danger that a resurgent nationalism will wreck efforts at European federation begun by political and economic elites during the Cold War. Nonetheless, the example of the Eastern European revolutions may provide important resources in the coming struggle against the Western European state system. The Easterners' success in mobilizing themselves for constructive political change may soften the brittle fears of revolution generated by the terrors of the twentieth century. If these Easterners can redefine the basic terms of their political existence, why not Westerners as well?

The answer given in the West will, in turn, have a powerful impact on the East. If Westerners mobilize and give deeper political meaning to the European Community, this revolutionary dynamic will reinforce those in the East who are working for liberal constitutional solutions; if Westerners relapse into a retrograde nationalism, the impact in the East will be devastating. At the same time, the fate of the constitution-building project in the East will rebound onto the West. If liberal democracy fails in the East, the West will find itself reeling under the pressure of millions of asylum seekers trying to escape a new round of authoritarianism and impoverishment;

mass migrations, in turn, could inflame nationalist sentiment and tip the balance in the western struggle between liberal federalism and retrograde nationalism.

Both in the East and in the West, the Europeans' success or failure to capitalize on the revolutionary possibilities opened up in 1989 will shape the destiny of the entire planet for a very long time to come. This is the reason why I have added an American voice to the ongoing European debate. Neither the Atlantic nor the Pacific are big enough to insulate the rest of us from Europe's blunders and triumphs. We are all interested parties.

As the struggle over European identity proceeds apace, 1989 will also have an immediate, if subtler, impact on others' efforts to define their own political predicaments. Can we begin to glimpse how the reemergence of liberal revolution is reshaping the terms of political definition in the rest of the world?

Beyond Europe

My essay began by rejecting the idea of total revolution. This is a notion that can admit only of a theological interpretation, as when Christ entered history and, in the eyes of believers, radically transformed the very nature of Being in the World. Liberal revolutionaries reject such totalizing trans-formations. They deny that mere mortals can coherently attempt radical escapes from history. Every new beginning is partial, carrying along with it much of the cultural and practical baggage of the past.

The revolutionary project is not therefore pointless; people aren't gods, but they aren't brutes either. Although they cannot escape history, they are not fated to repeat endlessly the habitual patterns of the past. The fundamental, if partial, critique and reorganization of social life will continue to distinguish human beings, and provide them with a significant degree of control over the conditions of their existence.

Perhaps this is not saying much, but it is about all I can muster when asked to state the general significance of the reemergence of liberal revolution as a world-historical possibility. Because liberal revolutions are always partial and depend on the local background of received practices and ideals, the meat of the discussion will always be found in the details, which I cannot provide here. Nonetheless, a few glimpses around the world may serve to orient future inquiry.

At present, the most revolutionary situation is in South Africa, which confronts challenges very different from Europe's. There is little danger that the constitutional moment will go underappreciated. To the contrary: negotiation over a new constitution provides the crucial mechanism through which politically mobilized blacks and whites will try to work out the terms of their new beginning together.

207

Both Mandela and de Klerk have been remarkably skillful in channeling the hopes and fears of their constituents in liberal directions. The question is whether this effort at constitution building will continue or whether it will disintegrate into mass violence and blind acts of retribution for past wrongs. Within this context, the image of Eastern Europe plays a modest, but helpful, role. Most important, it will soften the hard-line Marxist element in the African National Congress. The collapse of Communism in Europe provides a chance to retreat gracefully from the tired Marxist doctrines that have impoverished so much of Africa. With Communism so obviously on the retreat worldwide, hard-liners cannot easily pretend that a bright socialist future awaits South Africa at the end of history. Perhaps the working class should instead push aggressively for its interests within the constitutional framework of a rights-protecting, market-oriented, private property system?

Black acceptance of a liberal political economy will be an incentive for whites to continue their present course of interracial accommodation. De Klerk has brilliantly mobilized his own constituency at a crucial referendum in support of constitutional compromise. After gaining a decisive victory at the polls, he is now in a strong position to respond affirmatively if Mandela can credibly commit his movement to a liberal democratic constitutional solution. Even if the liberal center holds, both sides will still have plenty of extremists to deal with. But think how much harder the task would have been if the worldwide Communist revolution had continued to inspire ANC activists and to haunt the future for so many whites.

For all its importance, South Africa is a variation on an old theme: a revolutionary movement challenges an entrenched European structure, using the symbols of nationalism and socialism to mobilize the colonial population against oppression. As we look around the world, it is hard to identify many other places in which this story is likely to repeat itself. Peru? Cambodia? the Philippines?

In contrast, a new scenario is recurring with increasing frequency and importance. I will call it the "second-generation" dynamic. It involves nations that have successfully engaged in colonial revolutions during the past century. Some of these revolutions were straightforward applications of the Bolshevik model. But many had much deeper roots in local culture; the revolutions in places as different as Mexico and India, Israel and Algeria were all mass mobilizations originally inspired by a mix of socialist and nationalist ideas. Many other movements failed to generate the same level of active popular support but were nevertheless culturally distinctive – Baathist Socialism in the Middle East, for example, as well as many African socialist movements during the first generation of independence.

All these revolutionary enterprises confront a similar problem. The generation that won the earlier victories is dead or dying; the old proud nationalist and socialist slogans now serve as a cover for a corrupt bureaucracy. The challenge for a new generation is to renew and redefine a political direction. In this context the European revolutions of 1989 have a shattering symbolic impact. Here is the emerging scenario: the European revolutions, together with the local failure of central planning, encourage political elites to recognize the need for fundamental change. To win a liberal breakthrough, however, will not only require the sensitive implementation of market oriented, rights-protecting, liberal programs of economic and social development. Reformers must also gain widespread popular support if they hope to defeat the entrenched bureaucratic and economic interests that were built up in the previous round of revolutionary development.

The most promising experiments in such liberal transformations have been in Latin America. Both Mexico and Argentina provide variations on a typical situation: leaders emerge to head political movements – the PRI in Mexico, the Peronistas in Argentina – that had previously won revolutionary triumphs on the basis of nationalist and socialist goals. Nonetheless, both Salinas in Mexico and Menem in Argentina are attempting broad-ranging liberal reforms that increasingly challenge their inherited symbols. Will they be able to mobilize a large section of their traditional working-class constituency, together with the middle classes, to support a decisive liberal breakthrough? Even if such "revolutions from above" fail, will insurgent leaders emerge to attempt liberal revolutions from below, as in Poland and Russia?

At the moment, the United States occupies one of the few zones untouched by the threat or promise of liberal revolution. Americans may welcome the new possibilities opened by world transformation but seem curiously untouched – as if they were unmoved movers or self-satisfied voyeurs?

Since the Enlightenment, America has served as the leading exemplar of liberal revolution. James Madison, Abraham Lincoln, Martin Luther King, Jr. – these people and many others gained political leadership at the head of citizen movements for self-conscious change. After a generation of sacrifice and debate, the movements won the mobilized assent of a majority of Americans to a new beginning in their relationships with one another. Many of these collective acts of renewal have pushed the polity in a liberal direction-toward the separation of church and state, toward the protection of free markets, and beyond formal equality toward social justice.

I am the last to deny how far America falls short. Along many dimensions, it fails to assure a level of social justice taken for granted in European social democracies. Nonetheless, the American success in mobilizing citizen energies for constructive change during both the New Deal and the civil rights eras played an important role in the twentieth-century struggle against Fascism and Bolshevism. While traumatized European liberals like

Hayek were proclaiming that the pursuit of social justice was paving the road to serfdom, American liberals could remain more skeptical about apocalyptic antirevolutionary appeals. Whatever their substantive limitations, the New Deal and the civil rights movement gave tangible demonstrations of a different possibility: that men and women might work together to make new beginnings in their collective pursuit of a more just and free society.

How, then, to greet the great news from Europe? It could – should – be a reminder of the American past and a challenge to take up the burden in our own time. Surely, hoping for success any time soon would be foolish. Americans are living in a period of "politics as usual." At no time since the 1920s have the established political parties generated so little interest among ordinary Americans. But at least two movements beyond the parties have real thrust: environmentalism and feminism have mobilized broad publics and elicited sustaining political interest. Neither of these movements, however, has put its first priority on joining forces with more established civil rights and labor groups to deal with the single most pressing crisis: the disgrace of the American ghetto. Without an enormous effort to educate the next generation of ghetto kids, Americans will be confronting a pathological level of alienation from the civic enterprise early in the next century. A civilized liberal democracy will not survive if Americans allow their major cities to become centers of a proliferating underclass without education or hope.

We did not need the Los Angeles riots [of 1992] to make this obvious. The question is whether Americans have the political will to do something serious about it. Liberal revolutions are hard work, requiring millions to set aside their private interests to concentrate on the task of political renewal. In each generation, there have always been some Americans willing to make this sacrifice. But can they mobilize the majority of their fellow citizens in support of social justice? Americans will be in real trouble if they remain on the sidelines much longer, leaving it to others to carry the torch of liberal revolution into the new century.

The end of history

The defeat of Communism hardly represents the end of history. It is best likened to the end of a civil war between two children of the European Enlightenment. Despite their struggle, both communists and liberals agreed on many things: the separation of church and state, the repudiation of traditional caste, gender, and racial hierarchies; the rejection of xenophobic nationalism; and the pursuit of social justice. The battle raged onward because the combatants rallied behind very different versions of these Enlightenment ideals; when taken together, all their differences added up to a radically different understanding of the nature of state authority and the character of human freedom.

The end of the civil war, however, has left the winning side in a traumatized condition. No longer can it fight a negative battle against the transparent evils of bureaucratic totalitarianism. It must engage in a positive struggle to realize its own ideals of freedom and equality, and it must build a political order that will inspire dedicated support from a diverse and critical citizenry.

This must be accomplished in the face of resistance by formidable opponents. Religious fundamentalists in much of the world reject liberalism's separation of church and state, its insistence upon each person's fundamental right to define his or her own heaven and hell. Neo-Confucian societies in Asia resist liberalism's challenge to traditional hierarchies, its celebration of the right to be different. Indigenous cultures in Africa and parts of Latin America may find Enlightenment values even more difficult to appreciate.

Given this world setting, it is a thousand years too soon to suggest, with Francis Fukuyama, that victory in the civil war with Communism leaves liberals no choice but to return to the paltry consumerist satisfactions of market society.[1] The truth is very different if we seize the moment, if we expand the range of functioning constitutional democracy beyond the liberal heartland, perhaps we can provide convincing evidence that liberalism *deserved* to win the struggle in 1989. In history at least, nothing succeeds like success. Liberals in Germany succeeded in constructing a functioning democracy in the aftermath of Nazism – an achievement that, as we have seen, today serves as a model for further acts of constitutional construction. If liberals succeed today in Poland or Russia or South Africa, their triumphs will suggest to others that liberal revolution is not a hollow hope but a live political possibility.

Further successes may, in turn, inspire others in the more remote future to look back upon 1989 as a historical watershed. It was then, they may say, that the promise of the French Revolution finally began to be redeemed after the horrible false starts and shattered hopes of the twentieth century. Perhaps they will even indulge in the luxury of explaining to their children why the triumph of liberalism was historically inevitable.

But we know otherwise. As likely as not, the world of 2020 will have a very different appearance. It will contain a Europe of hostile nation-states and an America impoverished by economic nationalism, racked by ethnic division and the alienation of hopeless slums. This self-proclaimed First World will look out upon a larger complex of competing xenophobias and bitter proletariats while it gasps for breath in an environment that all have mindlessly conspired to destroy.

The promise of 1989 will have vanished like a dream, and this essay will serve as a bitter reminder of liberal illusion.

BRUCE ACKERMAN

Note

Source Reprinted by permission of the publisher from Bruce Ackerman, *The Future of Liberal Revolution* (Newhaven, CT: Yale University Press, 1992), pp. 113–23. Copyright © 1992 Yale University Press.

1 See Francis Fukuyama, *The End of History and the Last Man* (New York: Free Press, 1992).

11

THE LENINIST LEGACY

Ken Jowitt

American political scientist Ken Jowitt is well known for his unorthodox, innovative approaches to communist and postcommunist societies. In this article he insists on the importance of the Leninist "inheritance" for understanding both Communism's collapse and the aftermath of Soviet-style regimes. Cultural and political traditions, memories, and habits are critical in the making of the new polities. There is no reason to celebrate the advent of an open society as the only possible outcome of the Leninist wreckage. Indeed, as Jowitt argues (in agreement with Daniel Chirot, Tony Judt and G. M. Tamás), the region's traditions are not primarily liberal. Fascism, socialism, and peasantism (not to speak of clericalism and corporatism) were major trends within Eastern Europe's inter-war political cultures, and the possibility of their comeback cannot be easily discarded. In the same vein, Leninist authoritarian collectivist political and mental patterns will continue to affect these societies, in spite of the strong anticommunist rhetoric of the new elites.

Jowitt's sobering contribution complements the analyses of the revolutions of 1989 proposed by Chirot, Eisenstadt, and Ackerman in that he expresses serious doubts regarding the prospects for a fast and relatively smooth development of liberal democratic governments in the region. In his view, the absence of ideologically-defined political attachments leads to endemic political fragmentation and favors authoritarian developments (what he calls "liberal authoritarianism"). His warnings regarding the risk of isolating Eastern Europe from the West should not be underestimated: a liberal "fortress Europe" excluding the East will leave the postcommunist countries hostage to dangerous experiments of ethnocentric, authoritarian populism.

* * *

Conceptual geography

Eastern Europe's boundaries – political, ideological, economic, and military – have been radically redefined twice in less than a century. At the end of World War I, "the disappearance of the Austro-Hungarian Empire

213

(a truly momentous event in European history) left a huge gap in the conceptual geography of the continent. Of what did Central Europe now consist? What was East, what West in a landmass whose political divisions had been utterly and unrecognizably remade within a single lifetime"?[1] In 1989, the Soviet bloc became extinct; communist parties in every Eastern European country added the loss of political power to their earlier loss of ideological purpose during the phase of "real socialism"; and the Soviet Union, the "stern . . . impersonal, perpetual Center"[2] of this imperium, not only tolerated but instigated its collapse. The result is a gap in Europe's "conceptual geography" no less significant than that of 1918.

In 1987, Dan Chirot and I pointed out that "because of its historical experience, the diversity of its cultural traditions, and its vulnerability to big power interference, Eastern Europe has had, and will continue to have, a uniquely creative role in producing ideas and experimental solutions for solving the major problems of the modern world. Not only a number of key artistic and literary movements, but also political ideologies such as fascism, socialism, and peasantism received major innovative contributions from Eastern and Central Europe in the first half of the twentieth century."[3] The mass extinction of Leninist regimes in Eastern Europe in 1989 is a dramatic, promising, and unsettling event, and its immediate consequence is a direct challenge to the boundaries and identities of the region and its constituent parts. Whether the transformation is looked at as an imperative, process, or outcome, Eastern Europe is in the midst of redefining its cultural frames of reference, political and economic institutions, and political–territorial boundaries. Once again, Eastern Europe has become a laboratory in which a set of experiments are being undertaken under less than controlled conditions. The likelihood is that most will fail, but some will succeed, and many of those will have predominantly anti-democratic capitalist features. Whatever the results of the current turmoil in Eastern Europe, one thing is clear: the new institutional patterns will be shaped by the "inheritance" and legacy of forty years of Leninist rule.

The "inheritance"

Confronted with a turbulent environment, there is a quite understandable, predictable, and observable tendency by intellectuals to restore certainty idiomatically. That certainly is the case with Eastern Europe. One of its most pronounced expressions is the fetishlike repetition of the phrase "transition to democracy," as if saying it often enough, and inviting enough Latin American scholars from the United States to enough conferences in Eastern Europe (and the Soviet Union), will magically guarantee a new democratic capitalist telos in place of the ethnic, economic, and territorial maelstrom that is the reality today. One is reminded of Mephisto's observation: "Men usually believe, if only they hear words,/That there must also be some sort of meaning."[4] From the "transition to democracy" perspective, Eastern Europe resembles a historical blackboard written on with Leninist chalk for forty years, erased (largely) by Soviet actions in 1989, and waiting, tabula rasa, to be written on now in liberal capitalist script.

However, any substantial analysis of democracy's and market capitalism's chances in Eastern Europe must interpret the maelstrom itself, and that means coming to analytical grips with the cultural, political, and economic "inheritance" of forty years of Leninist rule. For Western analysts to treat the Leninist legacy the way Leninists after 1948 treated their own Eastern European inheritance – namely, as a collection of historically outmoded "survivals" bound to lose their cultural, social, and psychological significance – would be an intellectual mistake of the first order. All cultural and institutional legacies shape their successors. Peter Brown's creation of an age – late antiquity – rests on his rejection of a simplistic dichotomy of continuity versus discontinuity; on his appreciation of novel, not absolute, transformations of the Roman legacy.[5]

Some historical legacies positively contribute to the development of successor states. Karl van Wolferen presents a powerful (to me, compelling) case to support his argument that Japan's current economic success is directly related "to the authoritarian institutions and techniques dating from the first half of the twentieth century."[6]

The Leninist legacy is currently shaping, and will continue to shape, developmental efforts and outcomes in Eastern Europe – though not in a "Japanese" manner. Regarding the Leninist legacy, Timothy Garton Ash says: "Perhaps the beginning of wisdom is to recognize that what communism has left behind is an extraordinary mish-mash."[7] The comment is perceptive, suggestive, and self-defeating. The Leninist legacy is conflicting, confusing, and, fortunately, identifiable. Otherwise we are left with two inadequate and unacceptable alternatives: the simplistic application/ imposition of (a very theoretically thin) "transition to democracy" literature to the Eastern European/Soviet setting, or acceptance, following the Mock Turtle, of current events in Eastern Europe as Modern Mystery (i.e., not History).[8]

Private versus public virtues

In a curious, unintended, and highly consequential way, Leninist rule reinforced many of the most salient features of traditional culture throughout Eastern Europe (the Soviet Union and elsewhere). "Through their organization and ethos [Leninist regimes] have stimulated a series of informal adaptive social responses (behavioral and attitudinal) that are in many respects consistent with and supportive of certain basic elements of the traditional political culture in these societies," I argued in 1974. "In turn, these elements are antithetical to the appearance of a regime and society with an ethos and structure predicated on a complementary relationship between the public and private realms, on the viability of impersonal rules and norms, and on the value of egalitarianism expressed in the role of effective participant." Today I would put it more succinctly, but no differently: the Leninist experience in Eastern Europe (and elsewhere) reinforced the exclusive distinction and dichotomic antagonism between the official and private realms.

For forty years, regardless of the quite substantial developmental changes in the Party's relation to its host societies, ruling Leninist parties persistently defined and asserted themselves as the superior and dominant alternative to the nation-state, as the exclusive autarchic locus of political leadership and membership. The political consequence was to reinforce the traditional stark gap between a privileged, domineering official realm and a private realm characterized by mutual suspicion, resembling Montesquieu's description of despotic society.[9] No politically integrating nationwide public realm existed in the greater part of Eastern Europe (or the Russian, then Soviet, Empire) before or during the period of Leninist rule. The Leninist experience intensely reinforced and added to the already negative image of the political realm and the insular quality of the private realm. This reality expressed itself in a number of ways during the period of Leninist rule, and it persists more than inertially throughout Eastern Europe today.

To begin with, the Party's political monopoly and punitive relation to the population produced a "ghetto" political culture in Eastern Europe. The population at large viewed the political realm as something dangerous, something to avoid. Political involvement meant trouble. Regime-coerced political activity (not participation) sustained and heightened the population's psychological and political estrangement. At the same time, the Party could not be everywhere. So Leninist parties traded de facto privatization in nonpriority areas for active Party control and penetration of priority areas. This became particularly true during the Brezhnev period, when private egoism – *personalism* not individualism[10] – became the major sociocultural reality. As I argued in 1974, *dissimulation* became the effective (and ethically as well as politically debilitating) bond between the domineering official and societal supplicant during the entire period of Leninist rule. For four decades, dissimulation became the central feature of the population's (misre)presentation of its public or, better, visible self. Dissimulation reflected the fear and avoidance responses of a subordinate population: the need to deflect the Party's attention from possible or real underfulfillment of tasks, and its unchecked penetration of one's private and social life. Dissimulation also provided the means for an estranged population regularly to interact with a powerful, entrenched, and illegitimate regime.

The absence of a *shared public identity* as citizens, a role that would equalize rulers and ruled, and allow for truthful discussion and debate, had a second consequence: the central place of rumor as covert political discourse. In the *Agricola*, Tacitus says rumor "is not always at fault: it may even prompt a selection."[11] Maybe in Rome; not in Eastern Europe (the Soviet Union, or China). There rumor had and continues to have a debilitating effect in political life. It divides, frightens, and angers those who participate in what amounts to a chronic mode of semihysterical (pre)political speech. To be sure, its impact is much greater in some countries than others. If Romania could export its rumors, it would be more developed than Germany. But the political-psychological impact exists in the entire region, and its substantive thrust is clear: it strengthens the insular, privatized quality of social life and obstructs public discussion of national issues. The neotraditional secrecy characteristic of a ruling Leninist party; its corresponding distrust of an ideologically "unreconstructed" population; the invidious juxtaposition of an elite in possession of the real, but secret, truth about the polity, economy, world affairs . . . ; and a population living in the "cave" of political jokes and rumor are legacies that continue to shape the character of "civil society" in Eastern Europe and the Soviet Union. Civil society is more than economic and legal sociology; it is political culture.

In yet another way, the organization and operation of Leninist rule contributed to the difficulty Eastern European populations experience now in their efforts to create frameworks that relate their private, social, and political identities in a complementary, not fragmentary, fashion. Leninist regimes in Eastern Europe, the Soviet Union, and Asia organized their societies around a series of semi-autarchic institutions, the *danwei* in China, and *kollektiv* in the Soviet Union and Eastern Europe. Unlike liberal capitalist democracies, Leninist regimes "parcel" rather than "divide" labor. In Leninist regimes, the factory was (is) less a specialized institution and school of modernity than a functionally diffuse neopatriarchal provider: of houses, vacations, medical attention, food, and to some extent social activity for its workers.[12] The net effect was a division of labor that in important respects resembled Durkheim's *mechanical* division of labor, a "ringworm" division of labor in which each institution attempted to replicate the self-sufficiency of all the others.[13] Again the consequence was to juxtapose the polity and society antagonistically, and to fragment society itself. One corporate autarchic political entity, *The* Party hierarchically dominated and connected a set of semi-autarchic socioeconomic entities whose only common bond was a distant, different, and dominant official realm – the Party, *Them*.

The same pattern was created by the Soviet Union in its relations with Eastern European regimes. Remember Gomułka's interpreter's observation: "The men in power in the Eastern bloc talk constantly of 'internationalism,' but . . . no friendly neighbour relationship of the type that has developed since the end of the war between the French and the Germans has ever linked the Poles with the Russians or the Czechs or even the people of the DDR. They have remained 'stranger[s] to each other.'"[14] In the bloc, the Soviet regime occupied the same strategically dominant position the Party occupied in each society. Regionally and nationally, the Eastern European polities were fragmented, not integrated: fragmented into mutually exclusive official and private realms bridged by mutually deceptive presentations of their respective "selves." In this respect, Leninist regimes fostered the generic features of all despotisms in which people are "far too much disposed to think exclusively of their own interests, to become self-seekers practicing a narrow individualism and caring nothing for the public good. Far from trying to counteract such tendencies, despotism encourages them, depriving the governed of any sense of solidarity and interdependence; of good-neighborly feeling and a desire to further the welfare of the community at large. It immures them, so to speak, each in his or her private life and, taking advantage of the tendency they already have to keep apart, it estranges them still more."[15]

The Party's charismatic modus operandi also shaped the actions and dis-positions of Eastern Europe's populations. Leninist parties in this (and every) region were overwhelmingly concerned with targets and outcomes, with ends, not means; and they acted in a storming-heroic manner to achieve them. During the Brezhnev period, when they had exhausted their heroic-storming resources, capacity, and even inclination, they sub-stituted a corrupt set of personal patron–client relations to achieve their substantive ends. What no Leninist regime ever did was create *a culture of impersonal measured action*. The result is an Eastern European (Soviet, Chinese) population most of whose members have very little experience with regular, deliberate economic and political activity in a context of impersonal procedures; a population that in its authoritarian peasant and Leninist personas is more familiar with sharp disjunctions between periods of intense action and passivity than with what Weber termed the "methodical rational acquisition" (of goods or votes); a population that in its majority would find the tenor and operation of Ben Franklin's Protestant liberal capitalist way of life boring, demeaning, and, in good part, unintelligible.[16]

Ironically, even the remarkable discovery, articulation, and public expres-sion of human dignity and public ethics by exemplary political figures like Adam Michnik and Václav Havel, and civic movements like Solidarity and Civic Forum partially reinforce the antagonistic juxtaposition of a suspect political world and one of private virtue and ethics. In 1989, in Eastern Europe, one saw the charismatic efflorescence of public ethics: demands for and expressions of individual dignity as the "base," not the superstructure, of political life. In 1989, in Eastern Europe, ethics moved from the purely personal realm to the public realm; not in the form of an intrusive private standard for public performance (as in the United States today), but as an autonomous political criterion for public action, one that judges leadership in terms of its impact on and contribution to human dignity.

However, liberal democratic polities do not rest primarily, for that matter cannot rest primarily, on the charismatic permanence of politically ethical leadership or the private ethics of its citizens. They rest on "public virtues." Dahrendorf rightly emphasizes that in a society where "private" virtue is exalted, "the human personality, becomes a creature without a public life, and the formation of the nation is left behind. Many may well be quite content with this state of affairs. Their greatest happiness is found in private life, in the heights and depths of friendship, and familial harmony, in the satisfaction of imprecise reveries, perhaps even in the nearly metasocial bonds with others in unstructured collectivities."[17] Now listen to the Russian poet Andrei Voznesensky: "In Russia, I think we have... spiritual life. We can talk all day and all night long about all kinds of questions, immortal questions. That is the Russian style of thinking. I want our economy to be the same as in the West...But I am afraid to lose this Russian part of our soul."[18] Voznesensky's reflection, and for that matter the entire thrust of Hedrick Smith's description of Russian popular culture, speaks to the predominance of private over public virtues in the Russian population; and no great damage is done in generalizing his observations to the majority of people in practically every Eastern European nation.

Eastern Europe's pre-Leninist peasant culture and oligarchical authoritarian elites (at times cosmetically outfitted with Western political facades), the neotraditional features of Stalinist and Brezhnevite rule,[19] *and* the ethical charisma of 1989, for all their qualitative difference, combine to provide a remarkably consistent and continuous support for a worldview in which political life is suspect, distasteful, and possibly dangerous; to be kept at bay by dissimulation, made tolerable by private intimacy, and transcended by private virtues or charismatic ethics. To return to Dahrendorf: the "inner-direction of those oriented to private virtues is incomplete. *It is inner-direction without its liberal element, the carrying over of interest to the market of politics and the economy.*"[20] To put it bluntly: the Leninist legacy, understood as the impact of Party organization, practice, and ethos, *and* the initial charismatic ethical opposition to it favor an authoritarian, not a liberal democratic capitalist, way of life; the obstacles to which are not simply how to privatize and marketize the economy, or organize an electoral campaign, but rather how to institutionalize public virtues. Eastern European elites and social audiences have inherited what is for the most part a suspicious culture of mutual envy fostered by a corrupt neotraditional Leninist despotism that in good measure unintentionally reinforced a set of "limited-good" peasant cultures. The charismatically ethical antithesis provoked by "real socialism's" indignities – Solidarity being the paradigmatic instance – is by its very nature an unstable, inadequate base for a tolerant polity based on the complementarity of ethics and interests. Weber's observations are quite apt in examining the current fate of Solidarity in Poland and Civic Forum in Czechoslovakia: "When the tide that lifted a charismatically led group out of everyday life flows back into the channels of workaday routines, at least the 'pure' form of charismatic domination will wane and turn into an 'institution'; it is then either mechanized, as it were, or imperceptibly displaced by other structures, or fused with them in the most diverse forms, so that it becomes a mere component of a concrete historical structure. In this case it is often transformed beyond recognition, and identifiable only on an analytical level."[21]

The fragmentation of Eastern Europe

A good place to begin specifying the type of developments likely to occur in Eastern Europe is with a look at a special flag. The most vivid symbol of the Romanian uprising in December 1989 was the sight of the Romanian flag with its Leninist center ripped out. Eastern Europe in 1990 and 1991 is like the Romanian flag: its Leninist center has been removed, but a good deal of its institutional and cultural inheritance is still in place. In all of Eastern Europe, the Leninist extinction was as much a case of regime collapse as regime defeat, nicely captured by Garton Ash's term "refolution."[22]

And what one now sees taking place in Eastern Europe is more the breakup of existing identifies and boundaries than a breakthrough to new ones. Before the latter happens, political conflict in Eastern Europe will have to get beyond the "many are called" to the "few are chosen" stage, to a point where the antagonists are politically organized, not simply viscerally identified. Currently, the cleavages in Eastern Europe are neither crosscutting nor superimposed. They are diffuse, poorly articulated, psychological as much as political, and, because of that, remarkably intense. One reason for the diffuse manifestation of sociopolitical cleavages is the absence of established successor elites in these countries.[23] With the exception of Solidarity, prior to 1989, most opposition elites in Eastern Europe had minimal insulation from the intrusive punitive presence of their Leninist adversaries, minimal familiarity with one another and "politics as a vocation," and minimal success in bonding with a politically loyal social constituency. Only in Poland, over almost two decades, did a counterelite enjoy a Yenan-like protective/interactive experience; one that produced a contentious, but mutually tolerant and intelligible, elite that cohered, and even in its current divided and divisive state offers Poland something more important than either marketization or civil society: an "established" leadership. An "established elite" is one that recognizes

the legitimate places of all of its members in the polity despite genuine and
deeply felt party, policy, and ideological differences; has worked out civil
and practical modes of interaction; and can identify and organize a sociopolitical constituency in a regular manner. Excepting Poland, no Eastern
European country has an established (democratic or undemocratic) elite.
That means they are fragile polities – highly fragile democratic politics.

We can begin with Hungary. According to Elemer Hankiss, among the
new democratic forces "there is a certain confusion... they are rent by
inner divisions; they have not yet built up their national networks and con-
stituencies... they have not yet found their identities and their places in the
political spectrum. They have not drawn up their detailed programs and
have not clearly outlined the sociopolitical model they want to establish
in this country."[24] In Czechoslovakia, the ethnic splits between Slovak
and Czech leaders, the dramatic political entry of a religious authoritarian,
the Pope, in Slovakia (in April 1990) where one million (out of five million)
Slovaks greeted him, and the recent selection of Václav Klaus – a man
with little political connection to or affinity with the charismatically ethical
Havel – as finance minister, pointedly underscores the absence of an established elite. The political flux of Civic Forum's disorganized partisan con-
stituencies completes the picture of an attenuated, diffuse political
"constitution" in what many consider one of the most promising candidates for "transition to democracy."

In Romania the governing elite does form an established elite. However,
opposition elites (e.g., the Liberal Party, Peasant Party, Group for Social
Dialogue, and Civic Alliance leaders in Romania) fundamentally reject
the legitimacy of the incumbents. In Romania (and Bulgaria), one has
Dutch-like sociopolitical "pillars" without a reconciling consociational
political elite.[25] If that were not enough, there is evidence of serious
fragmentation within the governing parties themselves in Bulgaria and
Romania. The absence of democratic or undemocratic *established successor
elites* in Eastern Europe favors and furthers the maelstrom quality of life
throughout the area.

The difficulty in creating a democratic established political elite with a
tolerant culture is exacerbated by the "refolutionary" change that occurred
in 1989. Leninist personnel still play a prominent role in administrative,
economic (and, in the Balkans, political) life. In Eastern Europe, one sees
a novel evolutionary phenomenon: *survival of the first*, not simply the
fittest.[26] Former party cadres are exceptionally well placed to successfully
adapt themselves – and their families – to changes in the economic and
administrative order. Evidence of this adaptive ability abounds in Poland,
Hungary, and elsewhere in Eastern Europe.[27] Add to this the sizable portion of the population in Eastern Europe who in some significant way
collaborated with the Party and you have the recipe for a nasty social
climate, a climate of sustained, if so far largely contained, psychological

bitterness, in some quarters rage – a bitterness that expresses the *emotional fragmentation* of populations who can't find an acceptable political solution to the issues of Leninist survivors and collaborators.[28] Fragmentation is the dominant Eastern European reality.

Daniel Bell's observation that "most societies have become more self-consciously plural societies (defined in ethnic terms)"[29] certainly applies to Eastern Europe today. The case of Yugoslavia is compelling. On balance, there is more reason to think that Yugoslavia will not exist as a sovereign entity in five years than that it will. Civil war is a probability in good part because ethnic hate is a reality. The mutual hatred of Serbians and Albanians in Koscovo, between Slobodan Milosevic's Serbia and Franjo Tudjman's Croatia (and, for that matter between Serbs and Croats in Croatia), when combined with economic issues and the effective demise of the League of Yugoslav Communists favors civil war more than civic culture. The same might be said of the Soviet Union, where in one "Eastern European" republic, Moldavia, the political elite are "flirting" with Romania, while trying to suppress a secession movement by the Gagauz Turkic minority in the southern part of the republic and the efforts by its Russian population around Tiraspol to maintain Moldavia's ties with the Soviet Union. But the problem of *ethnic and territorial fragmentation* exists also in the northern tier of Eastern Europe – in Czechoslovakia where many Slovaks are demanding that Slovak be the official language in Slovakia, something quite unacceptable to the hundreds of thousands of Hungarians living there. The Slovak National Party demands full independence for Slovakia, and the rowdy reception given President Havel during his visit there in March 1991 is further evidence of the hostility felt by the active Slovak minority who favor independence.[30] Finally, should anyone need reminding, the territorial issues between Yugoslavia and Albania, Romania and Hungary, and Poland and its eastern neighbor are latent, not extinct. Today Eastern Europe is a *brittle* region. Suspicion, division, and fragmentation predominate, not coalition and integration. Sooner rather than later, attitudes, programs, and forces will appear demanding and promising unity.

In response to enduring economic disorder, popular desperation will – and already has – led to large-scale emigration that includes many of the youngest, most skilled, and most talented of the population. According to the *New York Times*, 1.2 million people left "what used to be the Soviet Bloc" in 1989. Seven hundred thousand were East German. Serge Schmemann quite correctly emphasizes that "nobody can predict . . . how the growing hardships in the East, and especially in Romania, Bulgaria, and Yugoslavia, will develop. What is known is that all economists agree that things in Eastern Europe will become far worse before they become better."[31] Like ethnic separatism and antagonism, emigration fragments a nation and will generate nationalist calls to end *demographic fragmentation*.

Unstable governance by recently formed ruling parties and coalitions – *political fragmentation* – also favors authoritarian developments. Poland, "tired but exhilarated after 14 months of a Solidarity Government, is bracing for a presidential election campaign that threatens to divide the nation and jeopardize economic and political change." The bitter conflict between Lech Walesa, Stanislaw Tyminski, and Tadeusz Mazowiecki took place in a country where "the standard of living has dropped 35 percent, unemployment is expected to climb to 1.5 million by year's end and there is a recession in industrial production."[32] In Hungary, "the ruling center-right coalition, in power for less than six months, took a beating in local elections.... The most severe blow was felt in Budapest, where opposition parties won 20 of the city's 22 electoral districts.... With inflation creeping past 30 percent, unemployment on the rise *and the political debate again mired in a barrage of accusations*, the mood in Hungary is grim."[33]

Past, present, future

I have presented a "catholic" not "protestant" argument regarding Eastern Europe's Leninist legacy and current fragmentation(s). I have obviously, if not explicitly, argued that the historical differences between countries and their current modes of transition from Leninism are not as important as the similarities. Poland is the one genuine exception, because of its "failure" to carry out a Stalinist anti-peasant and anti-Church revolution; the historically momentous emergence of a counterpolity, Solidarity; and its current ability to entertain passionate intra-elite conflict *and* sustained governmental action with social support. However, all but one of the other Eastern Europe regime "transitions" were instances of rapid and peaceful "decolonization" and consequently face the same problems as "Third World" successor elites, who transited to independence rapidly and for the most part peacefully: a very undeveloped capacity to cohere and govern after taking power.[34]

Now for the necessary genuflection to national differences: they exist. It is clear that different types of fragmentation will predominate in different countries, and that some will have lower thresholds of violence. But it should be equally clear that today the *dominant and shared* Eastern European reality is severe and multiple fragmentation.

Allow me to continue with my "catholic heresy" and suggest that in this setting it will be demogogues, priests, and colonels more than democrats and capitalists who will shape Eastern Europe's general institutional identity. Most of the Eastern Europe of the future is likely to resemble the Latin America of the recent past more than the Western Europe of the present. Irony of ironies, it may be earlier writings by American academics on the "breakdown of democracy" in Latin America rather than the recent literature on "transition to democracy" that speak most directly to the situation in Eastern Europe.[35]

Eastern European fragmentation offers a firmer foundation for transiting to some form of authoritarian oligarchy (in response to perceptions of anarchy) than to democracy. One likely area-wide response to fragmentation will be a growing political role for the Catholic Church. The pope and national churches are major actors, not only in Poland, where Walesa and his "Center," as well as the Peasant Party, offer firm political support, but in Hungary, Slovakia, Croatia, and Slovenia. The Church offers a hierarchically ordered community quite proximate in organization *and ethos* to the patriarchal peasant and neotraditional Leninist Eastern European experience prior to 1989; an international presence, something Eastern European populations and elites need now that their claim on Western European and American democrats and capitalists is losing some of its initial attractiveness; and a legitimating myth for authoritarian political rule in conjunction with a nationally unifying military. I should emphasize that, just as the Latin American case might be relevant after all to Eastern Europe – in its breakdown of, rather than transition to, democracy experience, in its Peronist more than its Alfonsin/Menem incarnation[36] – so the Spanish case might prove to be equally relevant – in its Franco even more than its Gonzalez stage of development.

One must be prepared to see Eastern European armies and their leaders become more self-aware, confident, and assertive as the maelstrom develops. The military will offer and receive support *if*, as is likely, these economies continue to deteriorate; *if*, as is likely, a clear pattern of "hustler" rather than market capitalism produces an ostentatiously wealthy consuming elite in societies that resent disparities in wealth and remain perplexed as to how one succeeds independently of a benevolent state – precisely the underpinnings of Peronism;[37] *if*, as is likely, Western Europe fails to provide a massive "democratic subsidy"; and *if*, as is likely, frontier and border issues become salient in a context of civil violence, even war, in Yugoslavia and/or in the Soviet Union. Already, the Romanian army provides whatever glue exists in holding that country together. The same is true of Yugoslavia. And, recently, in Bulgaria, a "regional judge in Haskovo registered the Bulgarian Legion 'Georgi Stoikov Rakovski' as an official organization. The group ... was founded to promote professionalism in the army and to campaign for soldiers' rights."[38]

However, in contrast to the shared quality of the Leninist legacy and fragmentation of Eastern Europe's successor regimes, the impact of the military and Church may vary decisively from country to country. Here we must be more "protestant." To begin with, even those countries with a pre-World War II history of political activity by the army, like Serbia, Bulgaria, Romania, and Poland, have now had regimes for close to half a century that have subordinated the army politically and denied it both a distinctive national mission and institutional elan. Second, at the moment neither the Czechoslovak nor the Hungarian army appears to have any significant place in the polity. As for the Catholic Church, it is not strong in the Czech lands or the Balkans.

The reality appears, then, to be decisively "protestant," diverse. However, if one adds a factor I have not yet touched on, the economic, the situation and interpretation of the area-wide role of armies and Church might change substantially. Currently, there is a debate in and outside Eastern Europe as to what type of government is best suited to deal with Eastern Europe's economic emergency.

"The immediate question . . . is: What variant of democratic politics can, on the one hand, provide sufficiently strong stable, consistent government to sustain the necessary rigors of fiscal, monetary, and economic policy over a period of several years, while, on the other hand, being sufficiently flexible and responsive to absorb the larger part of the inevitable popular discontents through parliamentary, or at least, legal channels, thus preventing the resort to . . . ultimately extraparliamentary means[?]" writes Timothy Garton Ash. He agrees with Al Stepan – one of the leading figures in the "transition to democracy" school – that "an unambiguously parliamentary system has a better chance of striking the necessary balance [between economic development and demographic participation] than a presidential one." I don't. The choices are not presidential authoritarianism, with the president either becoming a "weak president, because he bows to the majority, or a strong but antidemocratic one, because he does not," or Ash's "strong freely elected coalitions."[39] (In fact, given the current maelstrom of ethnic, economic, ecological, and political emergencies, any expectation of "strong freely elected coalitions" might be called utopian liberalism.) A third "option" exists – liberal authoritarianism.

In Eastern Europe, the immediate political imperative is economic. Any successful response to this imperative is likely to have an authoritarian cast. Take a "good" case for democratic capitalism, Czechoslovakia, a country that dismissed its communist defense minister, General Vacek, and where the Church is a political force only in the Slovak area. The economic emergency has led to Václav Klaus's dramatic political emergence. Klaus has a daunting charge, with traumatic implications, comparable to what was attempted in England when the Speenhamland public welfare system was abolished by the Poor Law of 1834.[40] And he must act on this charge without the advantage of (m)any shared substantive agreements or stylistic affinities within the Czechoslovak governing elite(s) or any well-delineated sociopolitical constituency to offer regular partisan support for his program!

What is likely to happen? Klaus's economic reforms will fail. What would it take to succeed? A Giovanni Giolitti, not a Havel, as president;[41] a Giolitti with a *dominant* parliamentary faction able to draw on a strategically placed and privileged voting constituency, with tacit but evident support from the Czechoslovak military and Catholic Church. In short, it will take the type of liberal authoritarianism that existed in nineteenth-century *Western* Europe. Both unambiguously freely elected parliamentary coalitions and presidents who rely primarily or exclusively on the military and the Church will be overwhelmed by emergency environments. I suggest that a form of liberal authoritarianism like the bourgeois regimes of nineteenth-century Western Europe[42] is a desirable alternative to the religio-ethnic, militant nationalist, even fascist regimes that might emerge from the maelstrom; and a more practical response than the utopian wish for immediate mass democracy in Eastern Europe.

The economic emergency in Eastern Europe is a social emergency, and the political responses to it are likely to draw on institutions, elites, policies, and orientations that in varying, but also shared, ways define themselves in terms of hierarchy and solidary and exclusionary practices – like the military and Church. The issue is not their participation, but on what terms!

The "Twain" had better meet

The Leninist legacy in Eastern Europe consists largely – not exclusively – of fragmented, mutually suspicious, societies with little religio-cultural support for tolerant and individually self-reliant behavior; and of a fragmented region made up of countries that view each other with animosity. The way Leninists ruled and the way Leninism collapsed contributed to this inheritance. However, the emergence and composition of movements like Civic Forum in the Czech lands, Public against Violence in Slovakia, the Alliance of Free Democrats in Hungary, the Union of Democratic Forces in Bulgaria, and the Civic Alliance in Romania bear witness to the reality of a modern citizenry in Eastern Europe. But it is one that must compete with anti-civic, anti-secular, anti-individual forces outside and inside itself. With the possible exception of Poland, no Eastern European country has a predominantly civic established elite and constituency. Question: Is there any point of leverage, critical mass of civic effort – political, cultural, and economic – that can add its weight to civic forces in Eastern Europe and check the increasing frustration, depression, fragmentation, and anger that will lead to country- and regionwide violence of a communal type in Eastern Europe? Yes! Western Europe.

The necessary, though not necessarily forthcoming, Western European response to the syndrome of Eastern European fragmentation(s) is *adoption*: of Eastern Europe by Western Europe. The fragmentation of Eastern Europe and the Soviet Union (where recently a district of Moscow attempted to claim sovereignty over the Bolshoi Ballet) is not a neutral, peripheral, self-contained event. It is already affecting political identities and relations in and between the Western and "Third" worlds. The disintegration of the former Leninist world and the ongoing fragmentation of its successor regimes can either be the stimulus for a parallel ethnic/civic confrontation in Western Europe (and the United States), or a stimulus for the West to attempt in Eastern Europe and parts of the Soviet Union what West Germany is attempting in East Germany: adoption.

This would require enormous imagination, coordination, and intrusion on Western Europe's (and, in a significant way, the United States's) part: a massive economic presence, provision for major population shifts on the European continent, and intracontinental party cooperation and action; all of which would substantially affect the current definition and operation of national sovereignty. One alternative is for Western Europe to become liberal fortress Europe and deny its "brother's keeper" responsibility. In that case, developments in Eastern Europe will degenerate in a frightening fashion.

Notes

Source Reprinted by permission of the publisher from Ken Jowitt, New World Disorder: The Leninist Extinction (Berkeley, CA: University of California Press, 1992), pp. 284–305. Copyright © 1992 The Regents of the University of California.

1 Tony Judt, "The Rediscovery of Central Europe," Daedalus 119:1 (Winter 1990): 25.
2 John Le Carré, The Spy Who Came In from the Cold (New York: Dell, 1963), p. 144.
3 Daniel Chirot and Ken Jowitt, "Beginning E.E.P.S.," Eastern European Politics and Societies 1:1 (Winter 1987): 2.
4 Goethe's FAUST (Garden City, NY: Doubleday, Anchor Books, 1963), p. 253.
5 See Peter Brown, The Making of Late Antiquity (Cambridge, MA: Harvard University Press, 1978).
6 Karl van Wolferen, The Enigma of Japanese Power (New York: Random House, Vintage Books, 1990), Chapter 14.
7 Timothy Garton Ash, "Eastern Europe: Après le Déluge, Nous," New York Review of Books 37:13 (August 16, 1990): 52.
8 Lewis Carroll, Alice's Adventures in Wonderland (London: Collins, 1973), p. 105.
9 I thank Veljko Vujacić for suggesting Montesquieu's observations to me. See The Spirit of the Laws (New York: Hafner Publishing, 1949), pp. 20–115.
10 I distinguish individualism and personalism in the following manner: individualism is ego restrained both by impersonal norms and an internal discipline of deferred gratification. Personalism is ego unrestrained by anything except external obstacle or internal disability.
11 Tacitus, The Agricola (Harmondsworth: Penguin Books, 1970), p. 59.
12 Alex Inkeles and David Smith, Becoming Modern (Cambridge, MA: Harvard University Press, 1974). On China, see Andrew G. Walder, Communist Neo-Traditionalism (Berkeley, CA: University of California Press, 1986), Chapter 2. Soviet and Eastern European factories are not the "total institution" the Chinese factory appears to be, but are more similar than dissimilar.
13 Emile Durkheim, The Division of Labor (Toronto: Free Press Paperback, 1964), Chapters 2 and 3.

14 E. Weit, *At the Red Summit* (New York: Macmillan, 1973), pp. 190–1.
15 Alexis de Tocqueville, *The Old Regime and the French Revolution* (Garden City, NY: Doubleday, Anchor Books, 1955), p. xiii. This book has a certain relevance to those interested in "transitions to democracy."
16 It is not enough to point out that most citizens in liberal capitalist democracies (certainly in the United States) themselves fail to vote and are poorly informed about issues and basic premises of democracy. The institutional framework, the practice and habits of elites, and the sociocultural constitutions in these countries assign critically different meanings to events in Western democracies and Eastern European countries.
17 Ralf Dahrendorf, *Society and Democracy in Germany* (Garden City, NY: Doubleday, Anchor Books, 1969), p. 293.
18 Hedrick Smith, "The Russian Character," *New York Times Magazine*, October 28, 1990, p. 30. Practically every observation Smith makes about Russian culture in 1990 is analyzed in my 1974 article on political culture.
19 On the Stalinist period, see Vera S. Dunham's *In Stalin's Time* (New York: Cambridge University Press, 1979); on the Brezhnev period, see Chapter 4, in Jowitt, *New World Disorder*.
20 Dahrendorf, *Society and Democracy in Germany*, p. 291; my emphasis. When Dahrendorf contrasts public and private virtues, in effect he identifies the difference between political and apolitical cultures. In analyzing the "transition" from Leninist rule, it should be kept in mind that it is easier to change political organization and behavior than to create a culture (elite or mass) that sees politics as a worthy (not distasteful) arena of bargaining, compromise, and principled and public individual action. Without such a culture, rooted in the material and ideal interests of strategic social strata, democratic life is fragile.
21 Max Weber, *Economy and Society*, ed. Guenther Roth and Claus Wittich (New York: Bedminster Press, 1968), 3:1120–1.
22 Timothy Garton Ash, "Refolution: The Springtime of The Nations," *New York Review of Books*, July 15, 1989.
23 See Ralf Dahrendorf's contrast of "established" and "abstract" elites in *Society and Democracy in Germany*. Dahrendorf emphasizes the shared socialization of established elites and how this contributes to tacit cooperation.
24 See Elemer Hankiss, "In Search of a Paradigm," *Daedalus* 119:1 (Winter 1990): 183–215.
25 On Holland, see Arend Lijphart, *The Politics of Accommodation: Pluralism and Democracy in the Netherlands* (Berkeley, CA: University of California Press, 1968).
26 My colleague in physics, Richard Muller, uses the phrase "survival of the first" in his discussion of evolutionary change in *Nemesis* (London: Heinemann, 1989), p. 14.
27 Bill Keller, "In Urals City: the Communist Apparatus Ends but Not the Communist Power," *New York Times*, December 13, 1990, illustrates very nicely how Party cadres take advantage of their positions to adapt to new environments. "In Sverdlovsk...the party is shoring up its positions by pumping its wealth into commercial joint ventures, small businesses and trading organizations," Keller points out. "The party owns the best hotel...has the best computers and printing services, and its 22-story office tower dominates the skyline."
28 If one takes Czechoslovakia, it has been estimated that some five of the fifteen million inhabitants have had some relation to the former Communist Party. So if one adds survivors and collaborators, one out of three Czechoslovaks are suspect to the remaining two. See Serge Schmemann, "For Eastern Europe

Now, a New Disillusion," *New York Times*, November 9, 1990; Burton Bollag, "In Czechoslovakia, Hunt for Villains," ibid., February 3, 1991; and Stephen Kinzer, "German Custodian of Stasi Files Insists on Justice," ibid., January 20, 1991.
29 Daniel Bell, *The Winding Passage* (New York: Basic Books, 1980), p. 224.
30 See Vladimir V. Kusin, "Czechs and Slovaks: The Road to the Current Debate," *Report on Eastern Europe* 1:40 (October 5, 1990): 4–14.
31 Serge Schmemann, "East Europe's Emigres Stall Just Short of West," *New York Times*, November 1, 1990.
32 John Tagliabue, "Poland's Elections Threaten to Jeopardize Change," *New York Times*, September 23, 1990.
33 Celestine Bohlen, "Hungarian Coalition Is Badly Beaten at Polls," *New York Times*, October 6, 1990; my emphasis.
34 In the "Third World," guerrilla counterelites who fought (the longer the better) against the colonizer constituted themselves as more cohesive successor elites. In this respect, Poland's Solidarity is more like the Algerian FLN, KANU in Kenya, and the Indian Congress Party than the "Ghanaian" rest of Eastern Europe. In Romania, where there was violence, it did not last long enough and was too anomic to generate a counterelite, let alone a cohesive one.
35 See Juan Linz and Alfred Stepan, eds., *The Breakdown of Democratic Regimes* (Baltimore, MD: Johns Hopkins University Press, 1978); and Guillermo O'Donnell, Philippe Schmitter and Laurence Whiehead, eds., *Transitions from Authoritarian Rule* (Baltimore, MD: Johns Hopkins University Press, 1986).
36 I find K. H. Silvert's "The Cost of Anti-Nationalism: Argentina," in Silvert, ed., *Expectant Peoples: Nationalism and Development* (New York: Random House, 1963), pp. 345–73, the most insightful analysis of Argentina's remarkable sixty-year failure to combine political modernity (i.e., civic nationalism) with an industrial economy.
37 In explaining Peronism, Naipaul quotes Eva Peron: "The strange thing is that the existence of the poor did not cause me as much pain as the knowledge that at the same time there were people who were rich"; and goes on himself to note that "that pain about the rich – the pain about other people remained the basis of the popular appeal of Peronism. That was the simple passion – rather than 'nationalism' or Peron's 'third position' – that set Argentina alight." (V. S. Naipaul, *The Return of Eva Peron* [New York: Vintage Books, 1981], pp. 176–7).
38 See Duncan M. Perry, "A New Military Lobby," *Report on Eastern Europe* 1:40 (October 5, 1990): 1–4.
39 Garton Ash, "Eastern Europe," pp. 54–5.
40 All of Eastern Europe (and the Soviety Union) are in a "Speenhamland" situation. (On the Speenhamland system in nineteenth-century England, see Karl Polanyi, *The Great Transformation: The Political and Economic Origins of Our Time* [Boston, MA: Beacon Press, 1965], esp. pp. 77–102, which emphasizes the social trauma associated with the introduction of a capitalist self-regulating market system.) In connection with Klaus and his reforms, see Henry Kamm, "Prague Reformers Reject Havel Bid," and Stephen Engelberg, "Czech Conversion to a Free Market Brings the Expected Pain and More" and "With No Controls and Little Competition, Prices Soar in Czechoslovakia," *New York Times*, October 16, 1990, January 4 and 30, 1991.
41 On Giolitti, see Richard Webster, *Industrial Imperialism in Italy, 1908–1915* (Berkeley, CA: University of California Press, 1975), in particular the Prologue and notes on pp. 346–7.

42 In this connection, see Theodore S. Hamerow, *The Birth of a New Europe: State and Society in the Nineteenth Century* (Chapel Hill, NC: University of North Carolina Press, 1983), Part 3; and Eric Hobsbawm, *The Age of Empire, 1875–1914* (New York: Pantheon Books, 1987).

12

THE POST-TOTALITARIAN BLUES

Jacques Rupnik

French political scientist and commentator Jacques Rupnik is one of the most knowledgeable interpreters of postcommunist transitions. In this essay he scrutinizes the cultural and moral dilemmas linked to the treatment of the former Leninist elites, the ambiguities of decommunization, and the daunting efforts to institutionalize democratic values and procedures. He identifies the split over continuity and change as being at the very heart of the main post-communist contradiction between decommunization and constitutionalism. Rupnik's discussion of the rise of staunch anticommunist fundamentalism that calls for revenge and retribution reveals the complexity of political choices and conflicts in these societies. His contribution is intimately related to Polish writer Adam Michnik's discussion of the ethical ambivalence of the "velvet restoration" included in this volume.

Particularly significant are Rupnik's considerations on the nature of the new political communities (presidential, semipresidential, parliamentary) as well as his forecasts about the future. Taking into account political, cultural, and economic conditions in different countries, he envisions Central Europe (Poland, Hungary, Slovenia and the Czech Republic) as democratically consolidated. In the Balkans and the former USSR, on the other hand, an incomplete and tottering transition is creating hybrid nationalist-populist regimes. In 1998 he appears to be right regarding Albania, Belarus, or the former Yugoslavia, but recent demo cratic changes in Romania and Bulgaria show the limits of such predictions given the extremely fluid realities of postcommunist politics.

*   *   *

The post-totalitarian blues are haunting the countries of the "other Europe." The euphoria that accompanied the fall of communism has given way to disappointment, social anomie, and the emergence of new dangers. The unity of the great mass rallies for democracy has shattered, and wide-ranging economic hardship has overshadowed political gain for most citizens. Instead of civil societies, one sees a splintered landscape teeming with corporatisms and resurgent communal loyalties. Václav

Havel paints a somber tableau of postcommunist political life that does not pertain to his country alone:

> Rancor and suspicion between ethnic groups; racism or even signs of fascism; brazen demagoguery; deliberate scheming and lying; political chicanery; wild and shameless squabbling over purely particular interests; naked ambition and lust for power; every kind of fanaticism; new and surprising forms of swindling; Mafia-style machinations; and a general absence of tolerance, mutual understanding, good taste, and a sense of moderation and reflection.[1]

Is this disenchantment part and parcel of any revolution? "Are all revolutions doomed to fail?" as Ralf Dahrendorf asks, hinging as they do on myths of unity, transparency, and innocence.[2] Is it inevitable that a drift toward varieties of nationalism and authoritarianism will follow the first elections?

While it is tempting for historians to compare the revolution of 1989 to others that started in democracy but ended in anarchy and terror, reasoning by analogy is not always the most illuminating method for understanding Eastern Europe's political dynamic, if only because revolutions are not what they used to be. Compared to the modem revolutions that began with the taking of the Bastille or the Winter Palace and continued for years in fire and blood, the negotiated transitions of 1989 were quick, easy, and nonviolent. In fact, 1989 brought to a close the era of revolutions precisely by its rejection of the idea of violence as a midwife for the birth of a new society. The revolutions of 1989 were unique in history because none of them claimed to bear within itself a new societal "project." With no new social utopia, there is little reason to fear the combination of virtue and terror typical of past revolutions. The transitions of 1989 took their bearings quite explicitly from both Western democracy and the precommunist traditions of their own lands. It is in this sense that François Furet speaks of "revolution-restoration," meaning the restoration of national sovereignty, the rule of law, and private property.[3]

The real question, however, is whether a revolution that is negotiated or "velvet" can rightly be called a revolution at all. This is no merely theoretical issue, but one that deeply divides the political landscape of postcommunist Europe. On one side are those who demand a radical break with the institutions and personnel inherited from communism; on the other are those who favor respect for the rule of law, and thus a degree of continuity. The first group emphasizes "restoration"; the second, imitation of Western constitutional models. The paradox is that the partisans of "permanent revolution" generally belong to the conservative (even nationalist) Right, whereas those who support an "evolutionary" approach in the name of law are moderate liberals, who often were former dissidents. In 1980,

Poland invented the "self-limiting revolution" in the name of geopolitics and the threat from the East; today, Poland practices it in the name of the rule of law and inducements from the West.

This split over continuity and change is at the heart of a double political game: that of *decommunization* and that of *constitutionalism*.

Justice, reflection, and old scores

We now know that communism dissolves in voting booths. Its sudden collapse, finalized by the holding of free elections, allowed new democratic institutions to develop. But if communism is dead as an ideology and a system of rule, its encumbering legacy continues to haunt the political and social landscape. Since the transition was gentle, the bulk of the old *nomenklatura* remains, attempting at every turn, as Elemer Hankiss puts it, to convert its old politically based privileges into new economic rights. This spectacle has fostered a diffuse but profound sense of injustice and tempted many to follow the radicals in demanding a settling of accounts with officials and the "collaborators" who ran the repressive machinery of the old regime. After a soft transition have come economic and social hardship and a search for those responsible for the crimes of the past and the difficulties of the present.

From the demand for justice it was but a step to a call for a purge, which was explicitly and effectively put into practice in the former East Germany; paid off relatively well in the Czech Republic; failed in Poland and Hungary; currently divides the noncommunist political elites in Bulgaria, Croatia, and Albania; and never made it onto the agenda in Romania, where the old regime's influence has remained strongest.

Supporters of radical decommunization cite a number of arguments. First, they invoke a moral imperative - truth and justice versus the lies and crimes of totalitarianism – that coincides with the need for a clean political break. In a speech to the Sejm in January 1992, then-Polish prime minister Jan Olszewski presented his short-lived government as "the beginning of the end of communism," thereby insinuating that the government of his predecessor Tadeusz Mazowiecki favored continuity. Olszewski contrasted those guilty of "betrayals, crimes, lies, and cruelty" with those having "clear consciences and clean hands." To forgo decommunization, he argued, would confirm the "cynicism of the guilty and discourage everyone else."

In Prague, security considerations were invoked alongside moral and political arguments. Not only was there the danger that highly compromised holdover personnel might be blackmailed; there was also the very questionable wisdom of entrusting the building of democratic institutions to former secret-police collaborators. To those who feared that the "lustration" law would lead to witch-hunts, supporters responded that it was not a penal procedure, but rather a professional ban affecting government posts and the upper ranks of the civil service for a period limited to five years.[4] The turnover of elites is supposed to serve as a guarantee against the return of the old regime. To permit impunity would be to invite that regime to start itself up again.

Moderate liberals reject the logic of "lustration" as the political exploitation of a moral question. To propose to society a few "guilty parties" is an act of political legerdemain that builds up the myth of an innocent society confronting the evil empire. In his speech marking New Year's 1990, Václav Havel stressed the links of complicity and adaptation that allowed the totalitarian system to function. Hence the importance of getting beyond a Manichaean vision, and reflecting upon the past rather than judging it. It is above all important to avoid compromising the élan of a society oriented toward the future out of some desire to settle old scores.

There are other, more pragmatic, considerations that one might add to these. After a negotiated revolution, it would have been awkward to suddenly turn against the very same roundtable partners who allowed the nonviolent transition to occur. While the moral imperative to oust collaborators or the *nomenklatura* is understandable, it could also undermine economic efficiency. Getting rid of the old economic officials, high-level administrators, and judges may be desirable, but who is to replace them? Dissidents? There were not many of them, and while they were surely virtuous, they are not necessarily qualified to manage the economy or modernize the state apparatus. For liberals, however, the most objectionable idea is that decommunization can provide society with a kind of collective catharsis. Communism's legacy in the structures and mentality of the society was decades in the making. The debate about the weight of this legacy thus leads to a pessimistic vision that extends beyond the reach of moral injunctions: the totalitarian experience soils the victim as much as it does the torturer.

Legality and legitimacy

Continuity or rupture – that is the issue which lies at the heart of the transition's most important dilemma, that of a constitution.[5] Should the transition toward democracy culminate in a democratic constitution, or is a democratic constitution the indispensable prerequisite for a democratic break with the institutions left over from communism?

Expressed another way, the issue concerns the relationship – indeed, the conflict – between legality and legitimacy. Democracy, as we know, needs both. But is it possible to create democratic institutions while respecting a constitution left over from a dictatorship? Conversely, is it possible to create the conditions for democratic pluralism by employing authoritarian methods? On the one hand, liberals, encouraged by Western advice, insist upon respect for the rule of law, and thus on constitutional continuity. Radicals, on the other hand, invoke revolutionary legitimacy and ask how change can be secured while the law remains something inherited from a system designed to control and manipulate society. Which is to be first: change *within* the law or change *of* the law?

The constitution thus lies at the heart of the debate between majoritarian democracy and constitutional democracy – the latter meaning the notion that all power, even the most "legitimate," must bow to the framework and the limits established by the supreme law embodied in a constitution. This classic dilemma, with democracy and participation on one side, and liberalism and law on the other, manifests itself in the postcommunist transition in terms different from those familiar in the democracies of the West. In the latter, to simplify, there are two teams whose players know the rules of the game and accept the intervention of an umpire when the rules have been broken. In the initial phase of the transition in the East, it often seemed as if everyone was running after the ball while changing teams and rules throughout the course of the game. In the West, one can identify the interests behind a proposed law; in the East, one can at best identify an institution or power center. In such a situation, elaborating a new constitution becomes extremely difficult.

András Sajo, an advisor to Hungary's President Arpád Göncz, notes that there is "a constitutional moment" that requires the kind of national unity appropriate to every great turning point in history.[6] If that founding moment is allowed to pass, there remains the procedure of amending the old constitution to allow for the new laws that are needed. Such was the method used in Poland and Hungary.

One must acknowledge that the only countries that succeeded in adopting new constitutions early on (1991), Romania and Bulgaria, are not necessarily the most democratic. The case of Russia seems to confirm this hypothesis. From 1991 to 1993, the Russian constitution was central to the struggle for power. In a slightly surreal struggle the first elected president in the history of Russia decided in early October 1993 to send in the tanks against a parliament dominated by communists claiming to defend – irony of ironies – the constitution and parliamentary sovereignty. By candlelight in September, the Supreme Soviet had designated General Aleksandr Rutskoi head of state. Clad in an Adidas sweatsuit, with a Kalashnikov on his shoulder, the general launched an assault against the Moscow television-broadcast building in a pitiable imitation of the taking of the Winter Palace. For Lenin, socialism was "soviets plus electrification"; democratization Yeltsin-style was the Supreme Soviet without electricity.

Russia must be the only place where the concept of a "democratic putsch" has been seriously broached. To be sure, the Russian conflict was resolved (elections were held after the tanks rolled back to their bases), but at what price? Can a president elicit respect from a legislature by shelling its meeting place? Was not Vladimir Zhirinovsky's electoral victory a high price to pay for the adoption of a made-to-order constitution whose democratic veneer is too thin to hide its authoritarianism (even if it is accepted by the West as a lesser evil)?

If the adoption of a new constitution does not necessarily guarantee a shift to democracy, the experience of Poland and Hungary does seem to suggest that constitutionalism can be a more propitious route to democracy. Poland was preparing a new constitution for the bicentennial of the May 1791 Constitution, but consensus proved unattainable.[7] Poland opted, therefore, for the "little constitution," a phrase used to refer to the gradual but ultimately rather large-scale amending of the old constitution. In Hungary, too, the old constitution was heavily amended. As Sajo waggishly puts it, all that remains of the original are the words: "The capital of Hungary is Budapest." Constitutionalism, guaranteeing the separation of powers and individual rights, rests on the existence of an arbitrating authority, a constitutional court. This court plays such an important role in Hungary (for example, it rejected the principle of retroactive justice in the matter of the new law covering crimes committed during the suppression of the 1956 rebellion) that some worry that it encroaches on "parliamentary sovereignty." Sajo interprets such coolness toward constitutionalism as a rejection of modernity in societies whose "social and intellectual structures (preserved and even reinforced under communism) are premodern."[8]

Despite fears of a "government of judges" and the risk of confusion and drift in a transition carried out by successive constitutional amendments, the Polish and Hungarian cases suggest two advantages. First, political players see that the construction of democratic institutions is an ongoing process that remains imperfect and incomplete. Second, the political habits of a majoritarian democracy evolve toward respect for the constitution and the legitimacy of its procedures. Governments and parliamentary majorities have time to get used to constitutional limits. Spreading out the making of the constitution in this way creates a *process* of constitutional education, a diffusion of constitutionalism's values among the political elites. In this sense, constitutionalism can become more important than the constitution itself, since it contributes to the transformation of political culture, without which the rule of law can never gain a solid foothold.

The territorial framework of politics

There remains the difficult question of the reciprocal links of legitimacy between the regime and the state. This issue has arisen with particular force in those federations that began to disappear as soon as communism fell. In these cases, the adoption of a constitution became an integral part of building a nation-state. The republics of the former Yugoslavia, for example, solidified their declarations of independence by adopting new constitutions (which often became the focus of controversies, as with the Serb minority in Croatia and the Albanian minority in Macedonia). After two years, the Czechoslovak parliament was unable to adopt a new federal constitution, but the Slovak legislature adopted one for Slovakia in August 1992. On the eve of partition in December 1992, the Czech legislature followed suit. The creation of a new state mandated the adoption of a new constitution.

One of the major problems of the transition to democracy in the post-communist world is the territorialization of the political. Whether or not the nation-state is the optimal locus of democracy, it remains true that the legitimation of some sort of formally structured state is a precondition for democratic transition. Juan Linz and Alfred Stepan have argued this in the case of Spain, and the former USSR and Yugoslavia confirm it *a contrario*.[9] All of these cases illustrate the crucial importance of electoral sequencing in the transition from dictatorship to democracy. It was vital that the first democratic elections in Spain encompass the entire country, even if this meant that the new constitution would have to include substantial transfers of power to Catalonia and the Basque regions. Likewise, in Yugoslavia at the beginning of 1990, the inability of Prime Minister Ante Marković's federal Government to hold free elections over the whole of the territory sounded the death knell for the South Slavic federation. The federal state was delegitimized as soon as the first free elections took place in the republics of Slovenia and Croatia. Power and legitimacy shifted from the federation to the republics, which soon opted for independence to complete their own democratic transitions. The end of communism became entangled with the end of Yugoslavia.

A similar sequence broke up the USSR, leaving the following large question hanging over the future of the Russian transition: How to establish a territorial framework for politics? This is very much a question about the Russian state and its consubstantiality with the empire. The great historian Vasili Kliouchevsky described Russia as "a state that has colonized itself." If that is the case, what is Russia without an empire?[10] For the time being, no one knows. But it seems that Yeltsin and the moderate democrats, under pressure from the military, are already formulating a Russian "Monroe Doctrine" for relations with the "near abroad." The other option, that of Zhirinovsky's extremists, implies a redrawing of Russia's boundaries according to an ethnic definition of the nation. Since 25 million Russians live outside Russia's borders, this would provide all the ingredients for a recurrence of the "Serbian syndrome." This scenario would signal the failure of democratic transition not only for Russia but also for the other new nation-states that have risen from the empire's ashes.

The crisis of the Russian state is all the sharper because the loss of the Soviet empire is coupled with a crisis of authority facing the central

Government in Moscow in its dealings with the regions. The breakup of Russia will not necessarily follow the breakup of the USSR, but the question of decentralization will be decisive for both the cohesion of the state and the pursuit of a democratic transition. How can these two goals be reconciled? A decentralized (and therefore weak) Russia is, we are told, the precondition of a shift to democracy. Yet would such a Russia be viable?

The crisis of state authority – a palpable reality in most postcommunist countries – is entwined with a necessary redefinition of the state's role. After decades of the omnipresent, omnipotent state, there is a healthy propensity, especially in Central Europe, to diminish the state's influence by limiting the bureaucracy and liberalizing the economy.

How to redefine the role of the state, which is to say the very nature of the social bond? Around two dimensions of security. One is the state's role as protector, a function that is especially pertinent in countries where crime is increasing by 100 percent a year, and where the old institutions of "law and order" lack credibility because of their corrupt relationship with the old regime. This is indeed changing, if a 1993 Polish poll is accurate: it shows that the army and the police rank extremely high in the public trust, far ahead of the church. From this perspective, the turnaround since the days of communism seems to be complete.

The second dimension concerns the state's welfare role. Since the state is no longer taking complete charge of the individual "from cradle to grave," what role should it play in a society where there is more freedom but less economic security? Leaving aside the Czech anomaly (the liberal right's victory in a country that, along with Liechtenstein, has the lowest unemployment rate in Europe), it may be that the most recent Polish elections show the limits to efforts at a "rollback" (even rhetorical) of the welfare state. In order for economic liberalism to take root in Central Europe, it must retain a redistributive function for the state.

The state's disengagement from the socioeconomic sphere is therefore necessary to the ongoing transition, but its limits are already apparent: dismantling an omnipotent bureaucracy does not mean forgoing a competent civil service, for instance. The paradox of many postcommunist countries is that while everyone used to work for the state, the governmental apparatus itself remained relatively modest in size. In France, the Ministry of Finance employs thousands of civil servants; in Ukraine, it has just a few hundred. Ukraine's parliament passes close to 150 important laws every year (compared to about 15 in Western countries), but the government has no means of enforcing them. Breaking up monopolies and establishing a new fiscal system require an efficient civil service. The transition to democracy and markets requires more "government," in the true sense of the word, in order to have less "state."

Presidents or parliaments?

This redefinition of the state indirectly poses a question about the link between institutional choices and economic transformation. Is a strong executive more apt than a parliamentary system to speed the march toward a market economy while resisting destabilizing effects along the way? This seems to be the dominant idea in Russia (where liberal economists have bet on Yeltsin and a strong executive) but certainly not in Central Europe: the more advanced the economic transition, the more the political center of gravity has moved away from the president (Václav Havel and Lech Wałęsa) and toward the prime minister (Václav Klaus, Hanna Suchocka followed by Waldemar Pawlak).

Experts on democratic transitions like Juan Linz and Alfred Stepan believe that a parliamentary system holds more promise for successful transition than a presidential regime.[11] They note two principal drawbacks of presidentialism. The first is that it is not conducive to the emergence of a multiparty system, since presidentialism promotes a two-party system. This limits considerably the post-totalitarian political field. Second, presidentialism is vulnerable to authoritarian and populist temptations. In contrast, the rise of a Stanisław Tyminski or an Alberto Fujimori would be impossible in a parliamentary system. As for Yeltsin-style presidentialism, there is the con siderable danger that the supposed champion of democracy could become a "Bonapartist" if confronted with a recalcitrant parliament. As interesting as may be such theoretical warnings from political scientists, they have not really influenced the political choices of postcommunist Europe.

In the choice between a parliamentary and a presidential regime, Central Europe opted for the first, the Balkans and Russia for the second. Central Europeans' wariness about repeating their history of a strong, centralized executive, along with the evolving balance of political forces, ruled out the presidential option there.

In Hungary, the pre-electoral situation in the winter of 1989–90 shifted the new institutions in two important directions. The democratic opposition, thinking it was impossible to avoid the election of the reform communist Imre Pozsgay as president, insisted on the parliamentary character of the new regime and on granting considerable powers to the Constitutional Court as guarantor of personal liberties and human rights. Ironically, it was the candidate of the Alliance of Free Democrats, Árpád Göncz, who was elected president. Despite, or perhaps because of, his very limited powers, he became the most popular politician in Hungary.

In Poland, because of Wałęsa, the first totally free election (held in the autumn of 1990) was not legislative but presidential. Given the influence of Solidarity's leader on the Polish political scene, it would have been difficult to leave him waiting patiently on the sidelines (as his former advisors had hoped) while the people first elected a legislature and then considered

General Jaruzelski's replacement. Initially, the rupture that occurred within the core of the Solidarity movement was less a basic disagreement over political orientation than a dispute about power and the rhythm of change. Wałęsa polarized the field by proclaiming his readiness to accelerate political change while slowing economic change. The more important institutional debate became lost in the details of deciding whether to hold presidential elections before legislative ones. When Wałęsa was elected by direct universal suffrage, fears arose in Poland and the West of a drift toward presidentialist authoritarianism. At present, those fears remain exaggerated. True, Wałęsa did try to force an expansion of his powers on the Sejm, but he also knew how to limit himself and accept rebuff from a legislature that hopes to preserve the parliamentary spirit of the "little constitution." Today's fragmented political field and the return of the ex-communists since the autumn of 1993 could play directly into Wałęsa's hands as he seeks to play the "savior" and act as a rampart against the return of the Left in order to remain president.

The Czechoslovak case confirms this Central European ambivalence toward the presidential system. The prewar constitution had been parliamentary, and the communist constitution gave the president merely symbolic duties: real power lay with the general secretary of the communist party. In reality, from the time of the Velvet Revolution in 1989, Václav Havel was clearly the country's major political figure. The former dissident was made president in a late December 1989 vote by the communist parliament. His position was then confirmed in June 1990 by a democratically elected parliament. As during the interwar period under President Tomáš Masaryk, Czechoslovakia had a parliamentary regime on the books, but a semipresidential one in actuality. Since January 1993, however, the situation in the newly established Czech Republic has changed completely.[12] In a system now dominated by Prime Minister Klaus, President Havel is no longer at the hub of power and is more constrained by the constitution.

Whereas Central Europe favors parliamentary constitutions, the Balkans (like Russia) tend more toward presidential regimes: Romania, Bulgaria, and Serbia all held direct presidential elections. Some see this as indicative of a secret nostalgia for the days of the old general secretary – particularly since a goodly number of former general secretaries, from the Serb Milošević to the Ukrainian Kravchuk, have been able to stay in power thanks to universal suffrage. (Their success is also attributable to the extensive fragmentation of the political field and the ability of leftover communist *apparat chiks* to recast themselves as engines of nationalism.)

The use of proportional representation (PR), of course, reinforces political fragmentation. When a totalitarian system crumbles, PR is doubtless bound to enjoy a moment of predilection. The first elections are much like a census: each group needs to identify itself, to stand and be counted, and people expect parliament to reflect society's makeup as closely as possible.

The existence of substantial ethnic minorities in most Eastern countries is an additional argument in favor of PR. It would be difficult to integrate politically the Hungarian minorities in Romania and Slovakia or the Turkish minority in Bulgaria without some recourse to the proportionalist principle.

This preference for PR (Hungary excluded), like the preference for presidentialism, occasionally disturbs Western experts who sometimes discern therein the danger of a democracy weakened by political fragmentation and at other times espy the authoritarian temptation. The danger and the temptation do exist, but Western models and standards are not easily transferred to the East. The strict separation of powers in America, the "checks and balances," work because political actors and society at large have internalized a certain juridical and political culture that is understandably absent in lands just emerging from a half-century of communism. British democracy is admired from afar – the Hungarian parliament building in Budapest, built at the close of the last century, is a copy of the Palace of Westminster in London. Yet how can anyone transplant something that rests on a thousand years of tradition and an unwritten constitution? The French Jacobin model, giving the president primary power, seems to inspire certain adepts of power politics, particularly in the Balkans – not necessarily the democrats. The latter tend to prefer the German system, which not only is the closest geographically to the post-Soviet world, but also stands as a successful example of a democracy risen from the ruins of totalitarianism. Its electoral system (PR with a 5 percent nationwide threshold and a corrective dose of majoritarianism), the regional autonomy accorded to the *Länder*, and the important role of the Federal Constitutional Court – all these are elements able to inspire postcommunist constitutionalists.

What does the future hold?

In his book *The Third Wave*, Samuel P. Huntington places the East European democratic breakthrough in a comparative global context.[13] The first wave of democratization, for East Central Europe, began in 1848 and culminated in the aftermath of the First World War. The second wave (post-1945) affected the Axis powers while the other Europe succumbed to totalitarianism. The third wave, ushered in by the Portuguese revolution and the fall of Francoism in Spain in the mid-1970s, was extended by democratic breakthroughs in Latin America and Asia and touched East Central Europe starting in 1989. Looking through a comparative lens, one can examine the factors affecting the emergence and the prospects of the transitions now under way: (1) The international environment: it has been favorable since Gorbachev, but will it remain so? (2) The economic situation: a market-based economy is a necessary but insufficient condition for democracy, which has never prospered amid economic disaster. (3) Social conditions: "No bourgeois, no democracy," as Barrington

241

Moore put it; yet while a renaissance of civil society may take decades, democracy must drop anchor in the here-and-now. (4) Last, the cultural realm: all of the aforementioned democratic institutions have no chance of taking root unless a shared democratic political culture develops, both among the elites and in society at large.

This list of conditions is not exhaustive, but it does distinguish the transition in postcommunist East Central Europe from those of Southern Europe 20 years ago (with respect to the market and civil society). It also helps us to weigh the risk of reversals. Huntington notes that after each wave of democratization came a reflux. There is surely no danger, however, of the old communist regime reasserting itself. If ex-communists (now converts to "social democracy") are getting votes in Poland or Hungary, it is precisely because they no longer embody the threat of a return to totalitarianism. Other authoritarian and nationalist dangers, however, are certainly present, especially in Russia and the Balkans.

Several future scenarios may be envisioned, region by region: (1) Democracy appears to be on the way to consolidation in Central Europe (Poland, Hungary, Slovenia, and the Czech Republic – Slovakia's case remains doubtful in the wake of Vladimir Mečiar's return to power). (2) In the Balkans and Russia, an incomplete transition is creating hybrid national-populist regimes. Serbia represents the extreme version of a transition from a totalitarian to an authoritarian regime, with a fleeting interlude of democratization and with ethnic nationalism as the dominant new ideology. (3) The Baltic countries come close to the Central European model. Most other ex-Soviet republics are closer to the Balkan model. Bulgaria and Slovakia could go either way.

East Central Europe must construct in very short order what the West took a long time to build. This is an unprecedented experiment, and it is *not* being conducted in laboratory-like isolation (where there is leisure to observe, and to perfect theories about democracy). This is not only because the Iron Curtain has disappeared, leaving the Continent as a whole exposed to the destabilizing consequences that would surely flow from any serious check to the democratic transition in the other Europe, but also because the difficulties and crises of the new democracies are not foreign to us in the West. Shrinking public space, weak political participation, growing mistrust of parties and politicians, and failing confidence in parliamentary institutions are common problems in established democracies. Should we see this as a sign that Central Europe is at the threshold of Western democratic "normality"? Or should we shudder at the parallel, at the profound link between the political crises in the predemocratic societies of the postcommunist East and the postdemocratic societies of the West?

Notes

Source Reprinted by permission of the publisher from *Journal of Democracy* 6:2 (April 1995): 61–73. Translated from the French by Deborah M. Brissman. Copyright © 1995 Johns Hopkins University Press.

1 Václav Havel, *Letní přemítání* (Prague: Odeon, 1991), p. 95. Published in French as *Méditations d'été* (Paris: Editions Aube, 1992), and in English as *Summer Meditations* (New York: Vintage Books, 1993).
2 Ralf Dahrendorf, *Reflections on the Revolution in Europe* (London: Chatto and Windus, 1990).
3 François Furet, *L'énigme de la désagrégation communiste* (Paris: Fondation Saint-Simon, 1990). See also his *Le passé d'une illusion* (Paris: Calmann-Levy, 1995).
4 Voitěch Cepl, "Ritual Sacrifices," *East European Constitutional Review* 1 (Spring 1992): 24–5.
5 Andrew Arato, "Dilemmas Arising from the Power to Create Constitutions in Eastern Europe," *Cardozo Law Review* 3–4 (January 1993): 661–90.
6 András Sajo, "The Arrogance of Power," *East European Reporter* 7 (May/June 1992): 46.
7 Marcin Król, "L'autre bicentennaire," *Belvédère* 1 (April/May 1991): 84–90.
8 Sajo, "The Arrogance of Power," p. 47.
9 Juan Linz and Alfred Stepan, "Political Identity and Electoral Sequence," *Daedalus* 121 (Spring 1992): 123–39.
10 Marie Mendras, ed., *Un état pour la Russie* (Brussels: Complexe, 1992). See also Georges Nivat, "Russie: Le deuil de l'empire," in Jacques Rupnik, ed., *Le déchirement des nations* (Paris: Seuil, 1995), pp. 59–76.
11 Juan J. Linz, "Transitions to Democracy," *Washington Quarterly* 13 (Summer 1990): 153–4.
12 Václav Havel, interview by the author, in *Politique internationale* 58 (Winter 1993): 13.
13 Samuel P. Huntington, *The Third Wave: Democratization in the late Twentieth Century* (Norman, OK: University of Oklahoma Press, 1993).

13

THE VELVET RESTORATION

Adam Michnik

Adam Michnik's contribution to both the theory and practice of dissent in East and Central Europe cannot be overestimated. His Letters from Prison (Los Angeles and Berkeley, CA: University of California Press, 1985, trans. Maya Latynski) were rightly celebrated as crucial for the formulation of the oppositional strategy that eventually led to the end of communism in Poland and in the whole region. In this essay, Michnik discusses the fate of the revolution after the victory of the anticommunist forces and the ethical dilemmas generated by the return of former communist parties to power.

Opposing fundamentalists within both the revolutionary and the ex-communist camps, Michnik suggests that restorations are the inevitable consequence of the refusal to unleash terror. In other words, the democratic game is sufficiently permissive for the ex-communists to use it in order to achieve electoral victories and thus return to governing positions. The first issue is that the former rulers do not return to power through the old means (via coups and in contempt of law), but in a procedural way. Second, their communist mindset has fundamentally changed. The post-communist politicians in countries like Hungary and Poland, Michnik argues, have no ideological zeal and do not aim to build up the classless utopia. Marxism has long since ceased to inspire their actions: far from favoring the restoration of centrally-planned, command economies, these people are staunch supporters (and beneficiaries) of open markets.

Michnik calls for a patient and tolerant approach to restoration. He opposes the logic of exclusion and warns against the neo-Jacobin temptations among the revolutionary radicals for whom nothing would suffice but a complete political annihilation of the former communists. In his usually vivid way, Michnik calls these fundamentalists "anticommunists with a Bolshevik face."

*   *   *

When I read in the Polish press about "the return of communism," I sometimes think it would be worthwhile to imagine an actual restoration of the communist system. The banging on the door at dawn. The declaration of martial law, the dissolution of parliament, the liquidation of political parties, the confiscation of newspapers, the censorship, closed borders, thousands imprisoned, trials, and sentences. And over and over again on the radio, a speech by the Leader on the need for "law, order, and discipline." For a year now, a coalition of post-communist parties has governed in Poland. A similar coalition governs in Lithuania. And in Hungary, an ex-communist party recently won the elections. Nowhere, however, did the communist system return. What, then, do these "returns" mean?

In Poland, and in other countries of the region, a revolution had taken place: the system of totalitarian dictatorships in the realms of politics, economics, and international order was overthrown. Fortunately, that was carried out – in Poland thanks to the roundtable agreements – without barricades and guillotines. It was, as Václav Havel so aptly put it, a "velvet revolution."

But every revolution – even a velvet one – has its own logic. It releases expectations and hopes that it can never satisfy. Therefore, it has to radicalize its own language, devour its own children, eliminate the moderates from its ranks, decree successive "accelerations," lustrations, purges. The revolution is forever unfinished. That is why it causes frustration and bitterness. Somebody must be held responsible for the fact that manna has not fallen from heaven. The revolution finds the guilty ones. First the people of the old regime, then their defenders, and finally its own leaders.

The revolutionary camp always has its own "moderates" and "extremists." The former want to defend freedom in the name of the constitutional state and of the rule of law; the latter believe that defending freedom means annihilating the enemies of freedom – that is, the people of the old regime. That is their only way of showing their concern for the well-being of the wronged and humiliated who started the revolution. After all, the liberation from dictatorship brought freedom and happiness only to a few. The majority, left in poverty and despair, did not enjoy the fruits of victory. According to that majority, the revolution was betrayed by the "moderates" – the majority has to liberate itself once again. That is why "acceleration" and "completion of the revolution" are necessities. To achieve those, it is necessary to stop playing the rule-of-law game. Clear and firm decisions are required: with regard to the people of the old regime, revolutionary justice should be applied, since no other justice is relevant.

The Bourbon king was tried ostensibly for collusion with the enemy, but in fact it was because he was a king. The execution of Louis XVI was a sentence on the monarchy, "this intrinsic crime," as Saint-Just defined it. In the name of that logic, Constitution was losing to Revolution.

"Measured against the immense sufferings of the vast majority of the people," as Hannah Arendt characterizes Robespierre's thought, "the impartiality of justice and law, the application of the same rules to those who sleep in palaces and those who sleep under the bridges of Paris, was like a mockery."

Previously, the goal was the constitutionally guaranteed freedom of citizens; now justice and the welfare of the people have become the goal. A goal so defined divides the revolutionary camp in an obvious way: the "moderates" and the "extremists" begin to perceive each other as enemies. This conflict tears apart and exhausts the revolution. Can anything still save it? Yes – a savior, who liquidating both camps, reaches for his armor and the language of the diktat.

But would the masses follow that leader? Or would they rather choose restoration? The same guillotine cut off the heads of the king, Danton, and finally Robespierre. Revolution can give way to terror. It can also avoid it, but then it has to engender restoration. Every revolution either culminates in dictatorship or brings about a restoration.

Poland's velvet revolution gave birth to the velvet restoration. A restoration is never the return of the old regime and the old order. The restoration is a reaction to the revolution, a paroxysm of old-timers' comebacks, of former symbols, traditions, customs. Revolution feeds on the promise of a Big Change; restoration promises the return of the "good old days."

But the restoration, like the revolution, inevitably brings disappointment. First there is joy. Humiliated by the revolution, the people of the old regime live a moment of relief and glory. Justice has been done. The self-proclaimed revolutionaries are handing over power. Loyal crowds joyfully greet the legitimate monarch and his retinue. The royalists strive to outdo each other in right-thinking declarations. The "ultras" get ready to fill the posts. However, it soon becomes apparent that, as among the senators praising the House of Stuarts or of Bourbons, there are many who once voted to execute Charles I or Louis XVI. Therefore the "ultras" demand purges, restitution of property, punishment, and humiliation for the people of the revolution.

The legitimate monarch, returning from exile to assume the throne, utters the memorable words, "Gentlemen, nothing has changed. We just have one Frenchman more." As one witness of the period observed. "The easy-going manner, the worldly tone, the friendly dignity, in such contrast to the domineering attitude and the proud and overbearing responses of Napoleon, made a great impression on those present. We felt transported into some new world. We were coming back to fatherly rule."

Nevertheless, the very same witness – Talleyrand – noted that "soon, denunciations began, feigned zeal, resentments, forced displays of devotion.... A crowd of firebrands and plotters of all shades were jammed into his palace. Each of them had reinstated the monarchy. Each demanded to be rewarded for his devotion and for his services. All posts needed new people. Originally the king himself was against such a settling of accounts:

'Gentlemen.' he would say to the 'ultras,' 'I urge and oblige you to find as few people guilty as possible.'" But that did not satisfy everyone. Soon there appeared criticism of the moderate approach. The "ultras" demanded more radical action and just punishment of the revolutionary malefactors. The restoration kept losing supporters, and the defenders of the lost revolution were winning them back. Because, just as the revolution failed to keep its promises earlier, the restoration did not keep them later: the peace and order of the good old days did not return.

For a large number of those who voted for the SLD and the PSL [both groupings of former communists in Poland], this year of coalition rule has calmed things down. Fear of the craze for decommunization and lustration has ended, along with fear of the contempt and discrimination of those who called the PZPR [Polish United Workers Party] "paid traitors" and "lackeys of Russia" and who compared it to [the German Nazi Party] and the *Volksdeutsche* population that had supported the Nazis in the occupied countries. Now, prior membership in the PZPR has ceased to be something shameful, thanks to the hard work of the most "rabid" zealots in the Solidarity camp

The fear of change that brought success to the SLD and the PSL resulted in a slowdown of privatization and reform of local self government, the reintroduction of centralization and state monopoly, the raising of protective tariffs, subsidies for enterprises going bankrupt, credits for weak farms. The decision of the parliamentary majority concerning the concordat with the Vatican and abortion dealt a blow to the prestige of the Catholic Church.

Nevertheless, for a decisive majority of the SLD and PSL electorate, the last year has brought disappointment. The good old days have not returned: the welfare state, an economy without unemployment, free vacation resorts for employees, free education and health services. The time of that peculiar egalitarianism - when poor work was rewarded with a poor wage and even the very thought of personal wealth was eradicated as a harmful relic of capitalism – did not return.

The restoration, just like the revolution, has its moderate wing and its extremists, or "ultras." The moderates want to change the logic of the democratic state of law and the market economy in such a way as to become its beneficiaries. They do not, however, want execution squads, massive purges, censorship, closed borders, dictatorship, and the nationalization of enterprises. The ultras, on the other hand, desire revenge and a rejection of reform. The ultras, taking advantage of the rising anticlerical climate, desire the humiliation of the Church. The ultras are dangerous – it is not difficult to see that. Nevertheless, none of those observations justifies the thesis of recommunization and the return of the Polish People's Republic.

Talleyrand, theorist of the moderate restoration, characterized his point of view in *Memorial for a Monarch*: "When religious feelings were strongly etched in people and strongly influenced their minds, people could believe that the might of a ruler was an emanation of divinity. . . . In times, however, when those feelings leave slight traces, when the religious bond, if not broken, is at least significantly loosened, one does not want to recognize that as a source of legitimacy. Popular opinion today . . . says that governments exist exclusively for the people. From that opinion comes the unavoidable conclusion that legitimate power is the one that best guarantees peace and prosperity for the people. Therefore, it turns out that the only legitimate power is the one that has already existed for many years. . . . But if by some misfortune, the thought arises that abuses of that power are outweighing its benefits, the result is that its legitimacy is perceived as a chimera. That might still suffice – but it is also necessary to constitute it in such a way that all the reasons for anxiety that it could provoke will be eliminated. To constitute it in such a way is equally in the interest of both the ruler and his subjects; because today absolute power would be just as heavy a burden for the one who wields it as for those he rules."

Talleyrand was right, but he had to submit his resignation. Other people had won, those with more radical views. The French restoration was taking the path of revenge and repression. Those people led France to a new revolution.

The mark of a restoration is its sterility. Sterility of government, lack of ideas, lack of courage, intellectual ossification, cynicism, and opportunism. Revolution had grandeur, hope, and danger. It was an epoch of liberation, risk, great dreams, and lowly passions. The restoration is the calm of a dead pond, a marketplace of petty intrigues, and the ugliness of the bribe.

François René, the Viscount of Chateaubriand, was the enemy of the revolution and of Napoleon. He longed fervently for the restoration and did a great deal for it. At the same time, however, he called the people of the revolution "giants in comparison with the small vermin who have hatched from us." He noted: "To fall from Bonaparte and the Imperium to what happened afterwards was to fall from being into nothingness, from the mountain top into a chasm. . . . Generations that are crippled, without faith, dedicated to a nothingness that they love, are not able to grant immortality; they do not have the power to bring glory: if you put your ear to their lips, you will hear nothing, no sound comes from the heart of the dead."

He had contempt for the epoch of the restoration and its people: how to "cite Louis XVIII after the Emperor"? Of the Chamber of Peers he wrote: "For those assembled old men, dried-out remnants of the old Monarchy, the Revolution, and the Empire, anything beyond platitudes looked like madness."

One does not have to like the Solidarity revolution anymore, and it is easy to criticize it. There is a great deal of criticism of Walesa and Mazowiecki, Bielecki and Suchocka, Geremek and Kuroń, Balcerowicz and Lewandowski, Skubiszewski and Rokita are not spared either. I have been collecting the whole repertoire of attacks on *Gazeta Wyborcza*, and I myself do not spare the Kaczynski brothers, Olszewski, or Macierewicz. Many of those criticisms are well founded. Nevertheless, it was all those people, amidst errors, inconsistencies, ill-considered decisions, and demoralizing arguments, who carried out the historic task of the anticommunist revolution in Poland.

With that revolution, the time of Solidarity and Walesa had passed. The great myth turned into a caricature. The movement toward freedom degenerated into noisy arrogance and greed. Soon after its victory it lost its instinct for self-preservation. That is why the post-Solidarity formations lost the last elections to parliament. Let us emphasize this: it is not so much that the postcommunist parties won as that the post-Solidarity parties lost. They were unable to build an elementary preelectoral coalition – a necessity obvious to anyone who has read the electoral law – because they were mired in pettiness and lack of imagination. Thanks to that, the party that received 20 percent of the vote won a stunning victory.

Now, in the face of the crawling, though velvet, restoration, the parties of the anticommunist opposition that lost ought to undertake a critical accounting. There is nothing, however, to suggest that such a process is taking place. Aside from a few exceptions, we still hear the speech of tired words and worn-out phrases, a song that no one wants to hear any more.

The people of communist Poland returned to power. How do they differ from the people of Solidarity?

The people of Solidarity were of all kinds: wise and stupid, courageous and cautious, modest and boastful. What they shared, however, was the sense that some time ago, they had made the decision to take a more difficult life path. The memory of that decision gave them a sense of dignity and pride, the ability to act in uncompromising and nonopportunistic ways. They usually lacked experience, a lack that could lead either to amateurishness or to freedom of imagination. Yet politics was for them not only a game but also a choice entailing real risk – even though, later on, many of them were to become players of the sleaziest kind.

The people of communist Poland also come in all kinds: wise and stupid, modest and boastful. But their whole experience was different, built on being at the disposal of others, on obedience, on the capacity for conformist adaptation. The people of Solidarity had both the good and the bad features of revolutionaries, or of reformers revolutionizing their own times. The people of communist Poland have all the features of routinized bureaucrats. The people of Solidarity frequently made decisions that were risky and faulty; the people of communist Poland would like best of all to make no decisions except those regarding personnel. In accordance with the rule that "the cadres decide everything," the people of communist Poland consistently awarded all posts according to internal party rank. It is only a few steps from that to handing out perks and privileges.

The people of Solidarity pushed the wheel of history forward; the people of communist Poland have not turned the wheel back, but they are stubbornly putting the brakes on it.

I do not like restoration. I do not like its ethics or aesthetics, its shallowness or boorishness. Nevertheless, one cannot simply reject this velvet restoration. One has to domesticate it. One has to negotiate with it as with an adversary or a partner. One has to permeate it with the values of the velvet democratic revolution. Even though it is bad, the logic of the restoration is better, after all, than the logic of a Jacobin-Bolshevik purge, revenge, or guillotine. A consistent restoration is gray with boredom; a consistent revolution is red with blood.

Restorations, too, are sometimes bloody, but their shape depends on the strategy of their opponents as well. If the people of the revolution reach for violence and announce revenge, restorations will use the same weapons. That is when the "ultras" win, like Zyuganov, the leader of the Russian postcommunists. That is why one has to look carefully at the hands of the restoration and not turn one's back on it. Brauzauskas, Horn, and Pawlak are better, after all, than anticommunists with a Bolshevik face.

One must not forget that, although restorations do not bring back the old order, they can cause gangrene in a democracy. After all, neither a return to communism nor a return to Solidarity is possible. We are entering a new epoch, a world of new conflicts and new divisions. Walesa and Pawlak are both signs of nostalgia for the past, whether for the Polish People's Republic or for Solidarity. Who today is a sign of the future?

Somewhat timidly, I think of certain distinguished politicians of the ex-communist opposition, people of the Church, and people of the post-communist formation, who were once divided by everything and are still divided by many things today. But they nevertheless share a certain perspective on reality: they all look to the future. In the face of the ominous temptations of the contemporary world, in the face of class, ethnic, and religious wars and hatreds, those people are proposing a conversation about an ordinary Poland in an ordinary Europe.

This project is free of the utopianism that has usually accompanied great turning points. Yet this very project has been the utopian dream of several generations of Poles.

Note

Source Reprinted by permission of the author. Originally published in Polish in *Gazeta Wyborcza* in September 1993. English version (trans. Elzbieta Matynia) published in *Bulletin of the East and Central Europe Program of the New School for Social Research* (October 1994).

14

THE NEIGHBORS OF KAFKA: INTELLECTUAL'S NOTE FROM THE UNDERGROUND

Mircea Mihăieş

This article, by Romanian author and critic Mircea Mihăieş, was written in 1992, several years before the watershed November 1996 elections were won by the democratic forces. Mihăieş's essay captures the dismay of the critical intellectuals in his country and the sentiments of despondency among those who had hoped that Romania's exit from Nicolae Ceauşescu's despotism would mean the end of communism. Of all the East European revolutions, only the Romanian one was violent. It was also only in Romania that the former communist dictator was summarily tried and executed. Many in Romania and abroad thought that these circumstances would result in the instant emergence of a most resolutely antitotalitarian regime. Paradoxically, however, the post-1989 government was made up of former party bureaucrats who did their utmost to preclude a genuine break with the past.

The essay's contrast between Václav Havel and Ion Iliescu (Ceauşescu's successor) is particularly poignant and disturbing: whereas the Czech leader embodies the best traditions of dissent, Iliescu's whole career and mindset reveal a stubborn commitment to Leninist authoritarianism. Illustrating the regional disparities that are also mentioned in Jacques Rupnik's contribution to this volume, Mihăieş's essay personalizes and memorializes the immediate political complexities and moral torments of the postcommunist, that is post-1989, transitions.

* * *

I have gathered notes from my own personal underground. The town I come from is situated in a semi-imaginary space I would call the East of Central Europe. And I am someone who is proud to have lived in Pericles's Golden Century. From this point of view, my essay may be considered a report on the life during neo-Periclism. My essay, "The Neighbors of

Franz Kafka," is a semi-touristic and semi-political study. You soon will see why.

Not long ago, I happened to spend a few days in Prague and then a few days in my native Transylvania. My experience – purely that of a tourist – proved to be full of surprises. It especially cleared up a number of the unknown elements among which we have been living during the past two years. Undoubtedly, Prague is one of Europe's most beautiful cities. Perfectly preserved, it reigns in the middle of the continent, the undeniable capital of Central Europe. In between Franz Kafka and Václav Havel, the town has always proved to be a radiant point for European spirituality. And perhaps it was not by chance alone that Havel was brought to the Hradčany Palace, the official residence of the president of Czechoslovakia, which is just a few steps away from the Golden Lane, where at Number 22, one can find Kafka's house.

After the Second World War, Soviet-type socialism triumphed in Czechoslovakia, just as it did in Romania. In both countries, the troops of the Red empire blocked the natural mechanism of social life. As in the rest of East Central Europe, the sun rose from Moscow. And yet, what are the origins of the Czech abilities to preserve, unaltered, the distinctive marks of the past? Through what miracle did Prague succeed in surviving the steamroller of Communism, preserving its beauty? "It may be that the Czechs never had the money of a Ceaușescu to destroy their city," my American friend, Jim Denton, suggested with black humor. But the Czechs did have August 1968, when they rose against Communism – the year 1968 when, in Romania, in a bizarre reaction to the Soviet invasion of Prague, Romanian youths joined, massively and enthusiastically, the Communist Party! The Czechs had Charter 77; we the Romanians, the 1977 earthquake. They had Havel; we, the Iliescu–Roman duo.

One cannot forget these things. The fiber of the nation was imbued with them; they exist regardless of the ups and downs of history. By contrast with other countries of the region, Czechoslovakia's integration into Europe had nothing to do with mere political bovaryism. Czechoslovakia is indeed part of Europe and not only geographically. The country is confronting at this moment a series of problems, such as nationalism. But these problems are part of the legacy the Soviets left everywhere. I would call them the diseases that come from the absence of dialogue. Incapable of protesting in front of Big Brother, the country finds aberrations that are surfacing only now, when his all-seeing eye closed for a moment. Beyond the problems inherent in any state in the process of changing its political regime, Czechoslovakia breathes an air of normality that shocks a tourist coming from the lower Danube. Yet the surprise experienced when coming into contact with a country that has regained normality is by no means bigger than the shock of readapting to the convulsions one has left at home. One returns to a country whose president knows the official results of a constitutional referendum days before they are officially announced. One returns to a country where the same president disregards the laws with Asiatic contempt, to a country where the constitution has been voted on, although a large majority of the citizens did not know what they voted for; to a country where my old aunt, an ardent monarchist, said "Yes" to a republican constitution because she was asked to do so by those on television; to a country where the rural population was threatened with the prospect of being forbidden to buy food from state-owned shops if it did not vote for the current government.

What a difference there is between the vote given by the European citizens of Czechoslovakia to Havel and the one given by my country cousin in Romania to Ion Iliescu! "But why?" I ask with amazement, "have you still not realized, even after two years, whom you are dealing with?"

The answer comes like thunder: "It suits us!"

"How do you mean?"

"Iliescu won't dismiss us from our jobs, and that suits us. With him, we have peace. You saw the Peasant Party leader, Rațiu, how he showed up at the voting, wearing a peasant's coat and bow-tie. Are we to expect justice from him? Or maybe from the King, in fact the ex-King, who wants to divide the country among his flock of daughters?"

"Well, but what has Rațiu's bow-tie got to do with democracy and justice?" I almost shout, indignant at all these sartorial aesthetics on the mind of the Romanian peasant.

"We even liked it with the Communists," my aunt intervenes. "We fended very well for ourselves. We had everything we needed. And now, Iliescu gave us land as well. It was better at the cooperative farm, though."

No, there is not a trace of surrealism in these dialogues. I transcribed them as exactly as I could. But their truth is horrifying. For a large part of the Romanians, the idea of civil society does not exist. The only thing that matters is the small personal arrangement, the small, barely warm spot. Passivity and living with evil have defeated any kind of vitality.

In the past two years, a huge distance has divided Czechoslovakia and Romania. Heading decisively towards democracy, the Czechs and Slovaks cleaned up their country. In Romania, we are not willing to clean up our own houses. In Czechoslovakia, the parliament promulgated a law banning Communism. In Romania, the parliament rose up against a former prime minister who attacked – in highly moderated terms – the Communist structures still active in the society. In Czechoslovakia, a president admired throughout the world tries to establish consensus and bring social peace. In Romania, a president elected for the "tranquility" of the people, fishing in troubled waters, incites a fraction of the population, the miners, to ethnic extremism and national disintegration. If Czechoslovakia now has the chance to become the first ex-Communist country accepted into the

European Community, President Iliescu has created all the premises for Romania to remain the last Sovietized country of Europe. While President Havel's speeches are models of Europeanism and truth, the public speeches of President Iliescu are samples of schematized Bolshevism, offered in homeopathic doses to a population that has been forced into numbness by cold, hunger, and ignorance.

Such comparisons could go on forever, but they lead nowhere. How can one compare the greatness of St. Venceslas' statue in Václavske Namesti with the shanties and Stalinist blocks of flats found in downtown Bucharest? How to compare a people's decision to eliminate forever the remains of Communism with the guilty romance our brothers and cousins entertain with the National Salvation Front? The answer, desolate in its truth, is to be found in the reply, "It suits us."

Why does the National Salvation Front suit the Romanians? For a long time, I thought it was because they did not know the truth. I think now that it is precisely because they know the truth too well. A personal poll proved to me that the credible wing for the average voter is the Iliescu wing and not Petre Roman's reformist segment. What results from all this? Nothing, except the inertia of a large number of the voters – an inertia that goes hand-in-hand with a grain of dishonesty. All the rumors spread by television, by the disinformation network of the secret police, and by the trained men of the Party have an amazing effect on the masses. The most incredible slanders of the leaders of the opposition are repeated, commented upon, and amplified with a malicious pleasure that betrays, in many of us, the remains of a resentment susceptible to psychoanalysis: if we are dirty, then everyone has to be dirty. And the dirtiest of all, of course, are those in the opposition, because in the mind of the Romanian citizen, the opposition stands against him or her and not against an irresponsible power. That by tradition the Romanian citizen has always been on the side of the powers-that-be was borne out by the interwar free elections, where the winner was, in every case, the ruling party. Frail, cowed before history, seeking desperately the protection of the strong, Romanians fear any force that threatens to unbalance their relative inner comfort, a comfort which seems to be more than a desperate fight for subsistence but is, in fact, never more than just that.

The Iliescu regime has governed for two years, and the country has reached the abyss. Lies and corruption have seized the entire social mechanism. The current prime minister, Theodor Stolojan, speaks of economic and financial blocking. It would be more accurate to speak of the blocking of honesty and honor. The workers are driven to despair by the thought that foreigners will come and exploit them. At the same time, they envy the Czechs, the Hungarians, and the Poles, who are being helped by the West. We don't sell our country, but we require everything for free. This is the revenge of the old phrases, so familiar to us, "they give" and "they bring." Unfortunately, in today's world, nothing is given or brought anymore. Year after year, Romanian workers have been transforming our industrial plants into places of rest; now they are afraid they will lose their daily bread. They understand perfectly that if foreign investors arrived, they would get rid of a number of these unfortunate proletarians, who have already been transformed by Ceauşescu into pseudo-*lumpen*. They do not seem to understand that the great father of the country himself, Ion Iliescu, will be obliged to do the very same thing. Having reached the deadline, the country's economy now faces the choice of bearing a brutal surgical intervention or acknowledging, in the near future, its own clinical death.

What the large mass of voters does not understand is that, once installed at the helm, Iliescu and his team would not hesitate to sacrifice those who helped to invest them with such authority. Unfortunately, the constitution gives them every right they need to do so. The voters do not want to understand – because "that suits us as well" – that for the sake of power, the National Salvation Front leadership is ready to do anything. It proved it in January, in February, in March, and in June of 1990, and it proved it as well in September 1991, and it will do so in the future whenever necessary. The star of Iliescu rises, shining with a glow of unanimity, as the most precious stone of a regime for which any minority – national, intellectual, professional – is considered, *ex officio*, criminal. Taking advantage of the troubled international political context, Iliescu is, in fact, only a step away from assuming dictatorial powers. In a Europe divided by irreconcilable conflicts and torn apart by fratricidal wars, a little despot from an isolated country between the Carpathians and the Danube bothers no one. As long as he maintains peace, his support is assured. Playing from the very beginning into the hands of party activists and the former repressive apparatus, Iliescu was sure to put up the high card. In Romania, where the shamelessness of politicians has reached the heights, no one is bothered that the heads of parliament are two old wrecks of Communism. No one minds that what sets the majority of the parliamentarians into motion is fidelity to the ancient Communist party apparatus, not an attachment to the values of democracy. The graceful speeches of men like Vasile Vacaru, Marian Enache, Dan Martian, Gheorghe Dumitrascu, Alexandru Birladeanu, Romulus Vulpescu will lead us, in an atmosphere of merry National Salvation Front democracy, to where Ceauşescu wanted to lead us in a paranoic allegro: to the Asiatic border of Europe, into the land of enlightened dictators.

The most frightening thing in this situation is that the man of good will seems to have signed a treaty with the red beast. Deprofessionalized, underqualified, driven to despair by poverty and misery, living as if he were kept in a kind of reservation, always waiting to be told what to do, what to think, what to say, and what to eat, he is part of a perfectly maneuverable mass in a country of absolute cynicism. A television company in which disinformation has reached the acme of shamelessness is contributing fully to the moral ill-treatment of the mass of Romanian people. Meek and frightened, it will lose even the nothing it possesses and keep on voting for standing still in the communitarian utopia.

It is no less true, though, that the opposition did its best to amplify the fears of a population infantilized by a Communist regime, which in Romania rules with dehumanizing force. In a way, the opposition has been the didactic material for the clever activist propaganda disguised as the herald of democracy. "You see," the propagandists used to say, "you see where these enemies of the people want to lead you? They will throw you out of your jobs, and they will abandon you to the foreigners who come here to get rich!" Under these circumstances, dialogue becomes impossible. In all the other ex-Communist countries, Bolshevik reformists had power for only a few months. In Romania, amidst the applause of a majority too frightened to face the truth, neo-Communist dictatorship triumphs openly.

There is such a thing as the logic of history. In Prague, Václav Havel comes to power and installs himself in the palace that belonged to the Emperor of the Holy Roman Empire of the German nations. The palace is but a few steps from Franz Kafka's house. In Bucharest, the roulette wheel of history having been spun, accident is abolished forever. In a Kafkaesque Romania, Nicolae Ceaușescu is followed, quite logically, by Ion Iliescu.

Note

Source Reprinted by permission of the author from *Partisan Review* 59:4 (1992): 711–17.

15

IS COMMUNISM RETURNING?

Zhelyu Zhelev

A former dissident and Bulgaria's first noncommunist president, Zhelyu Zhelev examines in his essay the meaning of the former communists' return to power and why the ideological obsessions of the Stalinist era are forever defunct. Like Poland's Adam Michnik, Zhelev warns against panic-ridden outburst of indignation and calls for a realistic assessment of the political situation. In Zhelev's view, it is fundamentally wrong to think that communism, as a political, economic, and cultural system, could be restored. Recommunization, in the sense of a full-fledged return of the old regime, is a sociological and ideological impossibility. None of the former communists who returned to power in the post-Leninist countries is an old-fashioned "true believer." Unlike Michnik, however, who sees the velvet restoration as inevitable, Zhelev advocates the need to reshape the anticommunism of the 1990s into "anti-postcommunism." This means a struggle against the reassertion of the old communists' practices and mentalities. He portrays the postcommunist situation as marred by the following ailments: an inordinately centralized state; corporatism cloaked in nationalist appeals; the persistence in power positions of the old, corrupt elites; and an intense suspicion of the West. His views are in many respects related to other former dissidents' disquieting reflections on the "postcommunist nightmare." The main threat for them is not the resurrection of communist despotisms, but rampant cynicism, corruption, and mafia-style politics.

*   *   *

In early 1990, carried away by the carnival atmosphere of the time, students and intellectuals all over Eastern Europe burned effigies and held symbolic burials of communism. I still have a souvenir of those heady days: a small can that holds "the last breath of communism." Some of those who served as exultant pallbearers and gravediggers may be in this hall today; others, perhaps, cast their most recent votes for the parties of the ex-communists. One thing is sure: the specter whose haunting of Europe Karl Marx announced in his *Communist Manifesto* a century and a half ago looks less certainly laid to rest in 1995 than it did in 1990. Viewed in historical perspective, this should not be in the least surprising.

By the fifth year of the French Revolution, France had had two constitutions, Louis XVI had been guillotined, the Terror had devoured such darlings of the Revolution as Danton and Robespierre, and Babeuf had begun hatching his "conspiracy of equals." Napoleon and the Restoration lay ahead.

By the fifth year of the Russian Revolution, the horrible civil war had just come to an end, war communism had failed, Lenin had announced his market-friendly New Economic Policy (NEP), and grassroots Bolsheviks had begun heatedly debating whether the NEP was or was not restoring capitalism. Stalin and the gulag lay ahead.

In the context of this revolutionary chronology, the return of communism today is hardly surprising. Revolutions, even velvet ones, rarely meet the expectations that they raise. Disenchantment and pessimism creep in. This is when we realize that the old regime, whose death knell we have so eagerly sounded, is still very much alive. The euphoric sense that everything has changed is followed by a numbing suspicion that nothing has changed

It is appropriate for historians and journalists to examine historical analogies in search of social and psychological explanations for the ex-communists' return to power in Eastern Europe; politicians should be allowed no such luxury. I make this point because too many democratic leaders tend to act like political commentators, sociologists, psychologists, or cultural critics. They explain and analyze the emerging tendencies rather than trying in earnest to stem the tide.

After the victory of the ex-communist left in the 1993 parliamentary elections in Poland, an observer asked the rhetorical question: "Can you imagine Franco's adherents returning to power in Spain just four years after his death?" In the context of this question, the left-wing resurgence in Eastern Europe seems anything but reassuring. Yet the democratic process in our countries is irreversible as long as there are political forces committed to the consolidation of democracy.

Competing paradigms

There are two basic models for understanding the former communists' return to power. One is the paradigm of recommunization, upheld mainly by the party of decommunizers, which sees a conspiracy by former communists to regain control. The other is the paradigm invoked by moderates, who interpret the return of the ex-communists as a "velvet restoration" that is actually an extension of the revolution itself, or a sign of its consolidation. According to this second model, democracy is now so securely entrenched that even if the communists win an election and return to power it will not make any fundamental difference to the nature of the regime: they will not be able to put an end to free political competition or reassert totalitarian social controls.

Both paradigms are political rather than intellectual, and relate directly to the specifics of different postcommunist countries. In Hungary, with its consensus in favor of democracy and markets, the paradigm of recommunization has few supporters; this is not the case in countries such as Bulgaria or Romania.

The decommunizers see no revolution, but rather a simulacrum of change that has allowed the ex-communists to convert political power into economic influence and sidestep claims for retribution and justice. The credibility of this thesis has grown as former communist *apparatchiki* and secret-police bosses have redistributed national wealth into their own pockets by manipulating privatization, thumbing the public in the eye and creating once again a society for themselves.

In the final analysis, however, we must admit that the paradigm of recommunization is a perfect excuse for the failure of the extreme anti-communists' attempts to enact reform. The paradigm of recommunization and the thesis of a global conspiracy cannot be used to exempt democratic leaders from responsibility for the failure of their policy.

The "velvet restoration" model also exercises its appeal by making things appear predetermined. Just as four years under Prime Minister József Antall buried nostalgia in Hungary for Admiral Miklós Horthy, so four years under Prime Minister Gyula Horn's rule will be enough to bury any nostalgic feelings about János Kádár. Influenced by the example of France after its revolution, Adam Michnik believes that the velvet restoration is inevitable and even necessary. It is a lesser evil than a revolution that goes on beyond its bounds. Both Michnik and my Hungarian friends make some fair points. Yet what may be true of Poland and Hungary is decreasingly true of Bulgaria. The East European countries may have been alike in their revolutions, but they differ in their restorations.

My own theory looks neither to recommunization nor to velvet restoration. The problem, as I see it, is how to reshape the anticommunism of 1990 into anti-postcommunism. For what threatens Eastern Europe, and my country in particular, is less the return of communism than the ossification of postcommunism.

Communism in its classical version cannot possibly return, just as the slave labor camps are no longer possible. Multipartism, political opposition, and the freedoms of speech and the press cannot be abolished. The country cannot be closed and hermetically isolated, any more than the Warsaw Pact or COMECON can be resurrected. Communism in this sense is clearly defunct, as even its adherents know. The threats that we actually face now are the gradual replacement of democracy by a kind of multipartisan, authoritarian free-for-all and the replacement of fairly free and honest markets by a quasi-capitalist hybrid economy wherein crime, racketeering, corruption, political manipulation, and the mafia thrive. Communism is dead, but we must be careful not to let its still-twitching corpse pull the infant democracy down into the grave along with it.

A major difference between the France of the Bourbon Restoration and the Eastern Europe of ossifying postcommunism is that the former had an articulated ideology. It adhered to the idea of monarchy and to faith in the natural order of things. Joseph de Maistre, Edmund Burke, and Chateaubriand remained staunch opponents of change, resisting it not merely on grounds of political expediency but on principle as well. But the Restoration ultimately became untenable because, although French society pitied the guillotined monarch and felt nostalgic about him, it no longer believed in the divine right of kings to rule.

In the case of Eastern Europe, restoration has proceeded against the backdrop of ostensible reforms. Thus even while the need for reforms is proclaimed, old communist practices quietly return.

But what precisely is it that is returning? First, there is the overweening state. In Bulgaria today, the effort to concentrate control over economic and public life in the state is one of the most striking features of Socialist Party (i.e., ex-communist) rule. Gradually, two kinds of ownership are coming to vie with each other: "good" state ownership and "bad" private ownership. Private enterprise is having both its arms twisted: one by the government trying to impose centralized bureaucratic management, and the other by an organized criminal underworld that has its own rules of doing business. Moreover, there have been attempts to suggest that civil society, notably the nongovernmental organizations, erodes the very idea of statehood, thus giving the state a handy pretext for trying to dominate the non-governmental sector.

Second, a malign type of corporatism is returning that seeks to replace the actual competition of ideas and interests with deals between factions of the ruling party. Partisan space crowds out public space. Then, to provide cover, partisan and corporatist concerns are cloaked in nationalist appeals.

Third, the rhetoric of the old regime is returning – that neutered, wooden discourse that reeks of mold and state-sponsored optimism and harks back to Kafka's *Castle* and the corridors of communist power!

Fourth, the personnel of the *ancien régime* are returning. Incongruously called upon to supervise radical economic and political reforms, they go about this task seeking a revenge that is formally political but essentially petty.

Fifth, intense suspicion of the West is returning. The cultural tolerance inherent in the Bulgarian national tradition is being threatened by the official cultivation of xenophobia. Fears of spying are also being roused to a degree not seen since the 1960s.

Attempts to degrade democracy into a dictatorship of the majority provide yet another cause for alarm. Here, however, Bulgaria's Constitutional Court has offered vital resistance. By taking principled stands in several critical situations, it has defended society's right to be governed within the framework of the Constitution rather than by the political will of the majority.

Though all of this is bad enough, something worse still is returning. That is the sense that "we, the people," are of no consequence. Once again, we see political apathy and tense divisions between "us" and "them" – the anonymous, amorphous "them," with no political profile, yet empowered despite and regardless of the citizens' will!

Communism itself cannot come back, but some of its worst features are returning. Herein may lie the curious fate of postcommunism: a society in which communism cannot return but is in no hurry to go.

Note

Source Reprinted by permission of the publisher from *Journal of Democracy* 7:3 (July 1996): 3–6. Copyright © Johns Hopkins University Press.

INDEX